The Bitter Root

Pursuit of Freedom By a Man of Our Time

George:
Wemcats!
73
Olin M Salisbury

Oliver M Salisbury

The Bitter Root

Pursuit of Freedom By a Man of Our Time

By

Oliver M. Salisbury

Superior PUBLISHING COMPANY

SEATTLE, WASHINGTON

Library of Congress Cataloging in Publication Data

Salisbury, Oliver Maxson
  1. Salisbury, Oliver Maxson. 2. United States—Biography.
  I. Title.
  CT275.S3118A38   973.9′092.′4 [B]   80-23814
  ISBN 0-87564-825-8

Copyright © 1980 by Oliver M. Salisbury Author

All rights reserved. No part of this publication may be reproduced or transmitted in any form or by any means, electronic or mechanical, including photocopy, recording or any information storage and retrieval system, without permission in writing from the publisher.
First published in 1980 in a hardbound edition by Superior Publishing Company, 708 Sixth Avenue, Seattle, Washington.

Printed in the United States of America

ACKNOWLEDGMENTS

Cover by: Nat Schram
Frontispiece by: Nat Schram

Photos from the author's collection except the two North Atlantic Convoy pictures which are by courtesy of Yankee Books Inc., Dublin, New Hampshire, used by them in their current book titled, "World Wars Remembered," in which they published "Wolf Pack Attack" which appears as Chapter XX in The Bitter Root. Yankee Magazine published Chapter XXIV "The SS John A. Poor," as well as Chapter XX.

The author wishes to express gratitude to Lois and Gary Howard who listened to me tell these stories and encouraged me to put them to writing.

The author also thanks all of those good friends and relatives who have shown so much interest in my efforts to write this book and have waited patiently for its publication.

TABLE OF CONTENTS

Chapter		Page
1	The loud voice of innocence	1
2	Twin Lakes	5
3	The best year of my life	15
4	Our friend the cattle rustler	23
5	We move to Hamilton	28
6	Father comes home	34
7	I graduate and leave Hamilton	44
8	Return to the Bitter Root	54
9	North to Alaska again	64
10	I visit my folks	75
11	I'm involved in the birth of a union	88
12	I go all the way	98
13	A trip around the world	109
14	Strange places—new experiences	118
15	Long lazy days	126
16	Better days	132
17	I go left—the cost of it all	142
18	I hit the big apple	145
19	I go to war	156
20	The S.S. Charles Carroll	165
21	The land of my ancestors	173
22	We join the North African campaign	178
23	The second North African shuttle	184
24	The poor S.S. John A. Poor	194
25	The S.S. Front Royal	208
26	Insurmountable adversity	214
27	The saga of Sag Harbor	222
28	Caught in the back lash	229
29	First phase of transition	239
30	We settle in Seattle	250
31	Fight for my life and conclusion	255

Chapter One

The Loud Voice Of Innocence

When I was a six-year-old farm boy, in the year of 1912, I seemed to be blessed—or cursed—with a deep bass voice. It was a voice that never changed with adolescence.

Father called me "Fog Horn Ferdinandrew" after a character in a serial story then running in a popular magazine. I was too young to read magazines, so I never really knew whether this was praise or criticism. I had an idea it was criticism because the epithet was most often used by Father after I had burst into the house with an alarming announcement such as: "The baby ducks have hatched!" or some other earth-shaking bit of news.

Big Sister Winnie called me "Fowler's Bull" because it was a habit of mine to go about bellowing in sullen tones, imitating the neighbor's big red bull. I think I dreaded silence and fought loneliness by articulating sounds that I admired. Winnie said, "If only he could sing." She advised the rest of the family, "Ignore him. Don't laugh at him." This tactic only made the problem worse because it increased my need to break the silence.

Uncle George, visiting from the East, said, "Oliver has a job waiting for him in Chicago when he gets big."

Mother, always hopefully looking for talent in her children (she was the only one who called me Sunny Jim) asked, "And what might that be?"

"Calling trains at Chicago's Union Station. What else?" Uncle George replied.

Little sister Maxine called me "Blow Hard." She had me associated with the wind in some way. She wasn't old enough to be accusing me of bragging. Maxine had heard Father use the word to describe a neighbor and confusedly at the age of three thought it fit her brother.

Big brother Al called me "Blabber Mouth." I knew this was derogatory because he would say it right after I had made some pronouncement to neighbor playmates like: "Mother is going to have a baby." Which statement was completely unfounded and based solely on an assumption of mine after having observed Father taking Mother by the hand and leading her to the bedroom on a lazy Sunday afternoon. On a farm, a boy learns the facts of life early.

The day before starting country school Mother took me aside and said, "Sunny Jim, now you are about to go out into the world. I will no longer always be in calling distance of you. You are a lucky young man to be born in a free country where life, liberty and the pursuit of happiness are guaranteed to you. In school you will learn the value of those things and how to protect them even with your life if called upon."

Those were pretty heavy words to send a six-year-old off to school with, but at the time I thought I understood them, especially the "pursuit of happiness" part.

I started first grade in the country school which consisted of grades one to eight, all in the same room with one single teacher. During recess and lunch hours we school kids would swap stories about what was going on at our fathers' farms. If grandparents were visiting, that was big news. Visitors were the biggest news a kid could come up with. The more important the visitor the bigger the news, importance usually being measured by the distance the visitor had come.

The County Sheriff came to visit us. Not only did he come but it looked as if he came to stay. Mother put him up in the guest cottage and he had breakfast, lunch and dinner with us. The Sheriff was a big handsome man, clean shaven, with a shiny star on his shirt and a wide-brimmed Stetson hat and polished riding boots. Santa Claus didn't stir as much excitement in me as this sheriff did.

The Sheriff, recognizing my friendly attitude, said, "Oliver, why don't you show me about the farm?"

I thought this was odd, because I'd seen Father showing him all around and pointing out what seemed to be everything. But I liked to talk, and the sheriff showed a willingness to listen.

We looked at the brood sows, I said, "That's old Susy—she has nine shoats. Over there is Nancy, and she has seven sucklings. Those pigs over in that other pen have been nutted and they will be going to the market." I knew all the words, and kept a daily count on all that was going on around the farm. I added, "That's old Rufus over there. He's the father of them all."

I took the sheriff through the sheep pens, giving him a run down on the state of gestation of the ewes and introduced the sheriff to "Mr. Bumper," the ram and father of all the sheep.

By the time we got to the cattle barns and horse stables I was holding the sheriff's hand and was sure he was the nicest man in all the world. Who ever listened to me that much?

The sheriff wanted to see the farm machinery. With great pride, I showed him the new Avery tractor with the paint hardly smudged. "It is the first tractor in the valley, Father says."

The sheriff asked, "Does all this equipment belong to your father?"

"No. That big disc and the spray wagon belong to Uncle Max. The rest is ours."

The sheriff thanked me for showing him about. I asked him if he'd like to take my baseball bat and knock up some flies for me. He said, "Sure, Oliver, anything you want to do." He was good at it too. I liked him.

Next day at school lunch hour, I announced in my loudest voice, "Guess who's visiting at our farm?" Not waiting for an answer, I raised my voice even louder, "The Sheriff! He's staying in the cottage and he helps me to do my chores and plays baseball with me!"

Brother Al was kicking me in the shins and Sister Winnie was putting her finger to her lips and saying, "Oliver, Oliver, shush, shush!"

I paid little attention to the brotherly and sisterly admonitions. I had pulled off a big scoop, a sensation. Little friends were saying, "The Sheriff plays ball with you! I don't believe it!"

I said, "Criss cross my heart to die. It's the truth."

That night after dinner, Mother said, "Sunny Jim, we must have a talk, a private talk, away from the others."

I got up on my perch on the kitchen woodbox, Mother sat down on a stool. She began to talk in a serious tone, "Sunny Jim, having the sheriff for a guest is not an honor. In fact it is a shame. Your father has been forced to declare bankruptcy. Bankruptcy means that he has borrowed more money than he can pay back. Now his promissory notes are due and the bank wants its money. Therefore the bank has asked for a sheriff's sale. Under the law the judge has allowed it. The sheriff is here to see that we remove nothing, sell nothing or destroy nothing that is collateral for your father's notes. Sunny Jim, do you understand why the sheriff is here?"

"Yes, Mother. Can I still play ball with him?"

Mother said, "Of course, the sheriff is a fine man, just don't tell the kids at school about it. Your father has been in town the past three days negotiating for a new loan so we can keep the farm. A lot of talk around the valley about our problem will not help him. Sunny Jim, some things are family matters and should be kept within the family."

Years later, when I was an adult, Mother asked, "Oliver, what became of Sunny Jim? You were such a happy boy."

Mother, Father, Winifred and Albert. I am on Father's lap looking quite content while he squeezes the bulb to take this family picture. Albert watches the camera mechanism, intrigued. August, 1906.

Mother with Albert and me Sister Maxine showing in the near future. 1909.

Big sister Winifred with me at Lake Shetek, Wisconsin. Summer 1909.

The shanty Father moved our family into in the Bitterroot Valley, Ravalli County, Montana, from the big house on North Henry Street in Madison, Wisconsin. Father sits at the left. He loved carpentry work, though he was better fit for other things. June 1910.

The shack grew, with the addition of a tent to store Mother's fine mahogany furniture and a picket fence to protect the garden from deer and livestock. The barn is under construction. The light streaks are irrigation ditches. The shack later became the kitchen and dining room and the tent the master bedroom as the house was built around it. August 1910.

A big family picnic in Lost Horse Canyon. All kinfolk on the Pierce side of the family. No fancy station wagons or motor homes in those days. August 1913.

On the ranch ready for Sunday school. Mother is looking quite smug, having forced Albert and me to submit to severe scrubbing of face and ears.—apparently rubbing the smiles off our faces as she did it. 1911.

Mother with her crop of kids and our first harvest of big Bitterroot baking potatoes. October 1910.

The country school we attended. This is where the soup kettle cooking in the door of the coal-burning heater exploded, shooting steam and smoke into the room with a loud bang. Fleet-footed Mary Rennaker bolted for the front door, I was close on her heels followed by the entire school, with teacher screaming, "Come back, come back." Albert had to catch me, but Fleet-Foot Mary made it all the way home and did not return to school for two days.

Ready for the first day of country school. Note the homemade clothing and the tobacco box lunch boxes. Since Father didn't smoke we had to collect these boxes from our mountaineer neighbors. We had a mile and a half to walk. Some students rode ponies or came in horse-drawn carts. We were not so lucky. Father said Shank's mares were cheaper. I kept wondering when he was going to buy the mares. Albert, Winifred and me. Sept. 1911.

CHAPTER TWO

Twin Lakes

What seemed to be the saddest day of my life turned out to be the beginning of the best year of my life.

It was a hot August day in 1918, the second year of the War.

A little family group consisting of Father, Mother, elder sister Winnie, little sister Maxine, brother Albert and I stood on a lonely cinder platform with Mother waving a handkerchief to flag the Bitterroot Special. This was the train that once a day ran up the Bitterroot Valley and back from Missoula, Montana.

Father was leaving to accept a commission in the U.S. Army. We were there to bid him farewell. As Mother waved the white handkerchief the big steel monster that seemed about to devour my father came roaring 'round the bend.

I knew what the war was all about. Brother Al insisted on reading the battle reports out loud from his perch on the kitchen woodbox to Mother each evening. Being more interested in what was cooking for dinner, I remained in the kitchen and suffered through those early day 'newscasts.'

Father gave us all a kiss and a hug and boarded the train, looking very handsome in a starched high white collar, tie and business suit. The conductor gave us all a sympathetic smile as he picked up the step. I am sure he had helped up many a lad the length of that valley the same way for the same reason, and more than a few who were never to return.

I sobbed all the way home. I expect my age was right for that kind of emotion. The others tell me I was the only one that wept. I was just 12 years old. Al, 14, had read through all the Civil War histories and fiction and knew all about how brave Americans kept their chins up.

I made a fast recovery from my melancholy that very afternoon. Richard Wade, a playmate, came over on horseback and asked me, "Oliver, how would you like to ride along on a mountain pack trip to Twin Lakes with my father?"

I shouted, "Do you mean it? Wait here while I ask my mother!" I ran into the house.

Mother, who could be described as an early-day permissive parent, readily agreed that I could skip the first two weeks of school and make the trip. Having gained Mother's approval, it was a mere formality convincing my teacher, since now in my country school mother and teacher were one and the same person. Mother knew the Wades. Mr. Wade was a local carpenter and part time rancher. Mrs. Wade came in to help Mother with housework from time to time.

Father and Mother both believed strongly in expanding the horizons of their children. She felt I would learn more on the trip than I would in two weeks of school. Mother said, "Oliver, you go ask Mr. Wade if he really wants you to come along."

I ran out and jumped up behind Richard on his pinto horse and we galloped over to the Wade ranch to ask the question.

Mr. Wade warned, "You boys are big enough to act and work like men. I will expect that of you both." We were delighted to go on any terms.

Twin Lakes was a magic word. This was favorite big game hunting country for my father and his friends. Bear, deer, elk, moose and mountain goats abounded in the Twin Lakes area, not to mention game birds and fish. The only way to get into these lakes in 1918 was to travel 55 miles by saddle horse from the nearest ranch house.

At six o'clock on a very sunny September morning I arrived at the Wade ranch dressed in felt hat, dungarees and deerskin chaps, mounted on a smart-stepping black mare named Lady. I was told we were taking a pack train of supplies over the Stair Step Mountains for Bill Lears, an Idaho rancher, who claimed it was easier to come over the mountains into Montana for his supplies than to go to Elk City, the nearest town in Idaho, supposedly some hundred miles away.

The Wade ranch was alive with activity in preparation for the trip. It had the bustle and rustle and hustle of a military staging area in wartime.

As I approached, a half-mile away I could hear the ring of the smitty's anvil as he pounded out shoes for the mules' and pack ponies' front feet. Wranglers were lassoing ponies and putting pack saddles on recalcitrant mules. Huge mule-drawn wagons were pulling into the ranch yard with loads of goods and supplies to be transferred to pack mules and ponies. Packers lashed boxes to pack saddles. Richard and I were put to many uses.

Mrs. Wade and her daughter Isabel were cooking up a huge breakfast of hash browns, thick-sliced bacon, eggs and hot biscuits with honey. Eggs were scooped out of the platter and not counted by twos. Mrs. Wade was known in the valley as the "Cowgirl from Kalispell," which made her special for some reason I didn't understand.

Old Bill, as Mrs. Wade called her husband, was many years her senior. He had been a meat hunter for the railroads when they were first stringing the rails across the prairies.

Old Bill was as much my teacher as my mother was. He was building a privy for the country school and called me over during lunch hour while I was preparing to eat a big red Macintosh apple for my lunch. "Oliver, do you want to see how a Chinaman eats an apple?"

Being ever curious, I said, "Sure, Bill."

"Well." he said, "Give me that big red apple." I passed it over to him and he chomped the whole thing down.

I said, "I don't see anything different about that."

"There isn't anything different. A Chinaman eats an apple the same way anybody else does." It cost me my lunch apple but I remembered the lesson.

About 9, before the sun was too hot, our pack train of 35 animals plus Bill Lears, Bill Wade, three wranglers, Richard and I snaked out of the ranch yard and into the foothills, headed for Lost Horse Canyon.

The Lost Horse River flowing through the canyon was a good-sized stream, a tributary of the Bitterroot River. During the high-water season horses had been lost here in the process of fording the river.

The Lost Horse Trail followed the river for 40 miles, then crossed over and up through the Stair Step Mountains into the Selway Forest of Idaho. It was a little-used trail, and pretty much neglected by 1918. I knew the Lolo Pass and the Nez Perce Trail were more used and better maintained by the U.S. Forest Service. (I had a cousin, Ed Mckay, who was a Forest Ranger who used to tell us these things.) Old Bill said, "This trail is a short cut," when I had asked him.

In an hour or so we were in virgin forest. The winding trail generally followed along the river or high above it. Blue grouse were plentiful and would startle the lead pony as they 'motored' to the nearest low branch and sat like 'fool's hens,' which is what they were called. I could have killed them with a rock if I had been of a mind to. As the day wore on, when the trail permitted passing I galloped from one end of the pack train to the other. I noticed that some of the mule packs made a sloshing noise. I asked the wrangler, Mr. Smith, "What's that noise?"

He said, "Coal oil, boy, coal oil."

When we were well into the canyon, Bill Lears stopped the train and all the men strapped on six-shooters. "Just in case we meet a bear in the trail," he said. There were plenty of bear along the trail but they gave us a wide berth. Sometimes I heard them crashing off through the brush along the river.

We stopped for lunch by a stream in the heavy shade on this hot, early fall day. The pack animals were fed a little oats and not allowed to wander off. The pack pony with the fireless cooker was unpacked and we had hot baked pork and beans prepared earlier by Mrs. Wade and kept hot in the cooker. The beans were very sustaining and helped us ride the saddle light that afternoon.

Bill Lears told us we could make the Ohio Slide before sundown and camp there. The Ohio Slide was caused by a huge avalanche which had cut a quarter-mile-wide swath through the lodgepole for a half mile down the side of the mountain to the river. At the Ohio Slide the lodgepole was thrown up at either side of the swatch, like grain cut by a scythe. Old Bill said, "It's the work of Paul Bunyan." With handsaw and axe, the trail had been cut through these two windrows of lodgepole, creating a 50-foot tunnel on each side of the slide.

When we reached the Ohio Slide late that afternoon and passed through the first tunnel, tired as I was, I gasped at the beauty of the meadow which opened up in the path of the swath. Lush grass and wild flowers abounded, with huckleberry bushes showing ripe black fruit. The meadow ran down to the edge of the river at its lower end and was bordered at the top by high rock bluffs where the slide had originated. A campsite with a stone stove and baking hut, leveled ground and a path down to the river bank for water was at the foot of the meadow. By placing poles across the entrances to the two tunnels, we made the Ohio Slide into a natural fenced pasture for the night.

While we were unpacking the animals, one of the mules bucked his pack and put on a good show. When he had the pack off his back he continued to kick the boxes with his hind feet until they splintered in every direction and out came cases of whiskey which he continued to kick.

He did all this very quickly and the amount of salvageable whiskey was of little value. However, the men started picking up cracked and half broken bottles and drinking with a great sense of responsibility to save every possible drop. I asked Old Bill why we were carrying all that whiskey and he replied, "Medicine, boy, this here is medicinal whiskey."

Richard had been very quiet all day. I think the ride was hard on him. It didn't seem to bother me. I was stronger and more used to riding.

As the men settled down to consuming the whiskey, Richard and I quickly found out how useful we were expected to be. I was told to get supper and Richard was told to take the pack herd up the slope to the very top of the meadow so they would work their way down to the river when their bellies were full and be near the camp in the morning. One of the wranglers strapped his revolver on Richard and said, "Shoot in the air to scare off any bear that may attack the herd." That was certainly a comforting bit of advice to a 12-year-old heading out in the dusk and a half mile up on a mountain with nothing but animals for company—and the friendliness of some of them in question.

The men were more interested in consuming the salvage from the whiskey pack than they were in what I was cooking for dinner or when it was served. It was long after dark when I had finished cleaning up and packed the food away. I threw away the warmed-over beans and the sausages I had cooked, saving out a bit for Richard. By this time the men had consumed their fill of whiskey and fallen asleep on the ground under their saddle blankets—a deep sleep that only 10 or 12 hours in the saddle and saturation with whiskey could produce. They were all snoring loudly, sounding altogether like hogs in a wallow.

I was really preoccupied with my thoughts of the day's travel and the excitement of the general scene. The men's drinking and failure to eat the supper I had cooked did not disturb me.

The last man able to vocalize said, "Oliver, take a snooze and then get your horse and ride up to relieve Richard."

I tried to sleep but kept listening to the tinkle of the horse bell on the lead mare way up on the slope. The tinkle of the bell told me all was well with Richard. I was just too excited to sleep. I got up and saddled Lady who had been tied up with a picket rope and not released with the herd. All of the saddle horses were either hobbled or picketed. I rode out to the herd. Richard was sitting drowsily on his horse and glad to see me. After we had visited for a few minutes, he passed me the big six-shooter and returned to camp for his night's sleep.

Sitting up there on my horse with the pack ponies and mules for company I had a wonderful opportunity to study the stars. It was a crystal-clear night and the air was so brisk and pure I breathed deeply and relaxed. I felt closer to nature than I have ever felt since. I was not depressed by the conduct of the packers but was very exuberant about the communication with nature that I was experiencing up on the side of the Ohio Slide with the grazing animals that night. I didn't really think of the bears and mountain lions that might be around. I thought, If there is a heaven this is it. The dawn came too soon.

The men were very quiet the next morning as they packed the animals and prepared for the day's travel. Nursing such hangovers as they must have had, they didn't have much to say. Even a curse was too much exertion.

The day's travel was routine, and we made camp early in the afternoon again on the bank of the Lost Horse River. Old Bill said, "You boys and I will stay here for a couple days while the others take the pack train on without us. I need a rest. I'm an old man."

The next morning the pack train forded the river and started up the Stair Step Mountains for the crossing into Idaho. Those mountains were very precipitous even for the sure-footed pack mules. Animals had been lost on that ascent too.

Richard and I tried our luck at trout fishing, using willow sticks for poles and grasshoppers for bait. We had good luck and caught about 20 nice pan-sized cutthroat trout. The river ran slowly at this point, with sandy bottom and deep holes where it made its turns. There were some big lunkers in those deep holes but we weren't skilled enough to catch them. They would rise for the grasshopper but we'd get so excited at the sight of the big monster trout in the clear water that we would jerk the hook away before he could grab it. The big trout would see us and be too wise to make a second pass.

Old Bill had lolled around the camp, resting and sleeping. He did a bit of practice with his six-shooter, demonstrating to Richard and me that he could shoot bottles and cans off a stump at 50 feet.

On the third day after the pack train had left we broke camp. Old Bill said, "No need to follow them, we'd never catch up. How would you boys like to go up to Twin Lakes for a few days?"

I said, "I thought that's where we were going all the time." Bill didn't answer.

We forked off on to the trail to Twin Lakes. Coming up from the Lost Horse River to Twin Lakes the trail travels through a boggy area where the horses must walk on two parallel logs across what looks like mud, but would quickly drag a horse and rider down to oblivion. It was good to feel my horse was sure-footed at this point. Lady was so careful that when she forded a stream she put her nose down in the water almost to her eyes in order to see the boulders and avoid slipping or stumbling. After the boggy area the trail climbed steeply to the summit and the Montana/Idaho line.

Near the summit of that climb we came right out on the Lower Twin Lake. I gasped for breath at the magnificent scene. The lake was about a half mile square, in the center of 150 acres of natural mountain meadow. There were game trails in the sod around the lake a foot deep, cut there by centuries of the hooves of elk, moose, deer, big horn sheep and wild goat. This country had never been grazed or logged and only the rugged could visit it.

We then traveled on to the upper lake, which was slightly smaller and kidney-shaped. Here we stayed in an old trapper's cabin built of solid logs with a stone fireplace. We caught big cutthroat trout, shot blue grouse, and ate like gourmets. Richard and I rode the horses to vista points and swam in the lake. We watched great bald eagles circle, then plunge and come up with rabbits and rodents. We listened to Old Bill's tales of buffalo hunts on the prairies, Indians, and what I am sure were genuine stories of the Old West, surely embellished a bit and aided by Bill's seemingly inexhaustible supply of salvaged whiskey from the mule-bucking incident. Bill taught us to recognize the mating call of the bull elk, the moose, the cry of the timber wolf, the lynx and the cougar and many other noises.

These were great days and we lost count of them. One morning Old Bill awakened us with a touch and a shush. We slipped out of the cabin to see a bull elk standing up to his belly in the lake and bugling his mating call of, "Whooo, whooo, whoooo." He had a great rack of antlers and was wearing his summer coat, cream colored with a dark brown mane.

Bill said, "We need fresh red meat. I'm going to have him. You kids sit still and and watch." A small brushy wooded peninsula ran out into the lake. The bull was on the other side of the lake opposite the tip of this peninsula. We watched Bill stalk through the brush and saw the elk raise his head alertly as he heard a twig snap, not sufficiently loud to alarm him. Bill got to the edge of the peninsula, but didn't shoot the bull while he was in the water because we wouldn't have been able to pull him out. Bill fired into the water by the side of the elk to scare him toward the shore. The bull wheeled and plunged for the bank.

Bill fired, hitting him in the rump. The elk wheeled again and jumped into the lake, swimming across towards Bill and sending up a gusher of water in his wake. When the bull came out on

Bill's side of the lake he stood with head lowered as for a charge, while Bill stealthily walked toward him, rifle raised. The elk turned and jumped into the lake a third time. When he reached the opposite shore Bill fired several shots and the big bull fell. He lay right on the ranger trail.

Bill said,"We'd better cut him up and get him off the trail. A ranger might come through. It's not hunting season. No open season on elk this year anyway."

Cutting up an elk is like cutting up a horse. While Bill chopped up the elk with an axe Richard and I carried the meat about 200 yards back up the side of the mountain, piece by piece. Our limit of meat per load was about 30 pounds. It took us many backbreaking, bloody trips, with scratches and bruises from frequent falls. The head and antlers were the worst of it; we could only drag that part.

Old Bill cut out some fine roasts and steaks, which we refrigerated in a snow bank not far from the cabin—snowdrifts remaining from the previous winter for our convenience. He also cut the ivory teeth for himself. They would bring $25 to $50 a pair from Elks Lodge members who wore them as watch charms. About two o'clock in the afternoon we finally sat down to elk steaks. They were tough and gamey but we didn't mind. Richard and I were covered with blood and elk hair; our clothes were torn, we were pestered by deer flies and mosquitoes, and above all we were very tired boys.

That night and the next day we could hear the noise of wild animals having their own feast on that elk's carcass. We heard mountain lions, bears, coyotes and wolves by night and could see eagles, buzzards, magpies and crows by day devouring the remains.

After a few more days of enjoying our mountain paradise, Bill began to get nervous about packing out and getting home. The remains of the elk's carcass were beginning to smell a telltale story of its slaughter. Bill said, " This is a poor place to be camping if a ranger came by. He'd sure investigate that smell."

We wound our way back down the Lost Horse Trail and into the familiar Bitterroot Valley.

When I reached home Mother greeted me like she had never expected to see me again. "What's the matter?" I asked. "We're home early." I couldn't imagine what all the excitement was about, but I hurried into the house in all my filth, covered with blood, elk hair, horse hair, horse manure, garbage and body sweat.

Mother told Maxine to curry and rub down the horse. She began, "Do you know who Bill Lears is? Do you know that Bill Wade is in on it? What happened? Do you know Bill Wade's ranch is a staging area for the smuggling of whiskey from Montana over the mountains into Idaho where it is sold at premium prices? Wade and Lears have been carrying on this business for two years, ever since Idaho voted in prohibition. Oh my! To think I thought I was helping your education and training for manhood by permitting you to go! What will your father say?"

After I had told Mother the story of the trip she said, "Now you can see why the revolvers on all the men. You can see why Bill Wade camped at the foot of the Stair Step Mountains. He was there to intercept anyone that had tried to follow, lawman or hijacker. You're a lucky boy that you didn't get mixed up in a shoot-out."

That same fall of 1918, with the soldiers still away, Montana voted dry. With a big snow storm blowing, my mother told me to hitch up the mare to the buggy so she could drive the 17 miles to Hamilton to cast her vote for Prohibition and for Jeanette Rankin. She snapped the buggy whip on the little mare's rump and said, "I've waited too long for this vote to let a little thing like a snow storm keep me away." That day she helped kill Bill Lears' whiskey smuggling venture: Montana went dry.

Years later, I asked Old Bill, "Why did you all carry revolvers?"

He said, "Well, there might have been some outlaws who wanted all that whiskey. I wouldn't let anybody have that whiskey, or any nosey ranger or sheriff who might have passed by." I was glad we didn't have a shoot-out there at the foot of the Stair Step Moutains where Old Bill spent two days "resting" to intercept anyone intent upon interrupting Bill Lears' excellent service to the parched throats of Idaho. I expect a shoot-out there would have gone down in history along with "O.K. Corral."

Eagle's Nest—The Charlos club house built and used by the O. W. Kerr Company land developers and promoters, to accommodate guests brought out from East to see the wonders of the Bitterroot. Note the Brush automobile in front of the garage. The horse and buggy tied to the fence belong to Father, who took the picture.

View of the club house and Charlos Heights. Work on the Highline Ditch shows up but it was never completed. Camas Peak is at the upper right. Albert, Winifred and I climbed this peak one August day to celebrate Winnie's return from the University of Chicago. She dedicated the climb to her classmates. 1917.

Twin Lakes near the Montana/Idaho line. The lake was loaded with cutthroat trout, and the area abundant with big game. Note the trapper's cabin. Marten and mink were plentiful. 1910.

O. W. Kerr and party on the Lost Horse/Twin Lakes Trail. A road now replaces the trail. This is the trail I went in on with Bill Wade and the **whiskey train in 1918.**

CHAPTER THREE

The Best Year Of My Life

Mother had contracted to teach the country school again. She and Father had decided to dispose of the livestock. Mother, Maxine and I would move from Charlos Heights into the small cottage next to the Charlos school house. Sister Winnie would be away attending the University of Chicago and Albert would be attending high school 20 miles away in the town of Hamilton and boarding there.

I felt quite the man of the house and happily took on the burden of having all the chores to do.

I was delighted to have the saddle horse to myself. That is, to myself aside from Maxine's precocious bare-back riding, which exposed the myth I tried to perpetuate among my friends about the black mare. I told them "Lady has mustang blood and is a very dangerous and spirited animal." Just at the time of telling, Maxine came galloping by, bareback, guiding the mare with a hackamore, her sun-bleached hair waving in the wind. Maxine's tomboy tendencies embarrassed me many times.

Mother talked to her friends on the country telephone. Her conversations were of the war still raging in France, the Spanish influenza epidemic, Hooverizing, and the patriotic effort on the home front. We all learned to knit. I don't know how the hopitals ever got the wash rags that I knit clean. If a wounded soldier ever saw one coming in the condition in which it left my hands, he would think, "This is it!"

We sold the livestock, keeping two horses, two dogs, numerous cats, some laying hens, a milk cow and a few pigs. We moved into the little cottage near the country school. We were hardly settled, when the influenza epidemic hit the Bitterroot Valley with tragic force.

The authorities closed the country schools but kept the town schools and the high schools open, the theory being that there were doctors and hospitals in the towns and none available for country calls.

I was left in the happy situation of having guns, hunting dogs, saddle horse, no school and no work. Furthermore, no discipline from a strict father or domination by a big brother. My only responsibility was to enjoy complete freedom and the pursuit of happiness.

I liked milking the one cow and feeding the few chickens. Of course the dogs and the horses were a pleasure I did not want to be deprived of.

I became friends with the Ward boys, Sid and Sam, brothers and near my age. Their father owned a great stock ranch a couple of miles from where we now lived. My mother approved of my friendship with these boys. Their father and mother were graduates of the University of Montana and were cultured people. Mother feared the hillbilly jargon that I was acquiring at that impressionable age from some of my other associates. Mr. Ward was the son of an early Montana pioneer, George Ward, who had settled in the Valley about the end of the Civil War.

I'll always remember George Ward's funeral. It took nearly an hour to pass the country school. School was recessed for the occasion and we stood smartly at the front school yard fence, with the flag bearer of the school holding the Stars and Stripes straight and tall to honor this old Union soldier.

The funeral was all horse-drawn, every animal curried and brushed to as high a shine as the various and interesting rigs.

G.A.R. (Grand Army of the Republic) was well represented, for there were many Civil War veterans yet living. It was a scene out of the last century.

As it worked out, the action that year was at the Ward ranch. Several mornings out of the week the cowboys on the ranch would break colts to ride. Mr. Ward was involved in raising and selling horses to the U.S. Army, the army still having cavalry and horse-drawn artillery. Mr. Ward owned several hundred horses. He used quarter horse stallions to breed them, though some were crossed with Percheron stallions to give size and weight for artillery animals.

Mr. Ward seemed to be away most of the time on trips to the coast selling horses. This fact also expanded our freedom a great deal.

On these mornings when they were breaking colts we enjoyed a real wild west show. Perched safely on the top rail of a strong pole corral, we would watch these men mount a wild horse. It seemed to be a contest whether the rider would get his neck broken or the horse would be broken to the saddle.

Some of the horses were pretty fierce and would be turned loose again as not being temperamentally fit for the army. "Conscientious objectors" one might have said. I used to wonder what happened to some raw recruit getting on one of those living torpedoes. I presumed the horses received a lot more training before they were assigned to a trooper.

One day after the men were through with the corral, Sid, Sam and I decided to run in some young steers and try our own skills at riding. We lassoed a small steer and put a rope around its belly with a loop at the end. Sam mounted while Sid and I held the steer. Sam pulled the belly rope tight. I yelled, "Let er rip, Sam!" We let the steer loose, he jumped, bucked and twisted just like the wild horses.

When the going got too rough, Sam, though still on, released the belly rope and the steer stopped the violent bucking. Sam slid safely off to the soft earth.

Sid said, "That's no fun. No one got hurt." We all thought it a bit dull. We roped a yearling bull much larger than the calf Sam had ridden. Sid volunteered to ride this one. The young bull, unhappy and very feisty about the whole operation, pawed the earth and made threatening noises as a bull will.

Sam and I held the bull and Sid mounted, crying out, "Powder River let 'er buck!" We released him. Sid dug his heels in, the bull made a mighty jump and buck, flipping his hindquarters high in the air and releasing a stream of dung as he did. He made a circle of mad jumps around the corral, each jump higher than the last and more flying dung. As the bull completed the circle of the corral he made a grand violent effort which sent Sid sailing through the air.

Sid landed on his face right in the fresh manure. When he raised his head he was hardly recognizable for the complete mask plastered on his face.

The young bull, angered, took after Sam and me, just missing our britches with his horns as we scrambled for the high rails on the corral. Then he turned, charging Sid, who was just getting to his feet only to be knocked down again.

Old Nick, the big, red, shorthaired cattle dog, decided at that moment that Sid needed help. Old Nick sailed in and grabbed the bull by the heel, giving Sid a chance to make the fence.

Sam and I went into high hysterics at Sid's mask of fresh barnyard plaster.

Sid, made unhappy by the whole experience, distraught by the smell of his smudge, and mad as hell at our laughter, started to bawl like a baby.

With the mad bull bellowing, the dog barking, Sid bawling and Sam and me in fits, the volume of noise brought Mrs. Ward from the house.

We stayed with riding calves after that. Sometimes parents' admonitions are unnecessary. This was one of those cases.

Mr. Ward was also a foxhound fancier and breeder. He maintained a pack of 30 to 40 Kentucky foxhounds for hunting coyotes—considered a sport at the time. Mr. Ward would have a steer slaughtered every few days just for those hounds to feed on.

Well, some of the hounds started following us on our exploring rides. We looked for Lewis and Clark campsites, old homesteads, caves, canyons, uncharted ponds and all those intriguing things that young boys with free time and transportation love to investigate.

Picking up the coyote scent, the hounds would go off in hot pursuit with Old Queenie, the lead dog, bugling her musical call, which seemed to excite the rest of the hounds as well as us. The baying of hounds and the commotion we stirred up in that part of the Valley and the foothills were really awesome.

On one clear late fall morning I reported at the Ward ranch on my horse hoping for the usual exciting day. I was not disappointed. Sid and Sam were waiting for me.

Mr. Ward was away, the foreman and the cowboys were out in the hills rounding up horses. No restrictions. No one to say, "I wouldn't do that, boys."

Mr. Ward had a bunch of young foxhound puppies that he had kept penned up so they wouldn't get out and start to run on their own and develop bad habits such as chasing rabbits. "Good hounds must be trained," Mr. Ward had said many times.

On this morning, Sam said, "Let's take the pups today."

"Why not?" said Sid, as he opened the gate to their pen. The puppies, about four months old, came yelping out like a bunch of kids let out on the last day of school.

Sam decided to take his father's hunting horn. This was a long bull's horn with a strap on it that was used to call the hounds. Sam put it to his mouth and produced that deep lowing sound that meant to the hounds that a hunt was on. Hounds came leaping in from all the corners of the many outbuildings and sheds on this big ranch layout.

There must have been 25 hounds with us including the puppies. Old Queenie, the mother of many of them, was their leader. She was trained to stay with the riders until told, "Go get 'em, Queenie."

We headed out for Camus Creek, three riders and a big pack of hounds. Hard to tell who was the happiest, hounds or boys. Don't think the horses didn't enjoy it too.

Mrs. Ward opened a window and called out, "Be careful, boys!"

The only thing we were careful of was not to miss any fun. I think she knew that too. She must have enjoyed the sight even though it gave her anxieties.

As long as Old Queenie stayed with the riders the hound pack was pretty orderly, confining their activities to sniffing out the right of way and putting farm dogs that dared come out into fast retreat. A few neighboring farmers looked a little shocked to see that the hunters were three young boys. They were used to seeing the horses and hounds, but always with Mr. Ward. One old codger yelled out, "The hills are gonna be singin' this afternoon."

Camus Creek was a small valley about a half mile wide with a fair-sized creek through the center of it and surrounded by marsh and dense thickets. It was a great place for coyotes and frequently mountain lion. This area made a sort of half-way place for lion, bear and coyotes crossing the Bitterroot Valley from the Hellgate Range to the Bitterroot Range, half-way because these wild animals sometimes got caught by daylight crossing the valley and would hide out through the day in this great swamp.

Sam and Sid knew the techniques of hunting in this manner. They had gone with their father on numerous occasions and they were great listeners to their father's hunting stories.

When we approached the Camus Swamp, Sid commanded, "Queenie, go in and get 'em." Queenie bugled and streaked into the woods, all hounds and puppies in pursuit. The ground and marsh were frozen solid with patches of frost and some snow showing here and there.

We heard Old Queenie bugle again, followed by the excited baying of Big Crip and then joined by the baying and yelping of the entire pack. They were on a hot trail.

Sam hollered, "Come on, gang, let's ride like hell for the top of that ridge, that's where the coyote will cross over to the next canyon!!"

We put our horses into a mad gallop over the rough grounds, windfalls, chuckholes and huckleberry bushes ignored.

Big Crip was the biggest, fastest and meanest dog in the pack. Crip was a son of Queenie and was noted for fighting. Once he suffered a broken toe from the bite of a fierce coyote that made the mistake of electing to stand and fight. He indulged a slight limp as a result and thereby earned the name of Big Crip. Actually he was a young dog in his prime.

On a hot trail Big Crip, strong and fast despite the bad toe, would take the lead away from Queenie. You could tell by the baying how the chase was progressing. Of course, the puppies chimed in to provide an exciting chorus.

As we made the summit, we could hear the baying of the hounds coming towards the edge of the swamp and the beginning of the ridge. We were too slow in getting to the summit of the ridge. The coyote was loping across the ridge ahead of us just out of gun range. I had a 20-gauge shotgun loaded with buckshot. I jumped off the horse and banged away at him with the single shot shotgun. At the first shot the coyote abandoned his lope and streaked for the other canyon—laughing to himself, I'm sure, at those fool boys and the dumb hounds left way behind in the swamp.

We'd had our chance and blown it. Lack of experience on the part of us young hunters spared that coyote's life. He was a big handsome fellow, with his winter coat and bushy tail, almost the size of a wolf. The state had a five-dollar bounty on coyotes too.

Sam said, "Listen to those hounds. They're on to something again!"

"Come on!" I cried, "They're headed down stream. Let's intercept them at that old logging road through the swamp."

Again a mad ride down the hill, over the same obstacles, onto the old logging road and into the center of the swamp.

We dismounted and tied the horses so they wouldn't panic and get in the way of our shooting. We watched the road in both directions. We were making as much noise as the hounds.

Sid hollered, "Here he comes. I'll shoot him as he jumps the road."

Sam and I were watching to the right. Sid was watching to the left. As the baying of the hounds told us, they had circled the swamp and started up creek. Sam yelled, "He'll be coming our way now!"

We were expecting nothing less than a mountain lion or at least another coyote.

There was a loud bang. Sid hollered, "I got him! I got him!"

Sam and I wheeled around to see what Sid had shot. A big snowshoe rabbit was the victim.

With the leaves off the trees, the pure-white rabbits could be seen fleeing through the brush a hundred feet before they leaped the road. Sid had done a good job holding his fire until the rabbit made his leap.

As the hounds' baying came closer, more rabbits started jumping the road. We banged and banged away, killing ten rabbits before the hounds crossed the road. As we hurried to pick up our game before the hounds got to them, Sam shouted, "I killed a lion! I killed a lion! Look! Look!"

Sam was holding up a small wildcat or bobcat that was fleeing with the rabbits in front of the hounds. I said, "Sam, that's not a lion, that's a lynx, a Canadian lynx!"

Sid said, "It was an unlucky kitty to get shot for a rabbit."

Smelling the blood from the slaughter of rabbits and one little bobcat, the hounds started gathering around, barking and yelping at the trophies we were holding.

Then we noticed that our hound pack was the puppy pack. We could still hear Big Crip, Old Queenie and the rest baying way over in the next canyon, still sniffing out the tracks of Mr. Coyote, who was a good half hour ahead of them.

We were delighted with our day's bag and so were the puppies. We were having some argument about who killed the lynx. None of us were quite sure when the cat met its fate. Sam didn't know until he picked it up and then he thought it was a lion.

Sam blew on the hunting horn again and again in an effort to bring in the hounds that were still chasing the coyote. Old Queenie came in, as did others one by one. Big Crip was a stubborn one. He could be heard all that night clear down at the ranch house still baying after that coyote. He stayed on the trail for two or three days until his feet got so sore he came limping home.

We really felt like the conquering heroes riding into the ranch with all those rabbits dangling and dripping blood from our saddle straps, Sam claiming the bobcat for his. The ranch hands quickly identified it as a young bobcat and a far cry from a lion or a lynx. No doubt it was killed by accident crossing the logging road at the time of the rabbit slaughter.

When Mr. Ward returned from the coast and heard about the rabbit hunt, he was furious and forbade us boys to do any further hunting with his hounds. He said, "Now I'll have to give those pups away; they are worthless."

A small pack train on the Lost Horse Trail.

Mother on Lady. This is the fine mare that I rode into Twin Lakes and later raced with the Ward boys. Lady was a thoroughbred crossed with mustang and trained as a cow pony. 1913.

Lady with her colt June. June was sired by Uncle George's Hamiltonian stallion who was in direct line of descent from the mare Mother rode as a girl in Big Foot Prairie, Wisconsin, some fifty years before. Grandfather Pierce was a horsebreeder. June was the two-year-old colt that I rode on the trip with Dave Smith, the ex-cattle rustler.

Father with a goat, killed for a research study in his work for the United States Public Health service, where he was employed on the Rocky Mountain spotted fever project.

CHAPTER FOUR

Our Friend The Cattle Rustler

After a long severe winter of virtual confinement due to Mother's precautions against the Spanish influenza which was raging throughout the world, I stepped outside and took a deep breath of cool spring air.

I wondered what Sid and Sam were doing. I had not seen them since the Christmas holidays. Extreme cold, deep snow and no school had isolated us. Besides, there was the need to be continually sawing and chopping stove wood to keep our little cottage warm. Mother didn't like me to get very far away from home in that kind of weather.

Spring comes late in western Montana, but when it gets there you are overjoyed by it.

Mother called Mrs. Ward to be sure everyone was well there and that I would be welcome. Sid and Sam were elated at the idea of resuming our adventures together. I saddled Lady and once again took off for the Ward ranch at a fast gallop.

Things appeared dull on the Ward ranch. No horses to break, no calves to brand. Spring fever was in the air.

Dave Smith, one of the bronco busters, was a man of 40, still strong and active and always friendly to us eager youngsters. He was always ready to teach us the tricks of riding, lassoing and of generally becoming men as he saw it. Dave had only a few months before been paroled from the Montana State Prison at Deer Lodge. He had served nearly ten years for cattle rustling. Mr. Ward said, "He's the last old-time rustler to be sent to prison." Fences and changing conditions had eliminated the profession. Mr. Ward had gone Dave's parole and given him a job.

Everyone in the Valley knew Dave Smith and in spite of his prison record seemed to respect him. He was a nice guy. I can vouch for that, but just where he earned the respect he had, I don't know. My mother even liked him and said he was a good man. Of course, what made him exciting to me at that age was not the good things but the bad things I had heard about him. Mother said, "He is a kind of Robin Hood."

On this Sunday morning, Dave said, "How would you boys like to take a long ride today and see my old cattle rustling pens and hide-outs?"

We yelled in unison, "You mean it, Dave?"

Mrs. Ward put up lunches for our saddle bags. Another bronc buster named Nels volunteered to go along. Dave told Mrs. Ward it would be late, probably after dark, before we returned.

Mrs. Ward called Mother to advise her of the journey and get her consent. Mother, of course, gave her blessings. No doubt she worried some over possible hunting and riding accidents, as mothers will, but she always looked at the rewards of the experience and seldom said no.

Dave didn't allow the dogs to follow. He said the trip would be too tough for them. (He was talking about the two cattle dogs; of course the hounds were now forbidden to us.)

What could be more exciting than an ex-cattle rustler taking you on a guided tour of the scenes of his daring exploits? We crossed down through the river bottom from the Ward ranch and forded the Bitterroot River, swimming the horses. Dave showed us how to crouch low so as not to throw the horse off balance, and if the horse floundered to slide off and hang on to the saddle horn, giving the horse his free rein. Though there was little snow left in the foothills, spring thaws in the mountains had not begun and the river was low.

After crossing the river we started up through the ravines and low-lying hills to the Hellgate Range. Dave explained that sticking to the gullies kept a horseman out of sight to anyone in the valley scanning the hills looking for a rustler.

These foothills were bare of trees but covered with wild grass and some sagebrush. We came on a nest of rattlesnakes sunning themselves on the rocks, so numbed by the winter cold that they could barely move. The men jumped off their horses, picked up clubs and killed as many as they saw, but advised us to stay mounted.

We finally left the foothills and entered virgin timber: big white pines, tall, straight and majestic. We climbed all morning, finally coming to a ridge that dropped steeply off into a canyon with a small green valley below. It seemed as if the descent was straight down.

"Get off your horses," Dave ordered. "We go over here."

Leading the horses, we had to pull hard on the reins to get them to start down this steep descent. It was steep for man and horse. The ground was soft with humus and pine needles. We slipped, slid, plunged and fell. Sam cried out because his horse was standing on his leg. The ground was soft, though and the little horse's hoof hardly left a mark on Sam. We were scratched, bleeding and complaining bitterly.

Dave said, "If men were chasing you with rifles and a bounty on your carcass, you wouldn't be complaining."

We at last made the bottom of the descent and came out on a pretty little valley with a lovely stream, green meadows and buttercups popping out in their spring yellow.

"This is Little Sleeping Child Creek," Dave explained, "named after Sleeping Child Springs, a natural hot springs over in the next canyon."

We remounted and came to a little meadow that opened on the creek.

Dave halted. "We'll eat lunch here."

We dropped the reins to the ground and let the horses munch grass and drink from the stream while we also munched our own lunches. Dave said, "This is where I had little Sadie Jensen. I was alone, had ditched a posse looking for me over in the big valley. I'd just come down where we did, mounted and was crossing that meadow when I saw a young girl sitting here by this stream, playing in the water. Right where we are now.

"I stopped my horse; she hadn't noticed me. Wondering where she came from, I noticed a homesteader's house a few hundred yards down the little valley, also saw no wagon. H'm, I thought, folks in town. About that time time she looked up and saw me.

"Frightened, she jumped up and started to run for the farm house. It was then I noticed she was no child, but a young woman of 15 or 16. I sprinted the horse, swept her up beside me on the saddle. She was scared as a rabbit but did not scream, too scared to. I let her to the ground, dropped beside her, and—what would you have done? Well, I did it. I fucked her. She was not unhappy, just frightened."

We boys didn't know quite what the story meant, but the part about swooping the girl up into the saddle sounded exciting. Horsemanship, that's what counted with us.

Nels spoke up for the first time that day. "Was she plump?" he asked.

"I'll say she was. I went out of my way several times after that and stopped to see her with sweet results. She is married and living down in the valley today."

I wondered why Nels cared whether she was plump or not. Maybe he thought she would be too heavy to lift to the saddle.

The way Dave told this story it did not seem lewd or titillating or even criminal, but more like an innocent experience of the adventure-seeking, carefree lad that he must have been. Twenty years later he was still a handsome man, graying around the temples, in fine physical condition, and could still win prize money at the bronco riding competitions at the County Fair. At the time of his cattle rustling, he must have been the true character that Hollywood tries so hard to portray.

We went on down this little valley and then crossed a trail over another ridge, not so rugged, and then another and another, finally coming out on some meadows, a stream and some remains of old weather-bleached corrals.

Dave explained that this was where he would bring the rustled cattle and these were his holding pens. An accomplice would guard the cattle and help change the brands.

After they had gathered enough of them and the brands had healed, they would drive them through the Hellgate Range to Philipsburg and sell them there to be slaughtered for the tables of the miners of Butte.

No one questioned their origin and little dreamed that they came all the way from the Bitterroot Valley. The scheme worked until they were caught and sent to the penitentiary.

I expect if one took the time to search the Montana State Archives and read the court records of this case, it would not sound nearly as romantic.

We returned by country road, arriving home long after dark—tired, hungry and fascinated by the day's experience.

When I wasn't riding I was reading Hopalong Cassidy or Zane Grey's western novels. I was enjoying life so thoroughly I hardly missed my father, and barely listened as Mother read his letters from the Army camps. I did write him and ask for a picture with his horse and revolver. He sent me one, and I still have it.

Is it hard to believe this was the best year of my life? All play, no work, no school and all the tools with which to enjoy life, including good companions. Is it any wonder that in later years I resented time clocks and commuter trains?

CHAPTER FIVE

We Move To Hamilton

The end of the war found my father in New York City waiting to board a transport with his company. He was captain of a Negro labor battalion destined for France. Father was greatly disappointed, according to his letters, not to become a member of the A.E.F. (American Expeditionary Forces). He wrote to mother that he would soon be discharged and would be coming home. We then did not hear from him again for ten months. His allotment checks, which continued to come from Washington, were Mother's only assurance that he was alive. We were all deeply disappointed that he did not come home.

We Move to Hamilton

When we did hear, the news was received from Paris in a whole package of letters. Censorship was still on. Mail, transportation and communications were as disrupted by the end of the war as they were by its advent. Father had accepted a commission as Captain in the American Red Cross and was assigned to rehabilitation work in Europe. He was given responsibility for the distribution of tons and tons of war surplus goods then on the docks and in the warehouses of France. His job was to distribute these goods throughout the countries where they would do the most good. He stayed with that work until the spring of 1920.

Mother said, "He'll be gone for a long time. I'll never move back to that ranch. We are going to move into Hamilton where you boys can go to high school."

Sister Winifred was leaving for her senior year at the University of Chicago. Winnie said, "Mother, when I graduate I can live at home and teach school in Hamilton." Mother bought what we were to call the 'Little Yellow House.' It was a cute three-bedroom house with a nice yard and a big maple tree beside it where my friends could climb up to yell in my second-story bedroom window.

Mother held a farm auction and disposed of all the remaining livestock except the dog, Sandy. She sold all the equipment but the Tin Lizzy, a 1917 model Ford which even I at the age of thirteen had learned to drive.

Sandy was run over by a car the very first night in town, his leg crushed to pulp. I said to my brother, "Do we have to shoot him?"

Al said, "Hell, no! We'll tape his leg up with bicycle tire tape using rulers for splints."

Sandy trusted us so much he scarcely whimpered while we administered as veterinarians. We had some experience in this field, having patched up broken legs and wings of rabbits, ducks, chickens, songbirds, and whatever unfortunate thing had the good fortune to be found by us. Sandy's leg healed beautifully and he regained use of it without a limp.

"The bone is kind of bunchy," Mother said, "but I have seen worse jobs done by supposedly skilled physicians on humans."

I was now in the eighth grade of grammar school. We moved to Hamilton in late August, giving us a little time to adjust to living in town and to the ways of town kids. The kids were organized into North End, South End, and Finn Town or Mill Town the West Side, also by levels of culture and economics. We lived in the middle of town and I exercised my freedom to go both directions. Father's being a Captain and now something of a celebrity, and Mother's being a school teacher, put us in the center of the cultural and economic strata.

I had a feeling that city life, as I looked upon Hamilton, would be somewhat stifling. Sister Winnie had warned me of town bullies. I swore to myself not to be bullied and to give up none of my freedoms. I would continue to hunt and fish. I noticed the mill pond was full of muskrat; I'd put out my traps come winter as usual. I heard about kids having to be off the streets with the nine o'clock curfew. That didn't sound too good.

An early lucky break helped establish me in the neighborhood. Some North End kids and I were having a corn roast. We had the bonfire going and our sacks of sweet corn sitting around. A husky-looking kid rode up on a bicycle, looked over our operation, picked up my bag of corn and started to walk away with it. I jumped up, caught him, grabbed the bag of corn, gave him a shove and said, "That's my bag of corn!" The kid looked dumbfounded and got on his bike and rode away.

My friends said, "Don't you know who that is? He's the toughest kid in town." I didn't know who he was, but I knew he had my corn. This helped my status with the kids a great deal and the incident was to become greatly exaggerated. However, this tough kid turned out to be very nice and became one of my buddies for years to come.

Trouble started for me with the start of school and continued for some time thereafter. I was good in geography, writing, reading, history and art, all of which interested me. Arithmetic and grammar were bores and I really had a block on those subjects. I attended Central School where we had a different teacher for each subject. This was quite an arrangement for me, coming from a one-room country school where most of the time my mother was the teacher.

The principal of Central School was Miss Oberton. Anyone of my generation who went through Central School will remember her. She was like a witch; that was her reputation among the town's kids, and she lived up to it.

I called her "Old Miss Oberton" to Mother.

Mother said, "Why Oliver, Miss Oberton can't be 35 years old. She's one of the youngest teachers in the school."

"I didn't know a woman that young could be so mean," I answered. I was a country bumpkin and Miss Oberton decided to make me over.

"She has taken on quite a task if she thinks she can make you over," Mother said.

When I walked I had sort of a hike and a spring in my step, making me bob up and down, something I had developed climbing the hills of Charlos Heights. I wasn't used to walking on flat ground. Marching in step, my hike-and-bob motion sort of spoiled the looks of the marching line going from classroom to classroom. Miss Oberton would jerk me out of the line and make me march it over on an even step. The next day the same thing would happen. I think it got to where she quit reviewing the line rather than continue the temper-testing ordeal of jerking me out of the line. When I say 'jerk,' she really did. It would take a half an hour for my arm to settle back in its socket. She was verbally very cruel and castigating about it which never helped my ego a bit.

Frequently on weekends Mother would let me board the train and go up the Valley for a visit and a ride with the Ward boys. I said to Sid and Sam, "Gee, guys! You got fresh air and room to breathe out here." As if we didn't in Hamilton. I went on telling them how lucky they were, "No marching in line or nine o'clock curfews out here." (The truth was that on the Ward Ranch we were always so worn out from activity that we were sound asleep in our bunks long before nine o'clock ever came.)

Miss Oberton was also my grammar teacher. I had picked up a jargon from the hillbillies out at Charlos which she couldn't stand and was determined to get out of me if she had to pound it out. To make it worse, Mother had taken a job as a substitute teacher. Miss Oberton would throw this at me, saying, "You, a son of a teacher, should know better."

On a couple of occasions I was sent to the principal's office by other teachers. As you entered her office, it was Miss Oberton's practice to give you a bang on one side of the head, then another bang on the other side, and then say, "What are you in here for?" You were judged guilty on the fact that you had been sent in to her. This warranted two bangs on the head just for taking up her time.

Miss Oberton learned that Mother was a Christian Scientist and was forever finding excuses to try to embarrass me or make me sensitive about that. I can never forget the expression on her face the day I came to school when there was the big "SMALLPOX" quarantine sign on our front door. Earlier arrivals at school had already reported it to her. She didn't get near enough to me to bang my ears that morning but sent me home. This in spite of the fact that I had a certificate from the Public Health Officer saying I could go to school if my mother would isolate my kid sister, the smallpox victim, from my brother and me, which she did. The doctor did vaccinate us and I later came down with a light case of smallpox. That was the one time I came into Miss Oberton's office without getting my ears boxed. Miss Oberton ignored the envelope I was trying to hand her and screamed, "Oliver, you get right out of here and go straight home!"

She ruled by terror. Her ideas of how to handle a potential dropout or slow student was to tell him, "I'll send you to the State Reformatory and if they don't want you, the Army or Navy will."

There was some basis for this threat too, as it was common for a local judge to tell a boy in trouble with the law that he could have ten days to join the Navy or he would be sent to the reformatory.

We had a good Navy in those days, too. Those young hoodlums would come home on furlough strong, fine men and be heroes to us younger aspirants. They could box, swim a good overhand stroke, row a boat, dance well and romance with girls with tales of far-away places. The flowing black tie on the open middie, the flapping bell bottom trousers, crew cuts, scrubbed skin and clean shave had the smell of the sea. That spelled 'freedom of the seas' to me. I didn't understand the political meaning of that phrase.

The most exciting event during that year at Central School was the day the Ravalli Hotel burned down. The Ravalli Hotel was a deluxe place. It had been built by Marcus Daley, the Montana Copper King, to accommodate the famous guests he often brought from the East and from Europe on his special private train.

In later years I met many people, especially drummers selling everything from clothes to farm equipment who, when they heard I was from Hamilton, had said they'd been guests at the Ravalli Hotel. They told me when they were in that part of the country they would go out of their way to spend a few days there, relaxing and enjoying the social life.

The fire took place during school hours. Because the hotel was just across the street, it was necessary to evacuate the students quickly. The three-story brick hotel was completely gutted. It was never rebuilt. In recent years I visited Hamilton and was a guest at the Elks' Club there. They have a fine lodge on that site which, it appeared to me, was built from the architect's plans of the old hotel. One person present was surprised that I should recognize this fact. He also had been a student in the building and a witness to the hotel fire from the school grounds.

Hamilton was, in the early part of this century, a town of about 2000 residents. It had been the location of a large A.C.M. (Anaconda Copper Mining) Company lumbermill employing several hundred people. They had built a large mill pond covering 200 acres by damming the Bitterroot River. This pond, which was really a lake, provided excellent hunting and trapping for the young nimrods of the town. One had to be careful that the watchman or the A.C.M. Co. warden did not catch you in what they considered their private waters or you would end up facing the judge and the Navy. 'No Trespassing' was enforced.

This was during the period of the I.W.W.'s (International Workers of the World) and socialistic militant labor unions. The workers nominated a socialist mayor, so the story goes, and the A.C.M. Company warned the people of the town that if they elected this man mayor, the company would shut the mill down and move it away. The people elected the mayor and the A.C.M. Company kept their threat, moving the mill to Bonner, Montana, never to open the Hamilton mill again.

The mill was gradually dismantled and disintegrated; one night the wooden dam burned to the water line, thus shrinking the pond to a mere lagoon. It did leave a fine swimming hole for the young people of the town. I expect the truth was that A.C.M. had creamed the easily accessible timber from the valley and would have closed the mill in a year or so anyway. The story sounded pretty oppressive to me. Mother said, "It was a vicious thing for A.C.M. to do."

Would be Huck-Finns. in Father's Army hat, Joe Rennaker, Delbert Greenfield, and Arnie Kyle in the foreground. Arnie was a boy Mother agreed to keep while his widower father served his country in the American Expeditionary Forces in France.

I was all dressed up for picture-taking and listening to Caruso on the Victrola, wondering why the folks thought he was so great. 1917.

Our dog Sandy, not too happy at being harnessed to a cart. Wiggles looks on, happy that he is too small for a cart-dog. I am wearing my father's Army hat. Arnie Kyle and Joe Rennaker fill out the picture.

Lt. O. M. Salisbury Sr., QMC 420 Res. Labor Battalion, Camp Shelby, Miss., as Officer of the Day. I had asked for a picture of him with his revolver showing. I had been reading Zane Grey and Hopalong Cassidy stories and was trying to fit him into that image. Nov. 1918.

Father was acting captain of a company of black soldiers at Camp Shelby.

Hamilton High School senior lettermen, graduating class of 1924. Left to right, Jim Coulter, George Hayes, Fred Roberts, Donald Gordon, Ralph Meager and me. The two in back with heads chopped are Ted Cottrell and George Vogt, too tall to get in the picture.

CHAPTER SIX

Father Comes Home

From the Central School I went on to Hamilton High School. Miss Oberton graduated me from the eighth grade—I think to save her sanity.

Mother received a cablegram: "Will be home soon." At the end of my freshman year Father was returning from Europe. He had been in Albania, Russia, Czechoslovakia, Italy, France and other places in the reconstruction post-war period. The President of Czechoslovakia presented him with an inscribed and signed parchment thanking him for his excellent work there. Father's picture had appeared in Leslie's Weekly, a popular current events magazine. The picture showed him standing between two lovely Red Cross nurses. Neighbors rushed to call my mother's attention to the story. She was not the jealous type. She said to the neighbor, "If it bothered me there's little I could do about it from here."

On his way home Father had sent a letter from Chicago saying he would buy me my first long pant suit at Marshall Field's. Mother sent him my sizes. Marshall Field's was a big name in the Midwest and the Rocky Mountain areas. Anyone going to Chicago surely had to bring back presents to their loved ones from that great store. My first long pant suit was excitement enough. In the early twenties boys wore knee pants and long black stockings until their second year of high school. Needless to say this doubled my excitement and anticipation of seeing Father.

Al and I had some trepidations about Father's homecoming. It sounded like the end of our freedom. About all we remembered of him was his severe disciplinary policies. We were almost certain that the Army had not softened him in this regard.

During Father's absence, Al and I had developed tremendous tempers resulting in constant pummeling of each other. The differences in our ages was beginning to show by now. I was still a boy, but Al was now sixteen. He was very much a young man physically, and developing sophistication. I was a constant source of embarrassment to him. He was on the high school football team and a pretty strong lad. It got to where I didn't make out very well in fist fights with him. Very often it ended in one blow from Al knocking me flat to the ground. This was a little rougher than just a bloody nose and a few scratches as in our earlier encounters. It was becoming very discouraging to me.

The day before Father's return, Al was complaining to Mother during the lunch hour of some conduct of mine that had embarassed him during the general assembly at school. His telling the story so infuriated me that I grabbed for the bread knife to go after him. Mother seized my arm and they wrenched the knife from me, threw me out the back door, slammed and locked it, saying, "Cool off!"

I was so furious that I threw stove wood at the back door, splitting the panels. I then sulked off to the river bottom, not returning to school. I was never going to return home. I would go out into the mountains and become a trapper. I would join the Navy, the Army, be a bum but never, never go home. It was March, and as the sun got low and the temperature dropped, my thoughts and plans changed towards home. I came in sheepishly to be confronted by Mother. She was prepared for me. "Oliver, you do not want me to tell your father of your spectacle and show of bad temper, your disrespect for me and hatred of your brother. You will have to do some apologizing. Your father is bringing home a long pant suit for a young man, not for an ill-tempered boy. He surely will withhold the suit while you do some growing up." This was a tough and bitter pill. I did not mind the apology to Mother so much as the thought of apologizing to Al. I swallowed the pill and made my apologies with no reservations. I am sure that was the last physical combat that Al and I engaged in and to my memory the last time we ever quarreled.

Father arrived the next day on the little Northern Pacific passenger train that ran up the valley and back to Missoula once a day. All my friends in Hamilton were at the depot to meet Father, whom they had never seen. He was greeted and banqueted by all. Coming home so long after the war was a sure way of getting special attention. I got my long pant suit, my little sister her silk Paris gown. I said to Al, "What a waste on an 11-year old brat. She is our father's favorite, no doubt about it."

Father never seemed to run out of knickknacks that he brought home from war surpluses: jacknives, sewing kits, pack sacks, gadgets and gimmicks.

For a time after his return Father took on a lecture tour, telling concerned people about the reconstruction of Europe. Communications were not so thorough as now and his knowledge was early, first-hand news from those faraway isolated areas for whose freedom we had fought.

After a few months of lecturing he obtained a position as assistant to Dr. Ralph Parker, a noted entomologist, who had just been granted an appropriation by the U.S. Public Health Service to carry on a research program on Rocky Mountain spotted fever.

During his absence Al and I had enjoyed a great deal of freedom. We would show up once or twice a day at the poolhall to shoot a game and plan some mischief. Al was sort of a leader of his age group and I, less so, of the younger group. I was more prone to get in trouble, not because I did more mischief, but because I was less skilled than Al. We were famous for being out after curfew.

Al and I were soon to regret that Father had returned. He hadn't been home a week when he called us in and said, "Things are going to be different from now on!" He had tried to go into our upstairs bedroom and had difficulty opening the door. There were boots, skates, skis, snowshoes, traps, guns, fishing poles, raw pelts, a giant snake skin, dirty socks—and the odor you would expect. Father established military discipline: "Every morning before you leave for school your beds are to be made. I will make a daily inspection." He showed us how our boots were to be shined Army style, those we wore and those not in use. Everything extra was moved out to the woodshed to be stored, and even there in orderly and military fashion.

When he called us in the morning from downstairs, we were to "hit the deck." We soon learned that this sound could be produced by lifting and dropping our shoes and in that way getting an extra five minutes sleep. He said, "Out of the house when the first school bell rings, not with the last bell." He never was able to really get control of us again outside the home.

I even practiced deception and defiance to maintain the independence that I had learned to enjoy. Chuck Stanton, Ralph Peterson and I had planned a trip to Twin Lakes, a place I had been before. I had told my friends so many times of my earlier trip with the whiskey smugglers that we had promised ourselves we would go in when we were old enough to manage it. At the end of the summer after my sophomore year in high school we had been working at various summer jobs and had our own money to spend. We felt we were old enough. We rented three horses and planned the trip to Twin Lakes. Father said, "No siree-bob. You don't go to the Twin Lakes. You can go as far as Camp Two on the Lost Horse, but no further."

Well, we went and we went all the way. The other boys had told their parents they were going to Twin Lakes: "Oliver knows the way, he has been there before, no problem."

Word soon leaked back to Father. It was one of those situations where there was absolutely nothing he could do about it except kill me when I got back. I figured he would stop short of that and the trip and experience would have been worth-while, which it was. Twin Lakes was still 55 miles from the nearest farmhouse, so the likelihood of my father following us in did not exist. We were back there about 10 days and thoroughly enjoyed it as 16-year-old boys would.

It was not as exciting as the first trip but there was more freedom. It was a great place to spend ten days. The only incident was that Ralph's horse broke its picket line and went home. Coming out we had to use one horse for a pack horse and take turns riding the remaining horse. The runaway horse was waiting for us at the gate to the National Forest Reserve. Years later, during World War II, I had a touch of nostalgia crossing the Atlantic and wrote to Chuck saying when the war was over I'd like to find Ralph and have the three of us make that trip again. Eventually I received an answer from Chuck saying, "I'd like to make the trip, but we can now drive our cars in there."

In another incident of defiance, I took Father's new Ford roadster without his permission. On a previous occasion, he had generously let me use it for a date to a nice party that I had been invited to. At a later time I knew he would not let me have it, so I just borrowed the car and went to Sleeping Child Hot Springs with Tom Judge, Florence Holbrook and Jeanette Johnson. We had a big time and thoroughly enjoyed the day. I was a pretty big boy by then, a little too big to thrash. All he could do was scold me severely. I knew from that day I had won a degree of freedom from him.

That spring I had developed a crush on Jeanette Johnson and dated her whenever I could. She was popular and I had to ask first if I wanted to be first. That following summer Jeanette and I corresponded while I was away working in the woods at Victor—not love letters, but she was a charming letter writer and managed to convey just enough concern to be tantalizing. She dated other dudes from college, lounging around, not looking for summer jobs but looking for girls. This was frustrating to me, stuck away in the woods in a logging camp. I only got home on the Fourth of July and once in a while on a Saturday night.

I went to the country dances near the camp and carried on like I thought a man should, my examples being the lumberjacks. By my summer work in the woods I earned enough spending money to last me through the following school terms. If I ran short before the year was out I could sign chits in the local soda fountain and poolhalls. These I promised to pay off the following summer.

When I returned to a class reunion of the classes of The Roaring 20's forty years later, I was told by my classmates that they remembered me as 'Peck's Bad Boy.' I didn't remember that I was that bad but in prodding my recall talents I fail to come up with anything that was good about me. Now, in looking at the record, I see where the reputation came from.

In another incident that must have contributed to that reputation, I attended a high school party and got drunk on wine. Mind you, this was during Prohibition. A buddy and I made our own wine. He was a good chemistry student and had worked out a little still for making brandy from hard cider. We made dandelion wine as well. I don't remember what the particular concoction was on the night of the party, but it made me sick and I passed out. My buddy had a horse and sleigh tied outside. Friends took me out and sat me up on the seat of the cutter, wrapped me in robes and let me sleep there while they went back in to enjoy the dance. Everyone saw me out there including the principal.

Monday morning the principal announced in the assembly, "No more high school parties this year!" Everyone knew why.

This didn't help me with Jeanette. Her father called and said, "Oliver, I would like to see you."

I went to his photograph studio with my cap in my hand. Mr. Johnson started in by saying, "I don't think I want you to call on Jeanette any more." He then proceded to lecture me on the evils of alcohol. I was a member of the De Molay, a Masonic-sponsored order, and he was one of the regents. Mr. Johnson sort of had a double hold on me. I admitted to being impressed with what he had said, especially when he threatened to tell my father, who had not heard of the incident.

I said to Mr. Johnson, "If you will not mention our talk to Jeanette or to my father I will change my ways."

Mr. Johnson said, "Oliver, I believe in you. You will be welcome in my home." I never had any more trouble with Mr. Johnson. In fact he seemed to like me very much.

My infatuation with Jeanette was not very productive. She was extremely popular and went out with other guys. I could always have a date provided I asked her in time.

Jeanette was not a beauty but she was cute and sassy. She played the violin in concerts, was a good student and busy in all school activities. We had good chemistry for each other. She seemed fond of me but not to the exclusion of other suitors.

Mr. Johnson was a socialist and Jeanette liked to take radical positions. She was on the high school debating team and competed in state extemporaneous speaking contests.

Since Jeanette would not accept me as her steady I was forced to date other girls, though I carried a big torch for her.

When still a junior in high school, I led a mass hooky rebellion. It was a beautiful mid-April spring day. If you have never experienced the bursting out of spring in the Rocky Mountains, you haven't lived. Spring fever hits you like a tidal wave. The grass is its greenest; buttercups and wild flowers of all descriptions seem to come out as if a theatre curtain were raised on them. The birds suddenly are back, the meadowlarks and song sparrows are at their best, and accompanied by many others become a symphony.

We students lolling on the schoolhouse grass could see the lagoons forming in the green meadows from the high waters backing up in the river bottom a half mile away. Some kids said, "What a day to have to return to classes."

Waiting for the lunch hour gong to ring, I said, "Let's not! Let's go to the river bottom."

About 20 kids yelled, "Yeah!" We took off like stampeded buffalo and traveled that half mile in short time, stripped off our clothes and went skinny dipping in the warm back waters that were flooding the meadow. We stayed naked, played leapfrog, had a track meet, jumping and racing. "What an afternoon!" kids yelled. We could be heard clear to the high school, which brought about the reckoning.

Next morning I was called to the Principal's office. Mr. Powell said, "Oliver, I'm sorry to have to do this, but you were the only Junior in that group. I watched you with field glasses from the third floor and have identified all of you even though you wore no clothes. Since you were the only Junior, I must assume you were the leader. I should expect you to be more responsible. I must expel you from high school for the remainder of this school term."

Mother was able to get the expulsion reduced to a suspension, but I was not allowed to return to classes except to take final exams. With a lot of help from my schoolteacher mother, I passed those exams. Father, strangely, was not angry about this incident. He thought I was wasting my time in school, and about that he was right. He would have consented to my dropping out and going to work. Oddly, he did not value his own college education.

My only real sexual experience while I was in high school was when a friend of mine named John hailed me one early spring Sunday and said, "Hey, let's pick up a couple of girls and go to the river bottom."

I knew what he meant but was inexperienced and I think he was too. He was certainly more aggressive in this direction than I. I don't doubt in looking back but what the 'couple of girls' were prearranged by my friend. He had set me up.

Very shortly we ran into two pretty young girls of fifteen. We were seventeen. My friend John asked them, "Would you girls like to go for a walk to the river bottom?" All too readily, they consented.

My girl was a cute blonde of Finnish descent with a good figure. She seemed to have as good an idea of where and why we were going as I did. John and I had long before surveyed out a location for such an experience. It being Sunday and both of us being, by compulsion, churchgoing lads, we were dressed in our Sunday best. I had found that if I went to church I'd be pretty free for the rest of the day.

In searching for the ideal location for such an escapade, we had anticipated that it would take place on a Sunday, that being a kind of promenade day in a small town, especially on a balmy spring Sunday.

I can't remember her name but I well remember what she looked like in the nude. She was not a girl that I knew, but she must have been in the first year of high school. She lived in Finn Town, which was a chauvinistic word for the 'ghetto,' if one could use that term for the poorer section of a small town.

If a young man wanted to go out with the 'uppity' girls of the town, he could not afford to be seen with a girl from Finn Town. Therefore, the river bottom. The place we had picked out was down below the A.C.M. dam, a swampy area made up of lagoons, tall cattails, rank vegetation—a veritable jungle. There were old disintegrating dikes running through the swamp left over from the mill days. One of these dikes had deteriorated to a mere path which, being elevated, was dry. I expect hunters and fishermen used it to get to the lagoons and the river. This path opened up on a little knoll or island that was a sunny oasis in the jungle of the swamp. The trail and dry ground ended here. Hunters and fishermen would need to wear rubber boots and wade in the swamp to go further. The likelihood of disturbance or interruption was remote. The knoll was carpeted with green grass and soft moss. It was a beautiful spot to relax and even more beautiful for what we had in mind.

When we arrived at the trail entering this area, my friend John said, "You go on. We'll wait here for you and give a loud shrill whistle if anyone starts in on the path. When you come out, we'll go in." The girls never said a word though they seemed to be sort of twittering like birds, or that may have been all that I was hearing in my anticipation and excitement. I am sure if my girl had not spoken a word of English, we would have still understood each other as perfectly. The throbbing of her hand was like the electric pulses from a low voltage cycle generator, strong and steady.

When we arrived at the end of the trail and at the knoll, without any preliminaries she undressed and lay on the grass. She was a beautiful sight with her ivory white body shining in the warm spring sunlight filtering through the trees, her pubic hair glittering like a gem, catching the gold of the sun. She appeared very scared, but very willing. I am sure she was a virgin just as I was.

I undressed and lay beside her, also scared but eager. Just at that moment the noise of splashing boots came through the swamp not 200 feet away. We lay quiet and breathless, hoping the intruder would continue on through the swamp. I could see him by raising to my elbow. My little sweetheart's body shone like a lighthouse beacon. He spotted it and stepped behind a tree to witness what he hoped would be a titillating scene. Being already scared, this scared me stiff (a poor word to describe my physical condition).

We jumped into our clothes, out of there and back to our friends, who then also became frightened. The hunter might have been a big brother, father, neighbor or certainly a person who would like to tell the story of what he saw in the swamp that afternoon.

I felt robbed of a great and exciting experience. It was to have been a purely sexual one, but in looking back one never knows how that would have ended had the act been consummated. I feel that I was robbed but was more than likely spared. Spared what? Happiness? Perhaps! It certainly might have given a new direction to my life.

When I came home, Father asked, "Where have you been?" in that accusing voice of his with all its disciplinary severity. I felt very guilty and probably looked even more so, thinking that G.D. hunter had probably already reported me.

I said, "To the river bottom."

"In those clothes?"

"Well, I just went for a walk on dry paths."

"That's how you got mud on your shoes?" I thought sure I had been seen. Under direct questioning I dared not lie to my father. He asked, "Who were your friends?"

I said, "Oh, some kids from Finn Town."

"You know, son, if you are seen playing with those hoodlums you will not get that job in the bank when you graduate." There had been some talk with the local banker of one of my father's boys coming into the bank to work. Brother Al already had rejected that idea and after graduation had escaped to western Washington, where he hoped to enter the University of Washington after working a year. I had no intention, ambition or desire to spend my life as a small town bank teller.

I was convinced Father knew something. Looking back, I don't believe he did. He had just taken a shot in the dark. If the shot was an accusation of misdemeanor, I was generally guilty and would make a full confession. This time I did not, but I was sufficiently frightened by the whole experience that I did not attempt to repeat it or pursue consummation of the desire.

Just before my senior year in high school, Father left again. He resigned from the U.S. Public Health Service and went to Seattle, Washington to try to relocate the family in an area where he hoped to have better opportunities.

With his absence I was back on 'Freedom Road,' to use Howard Fast's title. As a Senior I began to mature a little. I was no longer a nightmare to the teachers; in fact, they seemed to like me. I was on the high school football team and in the senior play—in neither case a star, but I was there. It was fun. I began to give serious thought to what I would do when I graduated.

CHAPTER SEVEN

I Graduate and Leave Hamilton

Father's library on the ranch had been a vast one. Many of these books had been given Father by our uncle Isaac Petersen of Row Petersen and Company, a publishing house that was the beginning of what is now Harper and Row Publishing Company, one of the largest in the nation. Father worked for Row Petersen as a salesman. Petersen was his brother-in-law. When father was in the Army and we moved to Hamilton, Mother donated its 5000 volumes to the Carnegie Public Library of Hamilton. I recall the bugging eyes of an illiterate mountain man sitting in Father's study on the ranch and looking with fear at those books as if they might jump out and bite him.

Because of our isolation, Christmas and birthdays always brought more books from our generous aunts and uncles in the East. A book for us was a safe gift. I was not an avid reader by comparison to the rest of the family. I was forced to read. My inclination was to play cards or games, or rough-house with my brother or my little sister.

I Graduate & Leave Hamilton

After supper on the ranch all other members of the family would settle down with a book next to the bright white light of an Aladdin lamp. My interruptions would be treated with a rude "Shut up!" from my brother. Older sister, if she was home, would complain to Mother about my distractions; little sister would follow suit with, "Oliver is bothering me!"

Out of forced isolation I would go to the book shelves and take down a book. Once into it I would continue and finish. I never was the fast reader that the rest of the family seemed to be. My favorite authors were James Fenimore Cooper, Jack London, Rex Beach, James Oliver Curwood, Zane Grey, Joseph Conrad, and anyone that wrote about the sea or the far North.

When about ten, I read *The Autobiography of a Grizzly Bear* by Ernest Thompson Seton, which sent me wailing and weeping when the bear died. I read it a second time with the same result. Mother had difficulty consoling me, saying, "Oliver, it's only a story."

Out of this compulsory and later voluntary reading I did acquire a life goal. I decided at some point during those years that after I finished high school I would go and see that wonderful big world that lay outside of the Bitterroot Valley. I even formed a sort of itinerary. First it would be Jack London's country, the far North. Then it would be the Orient. I would do it as Jack London did—by being a lumberjack, a seaman, or whatever other occupation would provide travel, food, and, most of all, freedom.

I graduated from Hamilton High School at ten o'clock of an early May evening in 1924 and left at six o'clock the next morning for the Pacific Coast. Not because I did not love home, but because I had a mission to fulfill: to see the world. A classmate, Dick Peterson, whose family had moved to Wenatchee, Washington, and left him behind to finish his school term, had invited me to travel with him and stop over in Wenatchee as his guest.

I received $44 cash for graduation presents from uncles and aunts, eight five-dollar bills and two two-dollar bills. A ticket to Seattle was about $21. Fifty-some years later, I am still traveling on that $44. I mean that I never had to write home for money, though I sent a good deal of it home to help Father and Mother during their hard times.

Brother Al had gone to Washington State earlier and had obtained work out on the Olympic Peninsula as a milker and later as a bridgebuilder for the Milwaukee R.R. What he could do, I could do. (This wasn't always true, but I always believed it to be.)

Father had gone to Seattle in an effort to expand his horizons. He had become distressed with the politics in the U.S. Public Health Laboratory at Hamilton. Father had never been one to stay where he was unhappy or where there was friction among others close by. He was having a difficult time getting relocated in Seattle. A post-World-War-I recession was then in full swing. In response to my enthusiastic announcement that I was coming to Seattle after graduation he had written, warning me not to come and be a burden to him. Now, as a father of grown children I can appreciate his position; but at the time I knew, of course, I could not be a burden to anyone.

Mother, always operating on some kind of inner intuition, had said, "Oliver, you go anyway." She was planning to sell the house in Hamilton that summer and follow the rest of us over when she got word from Father to come.

Montana had not been too good to the folks. They had moved out there from a good middle-class life in Madison, Wisconsin, to the rigors of a ranch life up on the benchland of the Bitterroot Mountains in western Montana. Father had resigned from a fine position with Ginn & Company, publishers, to move his family to what he thought would be a more wholesome, freer way of life.

Though financially disastrous to our folks, the ranch life had been good for us children. Father and Mother had many fine friends through their association with the University of Wisconsin and through my grandfather, who was president of what was then Whitewater Normal School, later to become The University of Wisconsin, Whitewater. Professors from the great universities were our frequent summer visitors. President Guy Ford of the University of Minnesota was a summer visitor with us on the ranch. Professor Frank Smith, a naturalist from the University of Michigan, spent several summers with us. Sixty-odd years later, I still possess an autographed pocket butterfly book he gave me for Christmas, 1915. Father gave Al and me the summer assignment of showing Professor Smith whatever he wanted to see. He taught us to recognize the birds, the wild animals, the trees and flowers by their proper names and to love them.

However severe and sometimes cruel a disciplinarian my father was, that fact seemed to have nothing to do with the respect and love his peers held for him. Today Al and I often say, "The older we get, the more reverence we have for him." The strap marks on our backs quickly disappeared, but the interest he taught us in life has been retained.

My friend Dick Peterson and I left early the morning after graduation, taking the Bitterroot Special to Missoula where we transferred to a mainliner for Spokane. In Spokane we had to stay overnight to transfer from the Northern Pacific to the Great Northern in order to get to Wenatchee on the Columbia River. We stayed at the Davenport Hotel that night and went to a vaudeville show, the first I had ever seen. I was so impressed that before I went to bed that night I wrote Mother of my excitement and lamented the fact that we had lived in a little place like Hamilton and missed all the great fun in the world. I had an exhilarated feeling of freedom. I was on on my way.

We arrived in Wenatchee the next afternoon. Again, I was impressed with the tremendous size of the Columbia River. It was late May and the river was very high. I stayed on with my friend and his family for several days. They took me on a picnic to Lake Chelan, where once again I could not get over the size of things. What a big lake!

I went on to Seattle alone, arriving there in the early evening.

I had not sent word to Father. Mother said, "Surprise him." The King Street Station was, I was sure, the busiest place in all the world. Trains arriving and departing. Noise with train callers, hucksters, newsboys, train whistles, taxicab horns and the rushing sounds of a city, which in no way related to the sound of movement of leaves in the trees, the wind or the gentle sounds I was used to. I loved it though. It was invigorating. This was the world!

How to get out to Father's address? I took a taxi through a beautiful part of the city. The clustered arc lights in Seattle residential areas were soft and inviting. Rhododendrons were in full bloom and many other flowering shrubs that I had never seen before. It was fragrant and exciting.

When I arrived at Father's door, I paid the taxi driver. "Two dollars and fifty cents. Whew!" I exclaimed, noting my fast dwindling $44. I rang the door bell.

A woman who appeared to be the landlady answered the door. She called up, "Mr. Salisbury, a young man to see you."

Father came down the stairs. His greeting was, "What are you doing here? You can't stay here." I had expected this kind of a greeting. I had long ago ceased to fear him, though I was feeling a bit awed and lonely and would have welcomed a warm reception.

The landlady was kind and offered to put a cot in Father's room.

He thawed a bit and said, "Well, now that you are here, let's see what can be done about it, aside from sending you back."

The next day he called a friend of his, Mr. John Ryan, an old classmate from the University of Wisconsin and a successful lawyer in Seattle. Mr. Ryan invited me to come to his office. He was friendly and really exerted himself to help. He sent me to Mr. Rhodes of Rhodes department store, with a special note of introduction. Mr. Rhodes was not too impressed. I was wearing a high school sweater with the big H still on it. I was a yokel and it stuck out all over. Mr. Rhodes said they might have a vacancy in the dry goods department in a few weeks and that I could keep in touch. I asked where the dry goods department was. He told me and I walked through, seeing nothing but ribbons and yard goods. I made a mental note not to come back there. What would my friends in Montana think of me, a ribbon clerk? A far cry from the far North.

Mr. Ryan continued his efforts and introduced me to his son, Burns. Burns was a student at Broadway High School—a friendly and competent young man, city-wise and really with it. Burns invited me to spend some time with the Ryans at their summer home, a big weathered farmhouse on Mercer Island. Burns owned a catboat and took me sailing on Lake Washington. There were a lot of young people around and it was fun, but I was restless to get on with my quest of adventure and felt a little uncomfortable among all those rich kids, though certainly there was no lack of friendliness and hospitality on the part of Burns and the Ryans. These young people were all college-bound, and my goals were different.

I Graduate & Leave Hamilton

During high school vacations in Montana, I had held several different jobs in the woods. Now that I was in Seattle, I started hanging around the Skid road where workmen were hired. There were huge bulletin boards in front of 'crimp joints' where jobs were posted. Flunky, whistle punk, grease-monkey, bull-cook, and swamper were titles that I thought I could handle. When they posted these unskilled jobs, a great crowd would jam into the front of the employment office door. They always selected someone before I ever got in close to the man who did the interviewing.

The Alaska cannery crews had already been hired and sailed, so my ambition in that direction was frustrated for the time. I was not to see the Silver Horde (Rex Beach's salmon run) that year.

While I was standing gaping at one of those skid road bulletin boards, an Army sergeant tapped me on the shoulder. "How about the U.S. Army in the Philippines, young man?" he said.

I replied, "I'm a high school graduate. I think too much of myself to ever join the peacetime Army. The Army is made up of the scum of the earth." (The latter part of my statement was an alleged quotation from William Howard Taft, when he was Governor General of the Philippines.)

The sergeant said, "Oh! a high school graduate, eh!" Instead of being ruffled by the put-down he picked up on my ego. "What do you expect to do?"

"I'm going to Alaska."

"Alaska! How would you like to go to Alaska and have a dog team, a horse, a cabin, guns, food and all the ammunition you need for hunting and be paid well besides?"

He was now talking my language. "How can I do that?" I asked, my enthusiasm rising by leaps and bounds.

The sergeant was already leading me towards the Fort Lawton street car. "Well, we have a school right up here in the Arcade Building where they train ten students and teach them telegraphy, wireless and the whole bit. The school is nine months, then they send you up to a station like I've described. You must be a high school graduate to get into the school."

I showed a bit of courage and demanded that he show me the school before going out to Fort Lawton.

He took me up to the school where I was given an IQ test and a little examination and sent out to Fort Lawton in the escort of the sergeant. I passed the physical exam. Then, because I was only 18, the Army had to have my parents' consent. I gave them Mother's Montana address, thinking that I could explain it all to Father. The sergeant had said, "You aren't really in the Army, just sort of on detached service but you do have to be sworn in for three years."

Mother sent a one-word telegram back, "No!" I took Father down to the school and introduced him to Charles Murphy, civilian superintendent of the Washington Alaska Military Cable and Telegraph System, abbreviated WAMCATS. Mr. Murphy introduced Father to Colonel J. D. L. Hartman, officer in charge of the system. He gave his consent, and by correspondence with Mother obtained hers after several days' delay.

Mr. Murphy arranged for a hotel room and meal tickets on credit and right downtown. I was down to my last 60¢ of the $44 graduation gift and I escaped being a burden on Father or anyone else.

The WAMCATS school worked out very much as the sergeant had described. I went to school six hours a day, five days a week, wore civilian clothes, drew commutation and ration allowance, and lived where I wanted to. The cash money came to $81 a month. This was much better than the $60-a-month ribbon clerk job I might have had at Rhodes working a ten-hour day, six days a week.

The other students were compatible. They were my age, and most of them came from rural areas of the Yakima Valley in Washington, one student having recruited another. They teased me about going 'ba-a-a-a-a-ck to Montana'—referring to sheep country—and I learned to call them 'appleknockers from Yakima.' I liked telegraphy and studied and practiced hard at it, even coming back in the evenings on my own. We students were all anxious to get assignment to Alaska and to become apprentices on the cable, radio and telegraph circuits.

The U.S. Army Signal Corps operated the communications system to Alaska just as the Military Telegraph had in the frontier days of the West. The Army had laid a cable from Seattle to Sitka in 1901 that had been replaced by a new cable to Ketchikan in 1924. This made Ketchikan a big relay point for the rest of Alaska.

I Graduate & Leave Hamilton 51

I was a good typist, having learned that in high school, and had some advantage over those who had to learn typing in addition to telegraphy.

After only five months I was sent to Ketchikan as a student operator. It was raining heavily when I got there in October, and it never stopped until I left there the following July.

Calvin Coolidge was President and, typical of his party, he immediately began federal retrenchment programs. One was to heavily cut the budget of the Army, which caused the WAMCATS to reduce personnel. Each station was given its quota to transfer off the system. This was worse than getting fired, since they didn't discharge you but sent you out to a line outfit, the infantry or artillery, the Philippines or the Canal Zone. If you were transferred out in this manner you lost your ratings and ended up with $21 per month and no allowances. This was a disaster to a married man. They picked misperformers, malcontents, inepts and those who could not stay out of debt on the pay they got.

I did not fall into any of these categories; however, a young married man with three children, who (little wonder) could not stay out of debt, was selected to be transferred to the infantry at Fort Lawton for reassignment. I felt very sorry for this young man and his family. I thought it was awful and wished that I could help in some way.

The morning after hearing about it, I was walking down to the cable office in a pouring rain and cursing the wet with each sloshing step. I was thinking of the tragedy of this family and I thought, Why don't I go in his place? Get myself out of this G.D. rain, and do that couple and their little kids a great big favor.

When I got to the office I suggested this to the Chief Operator, who didn't like me very well anyway. He said, "O.K."

Mr. Quist, the Chief Operator, was a character himself. He was a warrant officer and was always saying, "I was made a Mr. by an act of Congress and they all call me 'Q'."

To put it mildly, I didn't like him either. This feeling stemmed from an incident that occurred when Secretary of the Navy Wilbur was due in Ketchikan with a flotilla of Navy destroyers and was scheduled to make an inspection of the cable office and radio station. I was working at the radio station three miles out of town. I heard the order coming in over the telegraph sounder just as I was going off duty. The order instructed all personnel to appear in full uniform and muster on the dock when the

Secretary came off the destroyer. The order was signed "Q, Chief Operator."

In the first place, I didn't have a uniform, as I had sold it, shoes and all, to a pawnbroker in Seattle; second, the order had not yet been posted, I only heard it by accident; third and most important, I had planned a duck-hunting trip that day. I took off like a shot with my gun for a mountain lake.

Mr. Quist was furious that I wasn't there for the muster and wouldn't accept my excuse that I din't know about the order. I suspect the bootlicker that copied his message down had told him I was there when it came in on the wire. I lied and said I couldn't read the Morse telegraph that fast. Mr. Q was dumbfounded and didn't know what to do. He threatened to court-martial me, but knew he had no way of being able to prove that I could read the message as it came in. He did nothing about it, but from then on he seemed to dislike me. He was not, in any case, unhappy to see me go.

Along with the other transfers from up and down the coast of Alaska, I came south on the old SS Northwestern. On board I met a 'performer,' a maverick, a character by the name of Cornelius J. Vernooy, also transferring out. He qualified for transfer for all of the reasons mentioned, but he was a veteran of the military services and was a master at 'goldbricking.' He knew his way around. Vernooy told me, "When you get to Fort Lawton, immediately ask for a three months' furlough. The officers there already have a problem of what to do with us and that will give them a solution. Since you won't yet have been transferred to another outfit you will continue to draw subsistence allowances and will have a nice payoff coming when you come back from furlough." Then he added,"By then the WAMCATS will need men again and you can go see Mr. Murphy. Since there is nothing against your record, he will send you back to Alaska if that is what you want."

It sounded like a diabolical scheme, but I followed his advice. It worked out just that way, except that I got chicken-hearted and only asked for two months instead of three. Two is what they gave me.

After a quick visit with my folks, I took off for Montana. I was a bit homesick for that place and still somewhat in love with my high school sweetheart, Jeanette. We had been carrying on a heavy correspondence while I was in Alaska. She had written of her plans to attend Montana State Normal School in Dillon, then teach awhile and go on to the University of Montana. There was nothing in our letters that indicated any great change in our relationship since high school but she did express care for me. I was anxious to see her. I was rather hopeful but had no plans for doing anything about it. I felt that I had to be in a position to support a wife before I could ask a girl to become one. The idea of marriage was in conflict with my plans for seeing the world. Jeanette sounded as though she had such long-range plans too; somewhere down the road we might later get together. This feeling on my part had never been articulated, but I thought maybe this summer I would do that.

A group of cable operators at Ketchikan, Alaska. From left to right, Charlie Arnold, Evald Hansen, me, Lloyd Steele, James Barnwell, Cornelius Vernooy and Eddie Krepper. 1925.

Sara Sjursen, a lovely girl friend in Ketchikan—but she married the other guy. We have been and still are life-long friends. 1924.

Jeanette Johnson, the girl I went back to Montana to see and ended up quarreling with. 1925.

With my first car. Mother and Father visited me in Ketchikan on their way to Klawock, Alaska, where Father became superintendent of the government school and Mother a teacher. 1926.

Relaxing in Golden Gate Park, San Francisco. Ellison Barber sitting while I am reclining. 1929.

CHAPTER EIGHT

Return To The Bitterroot

My elder sister, Winifred, still lived in the Bitterroot Valley in a village named Victor, about 15 miles down the Valley from Hamilton. When I arrived in Missoula, Montana was having a heat wave. I spent the night in the Florence Hotel. When the clerk saw me register from Alaska he said, "My God, what did you leave that country for at this time of year?"

I soon understood what he meant. I had to get up and take a cold shower every half hour during that night just to survive the heat. Next morning I called my sister and asked her to meet the train in Victor. Winnie said, "Oliver, what in the world are you doing over here?"

I replied, "Winnie, for the next two months I'm going to go where and do what I cockeyed well please."

After a day with Winnie, I went on to Hamilton. I found most of my friends were out in the woods or on the farms working. I soon became bored, having quarreled with Jeanette the second day after our reunion. I became too aggressive, thinking Alaska women had taught me something. Jeanette said, "Oliver, you may have changed, but I haven't." I walked off in a huff. I never saw her again, though we did resume our correspondence some time later; but nothing ever developed from it.

I then met a young fellow my age named Jack Curry who had moved to Hamilton from North Dakota. He was an adventurous, strong, good-looking young man, son of a dentist and a perfect buddy for me. His mother seemed to take a dim view of me, having heard of my 'Peck's Bad Boy' reputation and then the added worldly stories of adventures in Alaska that I was rapidly spreading through my circle of friends as we lolled around the ol' swimming hole.

Jack and I added an old friend of mine named Tom Judge to become a trio. Out of boredom we decided to go to the Big Hole Basin and work in the hay. Tom had a car. The Big Hole Basin is in the southwestern part of the state, about 90 miles from Hamilton. The elevation is so high that it frosts every night of the year, with the result that wild hay is the only crop that can be produced there. It is a big plateau covering thousands of acres. The little town of Wisdom is the post office. Wisdom was a natural for a Hollywood western set—ponies tied up at the hitching posts and an occasional flivver also parked in front of the hitching post. Messages came in from the outside world to the central telephone operator, who was the sole contact for the community.

These hay ranches were big spreads. The ranchers put up wild hay in huge stacks spaced out over their meadows. In the winter great herds of cattle were driven in to winter on the hay as it was fed out to them. The hay was grown from a native wild grass that grew so rank it was four feet high when cut. It was fine quality hay.

The ranchers owned large herds of nearly wild horses which were rounded up before haying season and broken to harness and hitched to mowers, rakes, bull rakes and wagons. These horses were never fed an oat in their entire lives. They survived on wild grass and it seemed to harmonize with their dispositions.

In earlier days the ranchers had killed off all the mustang stallions and replaced them with Percheron stallions to give colts of the mustang mares some size. These were the horses we made hay with. On this particular ranch there were 60 teams working (120 horses). Every night the horses were turned loose to graze in the meadows. Each morning the wranglers rounded them up and brought them into a big high pole corral where they were roped and harnessed for the day's work. This was the ranch that Jack, Tom, and I were hired on as hay hands.

Jack was a good man with horses. The foreman spotted that on his first skirmish in the wrangler's corral and gave him a team of spirited grays that had kicked and broken an Indian's leg and run away just the day before.

Jack hitched the team to a mower with the aid of the foreman. The horses were blindfolded with jackets over their heads while they were harnessed. When they were fully hitched, the foreman jerked the jackets off their heads and yelled to Jack, "You're on your own."

He took off out of that barnyard and down the half-mile stretch to the hay fields like a Roman chariot. After he got to the hayfield he cut a few figure eights in the field with the mower and then the team settled down and went to work with Jack, their master.

After watching Jack, Tom said, "I don't want a team." They gave him a job in the cookhouse, helping the women who prepared the meals for that big crew of hard-working men.

The wrangler lassoed a big pair of black mares for me. The foreman said, "Those two just foaled colts yesterday. They won't be two peppy or hard to handle. There are so many black horses, rip up a necktie and tie a piece on each mare's mane so you can recognize them and get the same horses tomorrow, then they will learn to work together."

He was right. They were fairly gentle, but the mule colts were hungry and pesky and in the way while I was getting the harnesses on. I let them nurse and fill their bellies. Then the dummies had all they wanted of their mothers and wouldn't follow. I left them in the barnyard.

I got along fine until about 11 o'clock, when the team became hard to handle. One of the foremen who rode around on horseback troubleshooting saw I was in difficulties. He came riding up and asked, "What did you do with the colts?"

I told him, "They became a nuisance so I left 'em in the barnyard."

He said, "That's your trouble; the mares' bags are tight. Bring 'em alongside the fence over there by that haystack and I'll milk them out." He did this with some difficulty since they kicked out at him viciously because their udders were tight and tender. He got out enough milk to relieve them. Late in the afternoon the same situation began to develop. The foreman again rode up and said, "Since it's four o'clock and near quittin' time, take 'em in to their colts."

I started them for the barn a half-mile away. A long lane led out from the barns toward the field, with an open gate at the field end and another closed at the barnyard. The mule colts were starved. Someone opened the gate at the barnyard and the colts spotted their mothers and came galloping down the lane. My team of mother mares saw them and broke into a dead gallop too. I was trying my best to hold them when a rein broke. We were hell-bent for election on that big bouncy two-wheeled rake, and I saw they would never hit that first gate straight. I jumped free without injury, but those mares hit the other side, knocking off both wheels. They then scattered that rake to Kingdom Come.

I didn't get fired that night, but the next morning I was showing some timidity in the corral with that big herd of horses plunging around and the foreman said, "I'm gonna let you go. I'm scared you'll get hurt."

I said, "You're not half as scared of me getting hurt as I am." He laughed and was nice about it and said he regretted that he was going to lose my buddy who was doing so well with the gray team on the mower.

Tom had already been struck by homesickness after peeling the first sack of potatoes and had left for home with his car, leaving Jack and me a note apologizing for stranding us in the Big Hole Basin.

My good buddy Jack quit his gray team of wild horses to join me in quest of new adventure. Jack said, "It's just a matter of time before those gray demons give me the same treatment they did the Indian. They watch me out of the corner of their eyes all the time. They were spookin' me."

The next day we went into Wisdom and were loafing around there, trying to figure out how to get back to Hamilton, when a U.S. Forest Ranger came in and said, "You, you and you come with me. There's a big fire up Canyon Creek." He had a commanding voice and we were curious and therefore willing. Besides, the sheriff was standing there with him.

Before we knew it we were on a truck headed for that big fire. We were dumped out of the truck and onto wagons and finally out of the wagons, loaded up with picks, shovels and gear and told to hike. We hiked for several miles straight towards the flames and smoke. By the time we got to the first fire, it had been brought under control and another fire had started farther back up the canyon. I got a dividend for dragging my feet since they told me and another fellow to stay behind to patrol the fire paths that had been cut around the first fire and make sure the fire didn't spread.

The ranger took Jack and the rest of the crew and went back up the canyon several miles to fight the new fire. I didn't see Jack for ten days. Those of us left behind were the first to get fed when the bull-cook came in with pack animals loaded with food in fireless cookers. The fare was usually hot pork and beans, bread and coffee, and sometimes home-baked apple pies donated by generous ranch wives trying to help. Jack later told me the fires he was fighting were so hot they didn't dare bring pack animals in that close, so they had very little to eat. I didn't have a thing to do except to take an occasional trip around a half-mile circle to make sure the fire didn't creep across the fire trail. At night we had to keep a log fire going to keep warm. After ten days they finally got the fires under control by building backfires, and then a summer shower did the rest.

Jack and I were told we would have to go into Dillon, Montana, to get paid for the fire-fighting unless we wanted to have our checks mailed to us. Jack and I had no way to travel back to Hamilton; besides we didn't trust government red tape and believed in the old saying of 'a bird in the hand....' We went to Dillon for the payoff, which we received in cash. We bought some new Levis and shirts, then went to barbershop and got haircuts, shaves and baths.

We decided to have a little fun and then catch a freight train for Butte. While we were walking around, fun caught up with us. A girl Jack had known in North Dakota came by with a cute girl friend. They had been attending summer school at Montana State Normal School. We had a nice evening with them and agreed to meet them in North Dakota sometime. I really got a crush on that little girl. Her name was Eloise Plunkett and we corresponded for years. She went on to the University of Minnesota and later married.

Jack and I hopped a freight into Butte, which was a division point on the railroad. We were debating whether to go back to Missoula and Hamilton or go to Reeder, North Dakota, where Jack had lived before and which he said was only 40 miles from where Eloise lived. I said,"If an eastbound train comes first, we'll hop it; if westbound, we'll hop it."

Jack said, "O.K." Just then an eastbound freight came around the bend. We hopped it. It's a long ride on a freight train across the state of Montana, but we enjoyed it.

Looking at a timetable that I had helped myself to in the passenger station in Butte, I said to Jack, "This train won't stop at Reeder. It's not a division point."

"That's all right. There's a long grade just outside Reeder. The train will slow down and we can jump."

Two days later, as we finally approached Reeder, Jack noticed that the grade had been taken out since he lived there. The train we were on was barreling along at a terrific speed. Jack jumped and the momentum rolled him over and over until he hit the fence at the edge of the right of way. It was harder for me to make the jump after seeing how it went for him, but I did, with the same result.

We worked for 30 days harvesting wheat in North Dakota under an August sun that never let up. I drove a bundle wagon and loaded it myself. Jack got a tough job again, feeding the bundles into the thrasher. It was a 10-hour day. We slept in a big tent on straw. I had to take care of my team before and after the 10 hours in the field. Jack had a bonus here, with no team to care for.

We were paid $5 per day and board and blanket on the straw. No deducts. The farmer gave me $150 in cash when I quit. Cutting a slit in my Levis to make it like a money belt, I tucked the money into the seam and was ready for the return trip. My only other possession was a toothbrush.

The farmer said he could pay us $5.50 per day if we would stay through the harvest another 30 days. Jack said he'd stay if I didn't mind going back alone. I had to be back in Seattle since I was on a 60-day military furlough from Fort Lawton—an oppressive thought at the moment, and a severe inhibition to my freedom of movement. I never did get to see Eloise, who lived at Mott, 40 miles away on a different railroad and highway.

The way back was long and lonely. I hopped what I thought was a fast-moving freight in Miles City, Montana, to wake up ten hours later still in the yard at Miles City. After we finally got moving I got off the freight in Harlowtown and walked uptown to get a meal in a restaurant. The sheriff arrested me and said I could have my choice: "Twenty days on the county rock pile or thirty days in the harvest fields." I explained to the sheriff that I was on a military leave and due back in Seattle on the day after Labor Day. He could understand that and said, "I want no part of the Army." Fortunately, I had a furlough paper in my wallet. He then said, "There'll be a westbound freight at six p.m. and I want you on it. If I see you again I'll put you in the lock-up and throw the key away." I made that six o'clock freight.

I made a friend on the empty boxcar that I had crawled into. A nice guy, he seemed. The next day when the train stopped and broke up to remake at a division point, he suggested we go to the river and have a swim and get cleaned up. I grew a very heavy black beard for a young man, which after a few days of not shaving didn't help my appearance. He loaned me his soap and razor and again got after me on keeping up appearances, citing the advantages of always looking neat. While we were dressing I noticed a forty-five automatic pistol lying beside his clothes. I asked him why.

"No bum is going to bother me," he said. I could believe that. We finally separated in Butte.

I lived in the jungles (hobo jargon for the edge of the railroad yards) all the way. Didn't dare jingle my money, let alone show that I had a hundred and fifty dollars.

In Deer Lodge a brakeman spotted me and said, "Kid, you can't ride this train unless you've got a card."

I asked, "What kind of a card?"

The brakey said, "A red card, an I.W.W. card! What do you do? Where are you going?"

I told him I was a telegrapher, had been working in the harvest fields, and was on my way back to Seattle to my telegraph job.

The brakey said, "Do you belong to the Railroad Telegraphers' Union? Why do you think you got that big money in the harvest fields? Us Wobblies [I.W.W.'s] drove the wages up on the railroad and in the woods and now the farmer has to pay more to get harvest help. See how it works, kid! I'll let you ride but think about what I've said."

I did a lot of thinking for a long time about what he said. I thought to myself, It makes sense at that.

As we came into Missoula, through the Hellgate Canyon, past the University of Montana, I hopped off the train to follow my friend's advice and clean up. I got down the bank along the South Fork of the Lewis River, took off my clothes and swam out. I went a little too far, and the current carried me a couple of hundred yards downstream to the other side. I then had to huddle, crouch and creep, naked, along the rocks, since the highway passed close to the river on that side. Finally, I got far enough upstream so I could cross and land where my clothes were.

I walked into Missoula City Center to a barbershop at five minutes before six. The barber said, "Don't think for a minute I'm going to start on you now!" I was again unshaven and my clothes and shoes were dirty. I decided to start hiking up the Bitterroot Valley and maybe hitch a ride. Just as I reached the city limits of Missoula, a couple of yokels came rolling by in a 1916 Ford flivver, brass radiator hood, no top and a homemade box for a truck bed. I recognized them as Luke Laugerquist and Jim Colter from Hamilton. I hailed them and they stopped like country bumpkins do, not recognizing me, but stopping anyway. Both were flabbergasted when they learned my identity. They were headed for Wenatchee, Washington, to pick apples.

I borrowed their car and rode up the Bitterroot Valley to Victor, where my sister lived. I had left my suitcase and good clothes with her. I had some very good clothes too. I thought I was Beau Brummel with Stetson hat, Hart Schaffner and Marx suit, and Florsheim shoes, all in the style and vogue of the day. I gave my sister $130 to send on for me in care of my folks. I kept $20 for expenses and took off.

My friends were waiting for me in Missoula and we were off for Wenatchee again. We slept in a strawstack near French Town, crawling into a hole eaten out by cattle. It was a cold night so we closed up the hole after ourselves. In the morning a great herd of cattle was at the strawstack, and the first guy to open up our hole stared a huge bull right in the eye. He quickly closed the hole again while the bull roared disapproval. The bull finally went away and we made it to our car.

When we arrived in Wenatchee, I looked up my old friend Dick Peterson and his brother George and spent a night with them. I really cleaned up, getting a haircut and putting on my powder-blue suit and matching Stetson. I bought a ticket to Seattle on the Oriental Limited and was waiting on the platform to board the train when my old friend from the freight train with the 'keep-clean' lecture and the forty-five automatic saw me. He said, "God! What bank did you hit? I didn't read about it! You learn fast, kid!" He was boarding the same train but riding the blinds, which on the Oriental Limited was very dangerous. I never saw him again, but I expect he made it to Seattle. The conductor was calling, "All aboard!" and I didn't have time to explain to him how I got the good clothes. I left him behind looking dumbfounded.

The trip was not over yet. I arrived in Seattle about 1 a.m. and, of course, broke. I had spent what money I had kept on me in Wenatchee for the ticket. I had a two-bit piece and I was starved. I figured a piece of pie and coffee for fifteen cents would leave me with a dime for streetcar fare out to the folks. All that I needed. Looking back, I think sometimes I pushed my luck.

There was an Owl—a late-night streetcar—running out to the University of Washington campus at 2:30 a.m. I figured that would put me out where my folks lived about three o'clock and I would walk around the University campus until five o'clock before waking them up. After I got out to the campus I remembered that I would have to wake the people downstairs to get up to the flat where Father and Mother lived, since I didn't have a key. I thought I'd better not wake the landlord up before six o'clock. I walked and walked and I'd been up since the morning before. Finally it was light and I went to the folks' address. I laid on the bell and the landlord opened the door. I explained who I was. He said, "Your folks moved a month ago. I have no address for them."

Well, holy mackerel! Here I was way out by the University, not a dime for carfare and what a predicament. I had a good watch so I figured I'd go down to the Skid Road and pawn it and get a room, get rested, then somehow find the family.

I started walking again. It was Labor Day and all traffic was outbound, very few headed for town. I couldn't hitch a ride, so I walked all the five miles to the Skid Road. The pawn shops were closed. I finally found one open and borrowed five dollars on my watch, picked up my suitcase at the King Street Station, and got a room at the old St. Regis Hotel on First Avenue, where the Alaska people liked to stay.

I went to bed and slept for 23 hours. When I awakened I remembered the name of my younger sister's girl friend. I called her and found out where the family was.

That was my idea of a vacation, doing exactly what I felt like. During the whole two months I had not given the future a moment of thought. Now I had to face up to it. Perhaps old Cornelius J. Vernooy was right. I'd go see Mr. Charles Murphy and ask to go back to Alaska.

CHAPTER NINE

North To Alaska Again

As the old trooper Cornelius J. Vernooy had predicted, immediately on return from furlough I was accepted back on the WAMCATS, who were again short of operators.

Mr. Charles Murphy, the civilian superintendent of the system, promised me that if at all possible he would let me stay in Seattle and work a six p.m. to midnight shift so I could attend the University of Washington. It was a perfect set-up for my working my way through college. Traffic on the Alaska Cable dropped off to nothing about nine o'clock in the evening. I would be able to study the remaining hours. Others had done this. The officer in charge, Colonel J.D.L. Hartman, and Mr. Murphy, the Superintendent, liked to help ambitious young men—which I presented myself as being.

This great hope was short-lived. My high school grades were below average and I could not get into the University of Washington. The registrar said I would have to take entrance exams in U.S. history and modern history and get a grade of 85 in each in order to bring my average up.

I had already moved into my brother's fraternity house, which was also my father's fraternity. The frat house president said, "Well, as long as you are going to enter in the spring, you might as well stay on here at the house."

I had fun for a few months of college life, girls, football, games and roughhouse without the burden of study. It wasn't a bad few months.

Spring came and I took the entrance exams without any cramming and made a grade of 75 in one and 78 in the other. I told the registrar, "That's pretty good considering I didn't study."

He said, "Mr. Salisbury, if that's the way you prepare for your examinations I don't think you will make a very good student at the University." That was 'Goodbye, college.'

A few weeks later an opportunity came up to go out on the cableship SS Delwood as a radio operator. Going up to Alaska aboard this cableship promised to be an interesting adventure, a chance to see how deep-sea cable was laid on the bottom of the ocean and how it was repaired.

The food aboard ship was horrible. They served chicken that must have been in the freezer since the ship was built. The cooks never bothered to pull the pinfeathers. I lived on cornflakes and condensed milk, those being the only things I could stomach. When the ship finally came into Ketchikan, I was lucky enough to find a homesick guy with the same specialist rating as mine and we arranged a job swap. He got out of Alaska. I got off that ship.

This began my second tour of duty in Ketchikan. By this time I had been promoted and was earning a little more money. I was also becoming a better operator and therefore was gaining a little status among the veteran operators. I continued to strive to perfect my skills in radio, land-line and submarine cable telegraphy, these being three distinct but closely related crafts. The mastery of the three crafts would increase my freedom of choice of employment and greatly widen the opportunity to travel and see the world which was still my goal.

I bought my first car and began to date girls seriously. The chief operator was still Mr. Q., the warrant officer, and he was great for having married men on his staff. If you got married on that pay with an enlisted man's rank, you were stuck there forever or at least for 30 years. You couldn't afford to quit and couldn't transfer. The men said, "Mr. Q. has you where the hair is short."

I had a steady evening shift at the radio station three miles out of town. One day Mr. Q. asked me why I didn't get married. I said, "How can a young man court a girl, when he's stuck on a steady evening shift? Now I have my eye on a pretty high school teacher and if I had a day shift I'd try to date her."

"Salisbury, you start day shift tomorrow," he sputtered. He spoke with a heavy Danish accent.

My buddy, Sammy Hatfield, said, "He spits every word even if it's in your face and he don't serve a towel." We kept our conversations with Mr. Q. brief.

I dated the schoolmarm; she was several years older than I, besides being engaged to a professor at the University of Washington in Seattle. She lived with two other teachers in a private house. We had a lot of fun together, but nothing serious developed. I learned a lot from her about how to treat a good woman. She was a fine dancer and taught me to play bridge, and we were getting on fine.

One day Mr. Q. stopped me and asked, sputtering, "Shalausberry, when are you going to marry the School Mom?" He could never get my name right.

I said, "I don't know, Sir. I haven't asked her yet."

"Shawlesberry, you are too damned slow. I'm going to put you back on nights and give some one else a chance."

He did too, which very effectively broke up my romance with the schoolteacher.

I fell into a real affair then. I lived in a small, clean, respectable hotel, and the owner-landlady closed up her office just at the time I was coming in from my evening shift. She invited me in for a hot toddy (rum and butter). That became a regular ritual and, of course, led to where we didn't stop with the hot toddy. She was nine years older than I, but that made her still a very young woman. She was fully experienced and a good teacher. This was my first mature experience, where there was sex, respect and love.

On June 5th, 1927, my enlistment in the WAMCATS was over. I was anxious to go outside to the states, try my luck at getting a job and be free for further travel. I took my discharge in Alaska and came south on the Princess Louise, a Canadian

Pacific Railway Steamer. Alaska was dry and Canada was wet, so Canadian ships were more fun. The trip down the Inside Passage was beautiful in June, the weather was fine and the social activity on the steamer was rewarding. I felt I was beginning to live. The WAMCATS and Mr. Q. had been oppressive to me. The fact that I couldn't leave if I wanted to, the lowly enlisted man's status, all seemed to push me down, gave me a feeling of unworthiness that didn't like; I wasn't free.

When I arrived in Seattle I immediately got a job as a telegrapher with Western Union Telegraph Company. They sent me down to Baker, Oregon, a small town in the eastern part of that state.

It seemed that every young man left those inland towns when he was 18 years old and never came back. The only time a new man came to town was when Western Union or the railroad changed telegraph operators. The result was that all the young, unattached girls who were left stranded in the town would find an excuse to come into the telegraph office and ask some irrelevant question, just to meet the new operator. Western Union did a good job of protecting me from involvements. I worked ten hours a day, from eight in the morning until one p.m., then returning at five p.m. and working until ten p.m. seven days a week. For this 70-hour week I received $110 per month. Very often the Portland relay office would not get around to clear me of night letters until five minutes before ten and I would have an extra hour's work getting the night letters off with no extra pay. Still, people said, "What a lucky young man you are to have a steady job," and I thought it was.

There were some rewards. I enjoyed telegraphy; the skill absorbed me and as I became better I developed vanity and pride of work. At that time there was no daytime radio broadcast reception in eastern Oregon. Everyone listened to "Amos 'n' Andy" at night on the Portland radio and then went around imitating them the next day. What a bore, I thought.

It was my duty to copy the baseball scores over the wire every day, and a crowd would gather around the telegraph office to see the scores as they were posted.

The second Dempsey-Tunney fight took place while I was in Baker. I was the only Tunney man in town and had the only ten-dollar bet on him. I had bet the same on the first Dempsey-

Tunney fight. I was a loyal Tunney man. These sportsmen took that as a defiance and a challenge to their manhood. The heat and tempers got worse as the day of the fight drew near.

At fight time, I was receiving the round-by-round report in Morse code from the ringside. The telegraph operator sending out the story was about a round behind the action. I was just copying the word "Tunney's down" (the famous long count) when a strange fist (telegrapher's jargon for a sender's style) broke in and said, "Tunney wins!"

I jumped up from the the instruments and yelled, "TUNNEY WINS!" The manager had been reading the reports aloud over my shoulder as I copied them down to the big audience up until then. I jumped around like a madman yelling, "Tunney wins! Tunney wins!"

The manager, also a Dempsey man, shouted, "Pay no attention! this lid can't read the Morse!" ('Lid' was a derogatory name for a student telegrapher.) The manager broke the circuit and asked, "Confirm Tunney wins?"

"Confirmed" came back the snappy answer. Pandemonium broke out with the crowd inside and outside the telegraph office. I thought I was going to be lynched. I must say they took their sports seriously out there in eastern Oregon.

The operator I was relieving finally got well and came back to work and to get married. His girl was a cute redhead, and she had seemed to think because I was taking her fiance's place in the telegraph office, I was supposed to take his place with her. She would come to the telegraph office every night at ten and wait around for me to close up and walk her home. She sort of went with the job. I was respecting his job and his interests the best I could, but how long could that go on? He came back just in time for me to go to Hoquiam, Washington, on another relief job.

Hoquiam and Aberdeen are twin port cities, and their reason for being is lumber. This was during Prohibition, but loggers and lumberjacks didn't pay much attention to that fact. The towns were wide open. Again I worked ten hours a day—a split shift spread over fourteen hours—and seven days a week. It left me no time for merrymaking, and it was about all the $110 a month I earned would do to pay my board and room. There were some cute girls who came into the telegraph office to file the evening telegrams for the lumber companies. They were what I called "the marrying kind." Looking back, this was no doubt a male chauvinist fallacy. Haven't young men always carried around a lot of taboos that screw up their lives, making them marry the wrong girls or failing to marry the right ones?

A lot of male ego was involved too, as if those pretty young secretaries would even want to marry a lowly telegrapher.

It rained 18 inches the month of November in Hoquiam and Aberdeen, so much rain that it couldn't run off. Southwest winds drove the ocean into Grays Harbor on the extreme high tides, and the wind and rain were so heavy that the tide couldn't recede, flooding the streets. I was getting sick of the wet.

One evening a radio operator off a lumber schooner came in and filed some telegrams. We exchanged a little talk about our related jobs. I told him, "I'm also a radio operator and a cable operator."

He said, "Whew! If you can do all that you should be in San Francisco working on the Transpacific Wireless for RCA. They pay good and you would have a great future."

I wish I had kept his name and address, because he changed the course of my life right there, and for the better.

I pondered his advice for several days, and then one rainy evening a man came in and sent a telegram saying, "Leaving at six a.m. for Oakland." I knew there was no train at that time.

I asked, "Are you driving, and are you crowded?"

He said, "I'll be glad to have company and someone to spell me at the wheel."

I got hold of the manager and arranged for a leave of absence. The manager was a nice guy and said he would take care of everything so I could go back to work for the company in San Francisco if I wanted to. I left.

My free ride from Hoquiam let me out in Oakland, California. I had only to take the ferryboat across the bay the San Francisco and I would be at my destination.

Crossing on the ferry on a beautiful morning in December, 1927, I caught the exhilarating spirit of the great city. I studied the skyline and the waterfront and the big ships at her docks. I thought with confidence, I'll soon be a part of it. It was a vibrant feeling and I was buoyant with enthusiasm and excitement.

What a contrast, I thought, to the way I had felt on arrival in Seattle from Montana only three and one-half years before. At that time I was traveling on trepidations and romance, all nerve and no knowledge. This time I was self-assured; I would call on those big corporations with a product to offer—my skills in communications, my youth and my ambition. I knew that I would be hired.

I had little more money than when I first arrived in Seattle, but now I was a skilled telegrapher and knew how short-handed Western Union would be just before the Christmas season. I would go there and get on a payroll, then I would research the international communications companies and make the best deal I could with the best company.

I applied at the Western Union main office the day after I arrived and was immediately given a job at $25 per month more than they had been paying me in Hoquiam. I was able to handle all the circuits and was soon assigned to the SF-NY cable wire—the wire running into the N.Y. Western Union Cable Company and strictly international traffic. The messages were mostly ten-letter commercial banker's cipher and demanded and developed a high degree of accuracy. This experience helped me a little later in getting into the Trans-Pacific radio communications business. I continued in the main traffic office of Western Union for several weeks after Christmas, not being dropped with the other extra Christmas help.

The Chief Operator came by and patted me on the shoulder and said, "My boy, we'll have something better for you soon."

I said, "Thank you, sir." I worked as long hours as they would let me, partly because I had nothing else to do and partly from ambition. San Francisco is a lonely city when you know no one.

I put in my application at the Commercial Pacific Cable Company, Mackay Radio & Telegraph Company and the Radio Corporation of America. I was given tests on their circuits and interviews and filled out reams of forms. All three companies told me that I would be hearing from them. I believed them too.

Western Union asked me if I would like to go to Reno in their commercial department and relieve a woman who was night manager there. She was to be out about six weeks with an operation. After that I was to go to Lake Tahoe as telegraph operator in the big winter resort hotel. I would be sending in the newspaper reporters' dispatches on the winter sports events and society news. At the end of the Tahoe winter season I was to go to Paso

Robles, California, as telegraph operator for the Pittsburgh Pirates baseball team's spring training camp. This promised to be an exciting itinerary, with travel and interesting contacts.

As the Western Union commercial superintendent said, "It will be a great experience for your career with us." I accepted.

In the meantime I advised the companies where I had applied of my Reno address. What I really wanted was to work for one of the international companies. They were the elite of the communications industry; that's where the future of the industry was.

In Reno I worked from three p.m. until one a.m. seven days a week. I was night manager and did no telegraphy. I paid out about a thousand dollars in cash every evening in money orders and took in several hundred dollars over the counter. It was a very good experience in handling money, supervising two young clerks and a dozen messenger boys.

The social life was dull, since with those hours there was no opportunity to date girls. I met plenty of young divorcees at the counter. The usual recipients of the money orders, they were always in the office, either sending for money or receiving it. They all seemed to feel it was necessary to tell their life histories and describe to me the cruel treatment handed them by their husbands.

I was a little too young to interest them in any other way. I had not yet had my twenty-second birthday. I looked on them as old women just because they had been married.

For entertainment, I went to the divorce courts in the afternoons. The young women put on quite a show for the judge. They would come into court weeping like widows, but when the judge slammed his gavel and said, "Divorce granted!" they would go skipping out the door like schoolgirls. This form of entertainment sort of jaded my young bachelor's outlook on the institution of marriage.

I started going down to the gambling tables after I closed the office at one a.m. The first or second night I was down there I won $120, almost a month's pay for me. I was then hooked. Fortunately, they closed the gambling joints at two a.m., and I played small stakes so I couldn't lose too much in the one hour that I had to play. After three months in Reno, the woman I was relieving recovered from her operation and returned to work.

As I boarded the train for San Francisco, I looked at my wallet and saw that I had just $25, the exact amount of money I had arrived there with three months before. I had worked ten hours a day seven days a week for three months, had not had a date with a girl, had bought no clothes, and was not one bit better off than when I came.

I said to myself, "I'll make it pay. I'll never gamble again. It's a waste and a bore, and if I live by that rule the three months hard work in Reno will not have been for nothing." I did live that way. I have never been a gambler since.

Because of the woman's delay in returning to her job due to her slow recovery from an operation, I missed out on the Tahoe and Paso Robles jobs and was returned to the main office of Western Union in San Francisco.

I had received letters from all three of the radio and cable companies saying that they had a job for me on my return to San Francisco.

When I returned, I went back to the Western Union main office traffic center and worked a few weeks while I determined which radio or cable job to accept. RCA offered the best pay, the most opportunity to travel to foreign countries and the best future. That is where I ended up, at about twice the money that I had been earning.

I really felt that I had arrived. I loved the work, I liked the men I worked with and there was an unlimited amount of overtime at time and one half after eight hours and all holidays. Being young, healthy and energetic, I worked double shifts several times a week and felt like a plutocrat when I received those big fat checks.

I moved out of the cheap hotel into a fancy hotel where they served breakfast in your room and catered to male and female singles. I had my suits tailor-made, bought my shirts and ties at Bullits, and quickly learned to spend all the money I was earning. San Francisco has always been a swinging city and in the late 1920's it was especially so. Speakeasies abounded. I had my private bootlegger and had a standing order with him for a gallon of bathtub gin to be delivered every Saturday.

For the next three years I pursued a purely hedonistic life. Girls, night-clubs, dances, golf and fun wherever I could find it. In retrospect I wish some wise person had gotten hold of me and made me aware of the real opportunities that were available and being offered to me. I turned down assignments to Hawaii and the Philippines because I didn't wish to leave the high life I was enjoying in San Francisco. If I had met and married the right woman at that time it might have slowed me down and made me aware of the golden opportunities for advancement and moneymaking that were all around.

It appeared to me that being a boss was a bore. Settling down to a wife and kids in the suburbs had no appeal as a way of life. I liked the freedom I was enjoying and felt that the opportunity to travel would come in time.

I gave up the resident hotel to share an apartment with two friends from Alaska whom the superintendent had hired on my recommendation. They were as wild as I or wilder. Ellison Barber was a heavy gambler and Niel Chambers a heavy gambler and drinker. We were very compatible otherwise. They would both be broke on the day after payday and I generally had to carry them for cash and eating money until the next payday. Not that I had money in the bank, but I was just not as careless as they were.

The stock market crash of November, 1929, hit and rocked the country. I didn't know what the crash was. When I came to work one day and everyone was talking about it, I thought San Francisco had had another earthquake and I had slept through it. I was strictly nonpolitical, even having voted for Herbert Hoover on my boss's instructions.

The big depression was on, and layoffs were right and left. Bread lines formed and people jumped from windows in distress from losing their fortunes. I was oblivious to all of that and never gave a thought to what I would do if I lost my job. Message traffic slowed and slowed on the international communication channels. The staff at RCA had been reduced to about half its former size.

One day a supervisor came to me and said, "Oliver, what would you do if you were laid off?"

"Oh! I would go to sea as a radio operator on a ship. I have a commercial radio license and have always wanted to see the Orient."

The supervisor then went to another single fellow and asked him the same question. Al Hoey said, "Oh my God! I don't know what my poor old mother would do. I'm her sole support."

The next day I received a note from the superintendent giving me two weeks' notice of dismissal. The note said, "It has become Company policy to lay off single men regardless of seniority, rather than lay off married men and work a hardship on a family. We feel you will be the least hurt."

I was young enough not to be flattened by the disappointment as were many men who lost their jobs. It was then the spring of 1931. After all, I hadn't been the first to be let go. I felt the Company showed compassion for family men. I approved my layoff.

The fact was that I had just become engaged to a very fine young woman named Marjorie Frost a few weeks before; but we had made no announcement and set no date for the event. We agreed that losing my job obviously imposed an indefinite delay to marriage plans.

I had saved a little money and did nothing about looking for a new job. I spent my time seeing Marjorie and haphazardly put in my application for a ship job. I didn't really believe there were any such jobs and, being deeply in love, I wasn't anxious to go away for too long.

CHAPTER TEN

I Visit My Folks

While I was enjoying unemployment I noticed a special rate to Seattle being offered by the Pacific Steamship Company's Alexander boats. "Round Trip To Seattle, only $25.00"—so read the advertisements.

I said to Margie, "It's three days and two nights up and the same back. I can see my folks in Seattle and I can hardly live in San Francisco for that number of days on that amount."

Margie said, "Oliver, go see your folks."

I bought a round trip ticket on the SS Ruth Alexander. They had the usual band and confetti tape farewell party at the dock. I waved good-bye to Margie, and as I turned from the rail a friendly fellow said, "I'm Jim McNalley, would you like to join me for a drink?"

"I've never turned one down, there's no reason to begin now," I replied.

Though Prohibition was still the law of the land, the fellow had amply supplied himself. We began a party that I think lasted off and on all the way to Seattle.

The morning of arrival, coming in through Puget Sound, Jim and I, by then sobered up, visitied a little. He asked, "What are you going to do in Seattle?"

I told him, "I just lost my job. I'm a radio operator and I'm going to see my father and mother."

Jim said, "I'm a lawyer and I represent a man by the name of Collins who is a material witness in a houseboat murder case. Collins is Chief Radio Officer for the Bureau of Fisheries and he's not going to be able to go back to Alaska because of the trial coming up. There might be a good job for you there." He gave me his card and I thanked him.

After several days of being home with the folks, Father—reacting to my visit as if he might have a free-loading boarder for the duration of the Depression—said, "Oliver, what do you plan to do? You know, Son, this is a serious depression. It is now the spring of 1931 and we're one and a half years into it with no end in sight. Things throughout the nation are getting desperate." Father managed a big apartment hotel and was working and feeling pretty secure.

I really hadn't paid much attention to things up to this time other than the sports pages of the papers. In trying to answer Father's question as to my future plans, I mentioned Jim McNalley, the friendly lawyer on the boat.

Father scolded, "You get right down there and see that man. That may be a real opportunity. You mean you have been home three days and haven't yet been down to see him?"

"Okay, Father, I'll go see him."

I took Jim's card and went down to the Dexter Horton Building to look him up. Jim acted like he didn't remember me. Steamship friends seem to disappear from your mind as you hit the dock. I think this had happened to him, since it had to me except for Father's prodding.

Jim remembered and finally warmed up. "Oh! yes," and he took me across the hall. He read the names on the doors and typically, lawyer fashion, picked out the highest title: Robert Russell, U.S. Fisheries Commissioner.

Jim opened the door without waiting for the secretary to announce him and said, "Hello, Bob, how are you?"

Mr. Russell, looked bewildered but responded, "I'm fine, and you?" Jim's face no doubt was familiar to him from riding in the elevators.

"I'm your Chief Radio Officer's attorney. He's in all that trouble connected with the Lake Union houseboat murder case, which seems to be the local *cause celebre*."

The way Jim said it, it sounded very ominous, like the title to Sherlock Holmes mystery. He followed that deep jab with the statement that Collins, the chief radio officer, would not be permitted by the court to leave the city until after the trial, which was set for July. Jim then introduced me as a qualified radio operator who could likely take Collins' place.

Mr. Russell said, "Well, if Mr. Salisbury is qualified and looking for a job, let him take this note to Captain O'Donnell out at the Bureau of Fisheries wharf." He scribbled a note which practically instructed Captain O'Donnell to put me in Collins' place.

I telephoned the good news of my job to Margie in San Francisco. We agreed to set our wedding date for the fall when the ship returned from Alaska.

Father and Mother were delighted and could hardly believe my good fortune. Father admonished, "You see, Son, it always pays to follow through every lead when you're job hunting."

Looking back 40-some years, I now realize just how tough things were and how wise my father was. I admit to being very lucky at that time.

That was the nearest I ever in my life came to being unemployed. I don't think I was ever off a payroll between RCA's severance and vacation pay and the day I was put on the Bureau's payroll.

There was a month of getting acquainted with the other members of the crew and the crews of the other Bureau boats. The dock was a clatter of activity whenever word came out that an official from downtown offices was on the way. Ship's officers dating secretaries in the main office served a dual purpose and provided us with an 'early warning system.' The trick seemed to be to get something torn apart so you could be sitting in the middle of a mess and look extra busy when officials were around. Most of the rest of the time was spent in the galley of one ship or another, swapping stories over coffee.

The summer promised to be an interesting one. With due credit to everyone's skill, when it came time for the ships to sail for Alaska they sparkled like yachts. This was in the depth of the Depression, and very competent and over-qualified personnel were available for every job.

The U.S.F.S. Crane was 90 feet long with a broad beam and a 14-foot draft, built of heavy timbers, designed by naval architects for the rough waters of the Bering Sea. There is an old sailor's ditty, "You have never been a sailor 'till you've sailed the Bering Sea." Whoever the author, he had been there. It is a big shallow sea and the weather and water can be abominable. We were heavily loaded with all kinds of cargo: groceries, lumber, nails, tools, nets and other materials for the summer operations of the Bureau. We also had aboard several passengers who were wardens, stream guards, and other classifications of personnel that we put ashore at their assigned locations. We went up the Inside Passage, and the ship and her diesels operated smoothly.

I spent a good deal of time 'chewing the fat' over the radio waves in wireless code with my friends at the radio stations along the coast. I wrote long letters to Margie describing the beautiful scenery as well as expressing my desire to return to her.

When we got out on the Alaska Peninsula, Kodiak and west, I made a habit of dropping in on the radio operators at the various coastal stations. It always helped to have friends in those key spots. They could be very useful passing notes to Margie in San Francisco. Most of them had ham rigs and could contact San Francisco direct.

I had a thirty-two special Winchester rifle along that belonged to my father, and whenever the opportunity availed I would fire a few rounds in target practice, firing at flotsam or targets on the beach. I became a pretty good marksman. Cap said, "Sparks, I wouldn't hesitate to go bear hunting with you." Sparks is always the traditional nickname for a ship's radio operator.

It was my ambition to shoot a big brownie, a Kodiak. There were many of them and one could spot them along the beaches with a glass as we sailed westward for Unimak Pass. The wanton killing of these great animals has in the last quarter of this century greatly reduced their numbers, and severe restrictions against the killing of them are now in force. At the time I was there they were considered predatory to the spawning salmon.

We sailed westward for Unimak Pass, known as the graveyard of the Pacific, so many hulls of wrecks are strewn along its beaches. I was personally able to observe five such wrecks. Twelve-knot tides run through this pass. Combine that with wind and heavy seas and a ship can be in deep trouble.

We stopped at the little town of Sand Point, which had been built out of the salvage from those derelicts over a period of many years. The Captain, the chief engineer and I were invited into old Captain Griswold's elegant home, which was occupied by his granddaughter and her husband. It was furnished to a great extent from the captain's cabins of wrecked ships, some dating back to Seward's Folly. The collection of artifacts displayed boggled the mind. The home was a veritable museum.

Sand Point was a fair-sized village for that part of the world. The old Captain had passed on, but his descendants kept the village shipshape, whitewashed every year. The cemetery where the Captain is buried, as are his several wives and many of his offspring, is well kept and planted with evergreen trees, a rarity in those parts.

This seemed to be a strange part of the world. We called it, "the jumping off place," the edge of the world. I once counted 17 gray whales spouting at the same time. My son Tom, now—47 years later—a crab fisherman on the Bering Sea, tells me it has been three years since he has seen a single whale.

At Port Moller on the Bering Sea, where we discharged the last of our cargo and passengers, an Indian chief on a big white horse greeted us from the beach as we approached the harbor. This was Bear River Charlie. He could say a few words in English, like, "Me Chief." The cannery crews told him, kiddingly, that any chief worth his salt and hides had to have a horse. Bear River Charlie was loaded with money, so he sent out to the States for the big white horse, which at the time was the only horse in that part of the world. He had hay and oats shipped in at great expense to carry the horse through the winter.

The chief also acted as pilot for the harbor of Port Moller. When he appeared on the beach on his white horse, Cap sent a work boat ashore for him. Charlie turned the horse loose to find its own way back to the village. Then he mounted the ship's bridge and announced, "Me Fish-Commish!" He had learned that word in English and how to attach it to the U.S.F.S. Crane's yearly visit. The responsibility of piloting this beautiful ship into the dock gave him great status. Years before, the old Revenue cutter Bear had moved an entire Eskimo village from the Arctic where they were suffering a food famine and reestablished them in Port Moller on the Bering Sea where food was plentiful and the climate milder.

This was the place where I decided to launch myself as a big game hunter. The winter watchman at the cannery told me, "A big brownie can be seen any morning lumbering down to a pool by the pump house to take his morning spring bath."

It seems that when bears come out of hibernation they like to soak the mange and filth off themselves by bathing. The terrain here was made up of level land, but pockmarked with little hillocks as if it had been bombed or shelled by artillery. This condition was the result of heavy freezing and heaving of the soil, I was told. The winter snow melted into these holes, making warm stagnant pools. The pumphouse was about a half mile from the cannery and willows had grown up around the springs there.

This bear would come out of the willows where he slept and settle in one of the warm pools for his bath. The watchman said, "Sparks, I'll guarantee that if you go out there you'll see a very big Kodiak."

I felt highly elated at the prospects of bagging this big fellow. What a story to write Margie about!

The next morning I announced, "Who'll volunteer to help kill that bear?" Much to my surprise there was no great rush on any one's part to join me. I finally persuaded one of the sailors by the name of Victor Robert—now a retired Standard Oil tanker captain—to join me. The only other gun on the ship was a 12-gauge pumpgun with buckshot for ammunition. We took off for the half mile hike across the pockmarked tundra with the good wishes of the rest. Cap said, "I'll notify your next of kin."

Vic said, "Thanks a lot, Cap."

Going through the Eskimo village we picked up another volunteer: a malamute pup, full grown, but puppy-foolish. He romped along with us. As we neared the pumphouse, our hearts pumping louder than the gasoline pump had it been running, the pup, loping along a little ahead of us, went over the hillock and flushed the big brownie from his languid bath. We heard a yelp followed by a horrible roar and great splashing of water. The pup, scared witless, came running straight to us for protection. We braced for the charge, guns at the ready, expecting the monster to jump clear over the hillock. The noise grew louder like thunder but the splashing continued. I looked at my brave partner and said, "How do you feel?"

Vic said, "Same's you!"

My legs seemed to be swirling and felt as if they were on swivels. I now knew what was meant by rubber legs, buck ague, yellow streak, cowardice or whatever weakness it was, and that I had it.

I said, "Let's go!" and we did. We didn't look back until we reached the cannery. Everyone said we showed good judgment as well as excellent speed. Big brownies had been known to travel a hundred yards with a bullet through the heart, and furthermore we should not have been hunting that bear with a thirty-two special and a shotgun. I said, "As for me, I wouldn't get that close to one of those bears again with a cannon."

I had another experience that summer with the same gun. (Incidentally, this rifle of my father's was the very one that I had taken on the Twin Lakes trip many years before, the one Old Bill had killed the bull elk with.) We were at Dutch Harbor and I had decided to climb Ballyhoo Mountain, a fairly high mountain for that area. It does something for you to climb a mountain, besides taking the kinks out of your muscles and getting rid of your sea legs. A famous climber said, "You climb it because it's there." I climbed Ballyhoo alone, saw many ptarmigan and bald eagles, and picked some beautiful wildflowers for the messroom.

Next day I called again for volunteers to climb the mountain and shoot some ptarmigan and eagles. Since I was only carrying the gun for small game this time, I was more successful. The mate and the chief engineer volunteered to join me for the climb. We climbed for half a mile, a very steep half mile. I shot two ptarmigan. Their plumage is gray and white in the summer, and they rely entirely upon their camouflage for protection. They do not fly quickly and we were lucky enough to flush a covey of them. They were sitting all around us 15 or 20 feet away. I am somewhat color-blind and therefore camouflage does not always fool me. I killed two shooting their heads off, while my companions were exclaiming, "Where are they?" At that close range with a thirty-two special there would have been nothing left of the body had I shot them otherwise. They were fine eating and a nice relief from our steady fish diet.

Part of the project of climbing the mountain was to shoot bald eagles. Like the Kodiak bear, the eagle was considered a predator of the spawning salmon, and at that time the Bureau of Fisheries paid a dollar bounty for every pair of eagle claws presented to the warden.

We watched the eagles soaring high above the water. As they spotted a salmon beneath the surface with their built-in bombsight, they would plummet from a great height, hit the water with a splash and come up with a salmon in their talons. Often the salmon would be so large that the eagle could not regain flight with it and would of necessity pontoon it to the beach where he could get the fish in shallow water and proceed to devour it.

My companions and I spotted what appeared to be an eagle in shallow water. I said to the others, "Is that an eagle?" We were high on the side of the mountain a quarter of a mile away and looking down. We all watched.

"It moved! It's an eagle!" We all exclaimed in unison. I took careful aim with the rifle, raising my sights to allow for the drop called for by the distance. I saw my bullet hit the water 50 feet beyond the target. I lowered my sights, fired again, and saw the bullet hit the sand 50 feet short. The third shot kicked the sand right at his feet. The "eagle" started, firing a gun in the air. It was the cook from the boat. He was wearing a white cook's cap, a black wool shirt and blue galley pants which blended into the water, giving the appearance of an eagle standing three feet out in the water, the torso and head being just the right height for a big bald eagle. If the cook hadn't been able to fire the warning shot, I'm sure my fourth bullet would have nailed him as I closed the range.

I was so shocked that I could make such a mistake that I ejected all the rounds of ammunition from my rifle and threw away what cartridges I had left in my pocket, swearing never to hunt again. I have often wondered what the testimony of the mate and engineer would have been had I killed the cook.

We spent a lot of time at Unalaska and nearby Dutch Harbor. While we were there a Japanese warship, an aircraft tender, tied up alongside us. The Coast Guard was also tied up at the same dock and they told us the Japanese had permission from the State Department to be there. The Japanese had planned an island-

I Visit My Folks 83

hopping goodwill flight to America, and this tender was there to service them when the planes stopped at that point.

Every morning Japanese officers and enlisted men in the Emperor's full naval uniforms would come ashore with survey instruments, fishing poles, cameras and lunch baskets to climb the mountains around Dutch Harbor. I was fully convinced that Japan was preparing for an eventual war against the U.S.A. I wasn't at all surprised when years later, not too long after Pearl Harbor, I saw a photograph in the New York Times, released by Naval censors, showing a bombed-out U.S. Naval Radio Station. Censorship had deleted the location, but having spent so much time there I recognized the picture for where it was and what it was. I was able to confirm this in later years. The so-called goodwill flight was never made—unless you could call the bombing run on Dutch Harbor Naval Radio "goodwill."

That summer the U.S.S. Vegas, a naval collier, was late coming north to pick up the pelts and the Fouke Fur Company crew. We were asked to take the fur crew back to Seattle when the pelting was completed. This was a great break for us. Several of the men on board had not seen Seattle in the summertime since they were boys, always spending their summers in Alaska. We sailed direct from Unimak pass to Seattle, open ocean all the way. Fortunately, it was beautiful August weather.

The radio operator at Squaw Harbor asked me, "Are you coming back?"

I said, "Yes."

He asked, "Will you get me a gallon of Christmas whiskey?"

"O.K., if we come back your way I'll have it for you."

It was still Prohibition, but I picked up a gallon of good quality moonshine in Seattle. No risk was involved; no one was going to search a government ship. On our return trip, as soon as we were within radio calling distance, my friend started calling to see if I had his "Christmas merchandise," as he called it. I reassured him. The chief engineer on my ship was daily bugging me to give him a drink out of it. I knew if I pulled the cork that would be the end of the jug. I told the Chief that if we didn't go in to Squaw Harbor he and I could consume it. As we neared Squaw Harbor, which is well out on the Aleutian Peninsula, a terrific storm came up that made it dangerous for us to go in close to land. My friend on shore could tell by our radio signal that we were not far from him in air miles. He asked, "What time will you pass the Unga Spit?"

I checked with the Captain, who advised me it would be about three in the morning. I told my friend.

My radio pal said, "I'll be out there in a codfish dory at three a.m., waving a lantern."

I set my alarm clock for three a.m. We were pitching and rolling and it seemed as though there was as much water in the air as there was in the ocean, but there was my friend frantically waving his lantern from a codfish dory that was pitching and rolling. He pulled alongside as we slowed down and I tossed him the precious jug and hollered, "Merry Christmas!"

I called him on the air the next morning to see if he got back to the radio station o.k. and to give him a message. He was there and I sent the message—official business from the captain to a Bureau warden at Johnson's Hole on the Naknek River. The radio operator at Port Moller, by prearrangement, was to keep his station open to a certain date just to receive this message and to send it by courier to Naknek; there the warden would send a runner up the river to signal the Bureau's ground crew working at an inland lake to come downriver and be picked up by us. It was a complicated arrangement, but workable if everyone played his part.

When we arrived at Naknek there was no crew waiting for us. The operator at Port Moller had not received our message; as arranged, he had then left for Seattle on the last cannery tender.

After we had been lying off the mouth of the Naknek River for several days, the Bureau's crew finally came down the river in Indian canoes. A barge from shore had been pulled out into the river and moored in the Upper Hole, a deepwater hole that could only be reached by ship on a certain tide. The timing of that tide was part of the overall plan.

We were madly unloading cargo onto that barge, and had been at it all day, everyone on board working feverishly since the coming low tide would be a minus tide. As the tide started to recede, we were completing unloading when the strong pull of the outgoing tide and the current of the river caused our anchor to slip on the sandy bottom.

We hit the sandbar and flipped over on our side. The radio room was on the underwater side; there was no way to get into it, and no power anyway. Worst disaster of all, our dinner had just been put on the table and we had worked all day without stopping for lunch. When the ship went over the dinner went with it. Bill, the cook, jumped over the side, landing on the sandbar with the coffee pot in his hand, and never spilled a drop. "At least we have coffee," Cap said. "Ration it!"

We lay there on our side until the next high tide, fortunately an extreme high tide, floated us. We got to hell out of there.

We were the last ship out of the Bering Sea before the freeze-up. We stopped at Squaw Harbor to see what had happened to our message. The Captain was furious. I suspected the Christmas whiskey had something to do with it, but he was doubting whether I had sent the message. I was glad to be able to prove that I had. We went to the radio station, and sure enough my friend had copied my message okay, but had then started sampling the jug and failed to relay the message on to Port Moller. He cost the government thousands of dollars in wages and nearly cost our country a very fine fisheries ship. As far as I know, he was never disciplined for his dereliction of duty. At least my friend was honorable enough to produce the message and clear me of any involvement, unless you want to blame me for bringing him the whiskey, but then he might have done the same thing on good old sourdough—the Alaskan's standby.

We were just nine men aboard the U.S.F.S. Crane, and whenever we pulled in to a cannery dock we had to play a baseball game with the local team. It was the only time I ever made a baseball team. We generally got walloped, but we would have had no face at all had we refused to play.

Our cook, Bill Grahams, had been the chef at the Olympic Hotel in Seattle but was an alcoholic and had lost his job there. Our mess was a beautiful thing. He could dress a salmon or halibut in may different ways. We all gained weight. The only time it was tough would be the first two or three days after leaving port while Bill was sobering up.

The ship proceeded to Seattle without further incident. Margie was waiting at the Government Locks for me. She was as cute as I remembered and was a joy for salty eyes. The gang aboard ship, of course, knew of my marital plans and were all eyes and all praise. They had been having a lot of fun with me all summer telling me which foods the saltpeter was being put in. I didn't know whether it was true or false but they had me almost afraid to eat anything for fear of being a failure on my wedding night. The Captain even wrote a radio message—official business, no less—and had me send it to the captain of a Coast Guard vessel nearby, asking for five pounds of saltpeter which they tossed over to us. It may have been rice or sugar for all I knew but I was sorry the sailor was a good catcher.

After the three-day waiting period in Washington, Margie and I were married. We were married by the Reverend Fifield, then an up and coming young Presbyterian minister. The wedding took place in a small room in a restaurant on Union Street. Father and Mother and my brother Al were the only witnesses. I gave Margie an Alaskan red fox scarf for a wedding present. I had bought it from a trapper at Port Moller and sent it down to be made up for her. She was a chic and happy bride.

I was supposed to go back to Alaska for two months for the southeastern Alaskan salmon season. Since it was not my idea of a honeymoon to be out on a ship with my bride in Seattle, the day before sailing I went down and quit. When I came home and told Margie, I expected her to jump up and down with joy, but she was Depression-weary too and said, "What kind a nut have I married! Now what'll we do?"

In a few days I decided to weather the depression by signing up in the WAMCATS again. The Washington Alaskan Military Cable and Telegraph System was glad to have me. They promised, insofar as they could personally adhere to it, to keep me in Seattle unless there was a vacancy in a one-man station up in the Alaskan interior available. Those one-man stations carried extra pay from other government agencies since the operator could serve as U.S. Marshal, Postmaster, and weather observer and the operator's wife could be the village teacher if she qualified. These were pretty good jobs if you could corral all of the extra roles. I was then so qualified and Margie could teach.

We had orders to go to Eagle, Alaska, on the Yukon River. The personnel officer had bought our tickets and we were getting ready to go shopping for red flannels and other frontier supplies when Sergeant Knight, the man on the job at Eagle, decided to stay. Colonel J. D. L. Hartman, the officer in charge of the WAMCATS, had given him special permission to run the big bulldozer he had bought and contracted roadwork for and to keep his job in the radio station. I can't blame him for staying. I heard years later that he came out of there a very rich man. Margie and I were greatly disappointed not to get that assignment. In looking back over the many years I find it remarkable that such opportunities were offered a young couple.

We stayed in Seattle. A year and a half later I received a telegram offering me a job in San Francisco with Mackay Radio and Telegraph Company, an I.T.&T. subsidiary. They were opening new trans-Pacific circuits and greatly expanding their operations. I accepted the offer and bought out of the WAMCATS (for a price in peacetime you could buy a discharge). We returned to San Francisco to live, starting a new and different life.

The U.S. Fisheries Ship Crane and her crew. Top row, left to right, Bill the cook, Stan, 2nd engineer, Ernie, chief engineer, me, Captain Odonnel, warden, Bud, ordinary seaman, Floyd, mate, Vic, able seaman, and Captain Lowell Smith. 1931.

Sunny day aboard the U.S.F.S. Crane anchored off St. Paul Island in the Pribilofs. Ernie Sigurdson, chief engineer, Captain Bow, Floyd Smith, mate, myself, radio, and Bud Anderson, seaman. 1931.

Unalaska, Alaska. Dutch Harbor is around the point to the left. Ballyhoo Mountain also rises to the left. 1931.

CHAPTER ELEVEN

I'm Involved In
The Birth Of A Union

I arrived back in the great city of San Francisco more mature by far than when I had first arrived there five years before.

I was now married and Margie was pregnant. The Depression was beginning to bottom out and I was fortunate to have landed a better job with the first sign of upturn. This was a good job, too, with a better future and more pay than I had ever earned before.

Up to this time, I had been absolutely non-political in my thinking and reading and had cast my first vote for Herbert Hoover for President. Now I was becoming aware of things. While on the U.S.F.S. Crane I had received a copy of "CQ" Magazine, issue No. 1. A chap by the name of Mervyn Rathborne was publishing it in Santa Monica, California, with his own money. It was radical, militant, well-written and to the point. Rathborne was lobbying for legislation to benefit the commercial radio operators, such as requiring a licensed radio operator to be a citizen. When a law to this effect was passed by

Congress, he claimed the credit. Rathborne had somehow obtained a mailing list of all licensed commercial radio operators. There were about 1400 of us on the West Coast alone trying to make a living out of 400 jobs. We all received the magazine. He suggested a union of radio operators. The appeal was strong, though I did nothing about it. Whenever and wherever I met other operators, they asked, "Have you seen a copy of 'CQ'?"

While I was still working in the Seattle office of the WAMCATS after having left the Bureau of Fisheries, I had begun to develop an awareness of politics and supported Franklin D. Roosevelt for President. F.D.R. became my hero. My politics had come about through watching friends, relatives and family suffer in the throes of the Depression. I credited the upturn in the economy to President Roosevelt.

The job with Mackay Radio in San Francisco was good. I was well qualified to handle the work and quickly rose to the top wage.

The Chief Operator, Mr. Jorgensen, was an ex-sergeant from the WAMCATS in Alaska and had known me up there in earlier years when I was a student operator. He said, "Oliver, we're glad to have you with us. I know your training. Mr. Murphy, your Chief Operator, gave you a good boost. Said I was lucky to get you. You are a hard worker no matter the assignment. I like your versatility of skills. I can use you in any position."

I felt I was the beneficiary of some favoritism. I was given preferred hours and better circuits and was encouraged to like the job. However, I couldn't help but be aware of the partiality being shown me and of the fact that it was at someone else's expense. I felt the injustice when a competent operator was taken off day shift and put on evenings so that I could have a day shift and be home evenings with my pregnant wife. This fellow had been there longer, worked hard too, and had his own personal life. A co-worker remarked, "He also was once the chief operator's favorite."

As I listened to the grumbling around me, I became aware that there were plenty of other grievances. We worked 48 hours a week. Overtime was straight pay and only began after the 48 hours; there was plenty of it and it was compulsory. About this time F.D.R.'s New Deal came out with the 'Blue Eagle,' the

National Recovery Act (NRA), the first of the alphabet soup. The NRA, among other things, gave the worker the right to organize into trade unions, made overtime after eight hours a day or forty-eight hours a week payable at time-and-a-half, and gave many other benefits to working men and women. F.D.R. said in one of his famous fireside chats, "If I were a working man I would be a member of the union of my craft!"

We started talk among ourselves, saying, "What are we waiting for?" There were some old timers who remembered the Commercial Telegraphers' Union/A.F. of L. from World War I days. It had never met with much success and its leadership seemed stultified. One of our fellow operators assumed leadership and contacted the C.T.U./A.F. of L., whose head office was in Chicago. They sent us application blanks and asked for initiation fees and dues.

Their president wrote, "We will send an organizer around if you show sufficient interest."

Fifty or sixty of us joined and sent in our $5.00. We attended many meetings. One militant fellow said, "I don't know what C.T.U. means by 'sufficient interest.' I'd say their response is kinda lackadaisical and typical of the A.F. of L."

We learned later the Company had already acted by recruiting labor spies from within our ranks. The Company had seen "sufficient interest." They were not lackadaisical. These labor spies paid dues, attended meetings and reported to the Company superintendent on each move. This was all brought to the light of day by National Labor Relations Board hearings and court cases several years later and is a matter of record. The Company was obviously very impressed, since they started fighting us from the beginning.

About this time American Radio Telegraphists' Association (ARTA) appeared on the scene. There was an unemployed ship's radio operator by the name of Wayne Paschal living at the St. James Hotel on Mission Street. Wayne's room was ARTA headquarters. He explained that this union had started in New York City. Its president was Hoyt Haddock, a Texan, a radio operator off a Standard Oil tanker. He and his pretty wife lived in the back of the office, existing on the $1.00 per month dues that a couple of hundred members paid. Willard Bliss was editor of "ARTA Magazine." The magazine was radical; even the slick

I'm Involved in the Birth of a Union 91

cover was printed in Russian-style lettering. This union was active and had already won and lost some strikes. Their militancy was appealing and we responded. Wayne explained the red lettering on the magazine by saying, "You could be chartered by the largest Christian church in America and if you disturbed the profits of industry you would immediately be called Russian agents." We felt he was right about that.

Wayne said, "You might's well get used to persecution; if you organize an honest, militant union it'll be bound to follow."

One of the ship radio operators, Fred Brockway, trying to help organize the union, went down to the NRA office and filed charges against Mackay Radio for violating the National Recovery Act. This resulted in the Company being forced to pay us back at time-and-a-half for all that overtime we had been working. Brockway did this on his own and the Company was furious, but we all received checks of several hundred dollars. I personally received three hundred big Depression dollars. Those who hadn't joined ARTA now did. It was a terrific stimulus to organization, not only in our company but in the whole industry.

That fellow Brockway performed a hero's service for us. Then, unofficially blacklisted on all shore jobs for that dastardly deed of making our company abide by the law, he was starved out and had to go back to sea.

About this time the U.S. Supreme Court threw out the Blue Eagle, carcass and all. Those window cards with the blue eagle are now, 40-some years later, rare collector's items.

Congress quickly passed the Wagner Act and set up the National Labor Relations Board with an agent in San Francisco. This did not happen overnight; it was more like two years.

ARTA kept changing organizers as they expanded. An energetic fellow of Danish descent, Volney G. Mathison, whom we called 'Volney G.', was sent out by the New York office to take on the organizing. Volney G. picked up where Brockway left off. Wayne Paschal also continued to give us a great deal of help, though he was primarily involved with organizing the ship radio operators. These fellows were audacious, not afraid of being called names, not afraid to work and not just interested for the sake of money or prestige. They had tremendous appeal to us even with their somewhat frightening militant approach. They were well read and well informed and that, too, made a hit.

Volney G. Mathison was an author of some reknown, and his wife was a Hollywood scenario writer. Volney G. had written a popular series of stories entitled "The Radio Buster" back in the early days of wireless. He had operated a shore station way out on the Alaskan Peninsula during the early 1920's. He had learned to speak Russian by 'chewing the fat' with the Russian coastal operators in Siberia and also from the Aleutian Island residents of the Alaskan Peninsula who spoke Russian, as many of them were descendants of the Czar's political exiles.

Around 1930 Russia had done some recruiting of American technicians, and Volney G. was one of them. The Soviet government was interested in establishing a worldwide communications system and invited Mackay Radio, through its parent company, I.T.&T., as well as other American companies, to send representatives to Moscow to make propositions to them. There was a meeting of communications ministers in the Kremlin, all seated at a great table, as it was described to us by Mr. Rodman, the Mackay Radio superintendent in San Francisco. He, too, spoke Russian, having been an American Army lieutenant during the Russian Civil War when our country sent an expeditionary force to Siberia. "Over on the Soviet side of the table," Mr. Rodman said, "who sat but your ARTA Commissar and organizer, Volney G. Mathison! Right there with the red Soviet Commissars!" Mr. Rodman told this to us in person at a committee meeting we held seeking recognition of our grievance committee. We got it all again through what turned out to be his agents—the story being told at a big union meeting, just in case anyone had missed it.

We were supposed to turn and run and throw in our "Red Cards," as Mr. Rodman called them.

We held a well-attended meeting and thrashed this information all out. To our credit, someone yelled out, "What's this got to do with us?" The members clapped and cheered. We decided that it was a plus for our organizer's talent. It couldn't have been too easy to get to sit at that long table with the Soviet Commissars.

Volney G. was working energetically in our behalf. He seemed to know the laws and especially the economics of the communication industry, which are very complicated.

I'm Involved in the Birth of a Union

Our union continued to grow in numbers and militancy. Leadership changed in ARTA and it changed in our radio communications center. Some very articulate and loquacious orators came forward. They would give leadership for awhile and then give up in disgust when the bickering got nasty and tough. The bigger we became the rougher it got. More dissension, more disruption, mostly coming from the Company's agents. These Company agents would nitpick at the meetings, creating chaos on every issue.

I would come home to Margie full of union talk. Margie said, "What happens if the Company refuses to deal with you?"

"We'll strike!"

"Then what happens to us?"

"We can't lose."

The newspapers and radio were all vociferously anti-union. Looking back, it is hard to believe in this day, when unions are a part of the establishment.

Margie was expecting the birth of our first child at any time. She was nervous, and my militant union talk didn't tend to put her at ease.

I rarely got a day off. When we did we took the ferry to Sausalito and the train to Santa Rosa. Margie's folks owned a prosperous fruit ranch in Sonoma County. I never talked union with my in-laws, but on Sundays they would have friends in, and the conversation among the fruit growers was all violently anti-union. I had to sit quietly while a blowhard rancher bragged how many union organizers he would shoot dead if he caught them on his property. While I was suppressing my feelings, Margie would sit trembling for fear that I wouldn't. She was torn between two loyalties, to her husband and to her father.

Margie and I were living in an upstairs flat out by the Golden Gate. When I think of Robby's birth, I hear fog horns. It was a very foggy morning when Margie started her labor pains and they seemed to be synchronized with the moaning of those horns.

On August 4th, 1933, our son was born. Margie had a difficult time and the baby was taken with instruments. She was in labor for 15 hours before the doctor decided to take it. Margie swore she would never have another. We never did.

Robby was a strong, healthy baby, blue-eyed and yellow-haired, picking up those traits from Margie's Scotch ancestors, though Margie herself was dark-eyed and dark-haired, as am I.

The Pacific Coast waterfront strike took place in the summer of 1934. Mackay Radio & Telegraph's operating rooms were on the seventh floor of the old Postal Telegraph Building, about where a great hotel now stands. From our seventh-floor vantage point we witnessed street fights between strikebreakers and longshore pickets. We heard the shots fired at the 'Battle of Rincon Hill,' which was a 'shoot-out' with the police. The police did all the shooting, having the only guns and horses, and several longshoremen were killed. The anniversary of that 'battle' is still honored by the longshoremen.

The waterfront strike was followed by a general strike in which all labor in San Francisco struck for several days in support of the longshoremen. Nothing moved. Since we were not organized to a degree where we had been recognized by our employer, we were advised by the General Strike Committee to stay on our jobs. Streetcars didn't run; we were put up in a hotel by the Company and given meal tickets in a restaurant that was being kept open by the employers. You can imagine the parties that went on in those hotels with all the Western Union and Postal Telegraph girls and fellows in the same hotel with us. I got food poisoning from badly prepared food and was sick and, therefore, missed out on the big party. The absenteeism during the strike was about 50%. We were not supposed to be strikers!

The stimulus that these great militant strikes had on us in our very infancy as a union was tremendous. A lot of things became clear out of these struggles. The phony labor leaders exposed themselves, taking the side of industry and fighting only when it was to protect their own pie cards ('pie card' being jargon for a high salaried union job). Others, who were fearless fighters for their members' interests, were pushed forward to become, in several cases, the great labor leaders of this century. Harry Bridges, Walter Reuther, and Joe Curran were just a few who sprung from that era.

I belonged to the union, went to the meetings, listened and read all that was printed in the newspapers. I sat silently watching our local radio union leaders mislead and make mistakes. I witnessed the squabbles but did not take a forward part. I was backward about speaking up. To second a motion was a bold act for me.

The Great Pacific Coast Waterfront Strike of 1934 ended in a great victory for the longshoremen and the maritime unions, including ARTA. ARTA had supported the strike most solidly and had been one of the thorniest problems for the ship owners to overcome, since the law prohibited a ship from sailing without a licensed radio operator. Radio men had to be licensed by the Federal Communications Commission. This was not an easy examination to pass.

Prior to this, radio operators aboard merchant ships were getting $55 a month and doing purser's work, gangway watches and whatever the company asked of them. Two operators stood 12-hour watches on passenger ships. Radio operators were employed by the radio service companies that owned and leased the radio equipment to the ship owners, though the ship owners paid their wages.

Part of the sales pitch for winning a radio equipment contract for the service company from a steamship company was the low wages for which they could supply any operator.

The service company agent that hired you would take you down to a uniform store and outfit you with all the clothes he could conceivably pile on you and make you sign a payroll deduction for it. He later went back to get his kickback from the uniform store. The agent wouldn't let a man stay on a ship very long, since he wanted to make another kickback deal on the uniforms. Some of these agents went so far as to take a commission fee off the radio operator for the assignment and then later take another fee to leave him on it.

As the union became stronger and started winning labor contracts, we quickly corrected these situations. One of the first demands was, "Throw away the little black book," meaning the black list, the list of union activists. They did, too, and sometimes we were able to see the actual book. All this material surfaced as the union gained strength. We became militant, radical and, yes, some even became communists.

In writing about things that happened 40-some years ago, the memory has a tendency to telescope events and even years, but one does not forget the harsh things. I am trying here to let the reader understand what made me think and go the way I did.

Margie, son Robby, and I moved to Mill Valley, across the bay from San Francisco, during this period. We lived well up on the side of Mount Tamalpais in a rented bungalow. It was easy for Margie to visit with her folks in Sonoma County and vice versa. Mill Valley is a charming and inspirational place to live. Of course, I climbed Mt. Tam early and often during the year that we lived there. My son was then two years old. We had a Scotty dog named Bonnie. Margie did not work. We had a nice life. Nearly every weekend we would have guests over and spend the evenings playing bridge, the days hiking and visiting. We appeared to have everything going our way, yet I was very disturbed by all of the labor problems which I have been describing.

I rode the ferryboat (the Golden Gate Bridge had not yet been built) with a fellow worker and radio operator, Leo Bash. He was well read, radical, and had traveled the world. Like me, he also had a wife and a little boy. He was a Jehovah's Witness and worked hard at his religion. On the ferry coming home he would mount the steps and give an eloquent sermon almost every night. He had overly long, wavy hair, suggestive of Leo the Lion. He played a mean game of payday poker and blackjack, generally winning. Those locker room games were sometimes big: it was nothing for a man to lose his two weeks' pay and then go to a loan shark so he could bring home grocery money to his family, facing the day of reckoning later.

Leo held his own in those games. I didn't play; I was no longer gambling. I heard it said, "Leo isn't averse to taking a card off the bottom, and having been a dogface soldier in the Philippines he knows all the tricks." I can personally vouch that this 'godly' man could sure handle his whiskey. He and I could polish off a fifth on a Saturday night and he never had a hangover, but I did. Leo would say, "Oliver, if you'd go to church you'd never have a hangover." I never tried that for a cure, preferring 'the hair of the dog.'

He was a considerable influence on me. On the morning ferryboat ride he would lecture me on Marxist economics as interpreted by his version of Jehovah's Witnesses. He said, "Oliver, take leadership in the union! All your ideas are good. You're honest, popular and strong enough to do a real job if you only would." Leo reserved the ferryboat ride home for his unsolicited sermons. Unsolicited, yes, but on days he wasn't there the passengers would ask me for him and if he was well. He knew the Bible like Billy Sunday, backward and forward. Leo could field any question no matter how provocative, and he could do it every night. He surely had missed his calling; no question, Leo was talented.

I can hear him yet in his loud resonant voice from the steps of the ferryboat, "You will see God, if you see a baby in birth!" I don't know yet what that meant.

One night we went back for the union meeting and Leo convinced me to step up and say what I believed. To gather nerve to do it, we stopped at a bar just before going into the union hall and we both took a couple of straight belts of whiskey.

When the subject I wanted to speak on came up, I got up and gave my views. The men applauded and I felt great. I can't remember today just what I said, but I think I spoke of "planning and caution"—in that vein, I'm sure.

After that I never hesitated to speak up again. Before long I was being elected to committees. In time, I was elected chairman of the local. I was on the brink of a big change in the direction of my life. A shot of whiskey can be great therapy.

CHAPTER TWELVE

I Go All The Way

I was like a puppy seal: once having gotten wet in the sea of union work, there was no problem getting into the swim. I was swept along with the current and soon elected shop chairman of the San Francisco office of Mackay Radio, which included several stations and shops that were a part of the Company's operations. There were about 120 employees in this one company. The San Francisco Central operation was where the money was made.

As shop chairman it was my duty to collect dues, sign up new members and take the Union's position at all times. I was able to do this and work a full shift on the job. Generally I went to ARTA headquarters after work, ground out organizing letters, and mailed them to operators working for the Company in the several major cities where the Company was located. A few of these letters turned up in the hands of the Company attorneys at the Labor Board hearings some time later. I would ask on the telegraph key, "What's your name and home address? I want to write you a letter." A lot of organizing went on over these channels. I just took the chance that the guy at the other end felt like I did. As I later found out, that was not always true.

You would have to be a radio telegrapher to fully understand us. We were a small fraternity and the very nature of our work drew us together. If the operator you were working with in New York or Los Angeles or wherever was a good operator, you would assume that he was also a good person. Generally speaking this was true. The more intelligent and better the operator, the better the union man. One seemed to follow the other. This factor made it very difficult for the Company to fire men for their union activities. They were reluctant to cut off their right hand or the hand that served them best. Of course, Company officials tried to use this psychology in reverse by saying, "Are you going to kill the goose that lays the golden egg?"

We began to develop very rapidly as a union and formed a strong collective bargaining unit. The President of Mackay Radio and Telegraph Company, with head offices in the I.T.&T. Building in New York City, came out to San Francisco in response to our request to be recognized as the collective bargaining agent. Mr. A. Y. Tuel, the President, was an ex-telegrapher himself and had come up the hard way. He had brought the Company from a small Pacific Coast communications system called Federal Telegraph Company. This in turn had started as a fast telegraph service handling sugar quotations between the various West Coast cities; it had been owned by the Spreckels sugar interests. Mr. Tuel took the Company into the I.T.&T. System. It was named Mackay Radio and Telegraph Company after Clarence Mackay, who had laid the first cable across the Pacific in 1900. Mr. Tuel was a very competent executive and we found him to be surprisingly broad-minded.

A great deal of time in committee and membership meetings was spent drawing up our demands. These meetings were tough to handle, since the Company's agents were ever present to disrupt and we had plenty of dissension without that. A number of skills and classifications were involved, and many petty jealousies existed.

When we got all this squabbling behind us we asked the Company to meet with us, thus Mr. A. Y. Tuel's visit to the West Coast. We had a bold negotiating committee that formally presented our demands. Mr. Tuel started off with a friendly handshake to each of us and the remark that he had once been a telegrapher himself and had joined the Order of Railroad

Telegraphers. He said, "I think unions have done a lot of good. I believe in unions and think collective bargaining is the proper way to handle the matter of wages and working conditions. However," he went on after a pause, "I prefer a national labor agreement, and if and when you can satisfy me that you represent a majority of the the employees nationwide, I will negotiate such a contract with you."

We liked the sound of that program and belived he was sincere. I'm not sure that there was any choice to do otherwise, but we accepted his challenge.

Interest in the Union was great. Those who had not yet joined came to the meetings that we called. I addressed the meeting, saying, "Represented by the Union you will be free men and women. You will be the Company's equal! You can hold your head up with pride!" I added, "The President of our Company and the President of the United States recommend you join a union of your choosing! The Congress has passed a law making it legal for us and illegal for the Company to interfere! What are we waiting for?"

Those who had not joined did so. We went after the others in the other cities. It was not hard to get them signed into the Union, especially in places where we had direct radio circuits. Many of us were ham radio operators as well, and we used our private radio stations for this purpose too.

In a short time the national office of ARTA advised us that we had a comfortable majority. The San Francisco membership voted to send me back to New York City to represent them in negotiations with the Company. Mr. A. Y. Tuel had agreed to meet with us and proceed with negotiations. I asked for a leave of absence to carry on union work.

Mr. Tuel signed my three months' leave of absence, changing it to read, "...to do good and welfare work among employees." Otherwise, it was what I had asked for.

A week or so later I was advised that Mr. Ellery W. Stone had been appointed President of Mackay Radio, succeeding Mr. Tuel, who had died suddenly of a heart attack.

I received a letter from Mr. Stone stating, "Your leave has been granted and signed by Mr. Tuel, but if you will wait a few weeks for me to take over the office, I will advise you when I can be ready to meet with you and your committee."

I took my leave, feeling that I could use the time to strengthen our organization in New York and get set for the task I was confronted with. Mervyn Rathborne was then the paid business agent of San Francisco ARTA, Local #3, which consisted of ships' radio men as well as us. He bought me a one-way ticket to New York City with an upper berth.

Margie had acquiesced to my going with some trepidations. I said, "Goodbye," kissed her and my son and took off.

Mervyn met me for breakfast and took me to the train. He said, "Oliver, you are launched on a big change in your life. You will be fighting capital, industry, big business and sometimes government." He wished me good luck and said goodbye.

Crossing the country by train, I had a lot of time to think about what I was doing. I really felt that my efforts would be for my family's strength and freedom. All that I wanted was to accomplish the thing the members had entrusted me with. I had no other ambition beyond this purpose and a strong desire to get home and back on the job. I did not realize how profound Mervyn's remarks had been.

I was met at Grand Central Station in New York City by two union members, Dave Wingate and Bill Hathaway. They gave me a hearty greeting. Dave was carrying the ball for the Union in the New York Central Office and proved to be a fine and courageous person. He was a highly skilled radio operator and well liked. Bill was working temporarily as a clerk in the same office.

Bill Hathaway came from San Francisco, where I had known him as a messenger boy in the RCA. He had been fired because he had borrowed a set of headphones from the company to practice code in his room. He was accused of stealing the headphones. What a reward for a young ambitious kid! He was later killed in Spain, fighting with the Abraham Lincoln Brigade against Franco.

Coming into New York City was again a big moment in my life. I gasped, "The size of it!"

Dave and Bill asked, "Do you want a real cheap lunch?"

"Sounds great!" I added, "How cheap?"

"You won't believe it," Dave said.

They took me to a Cuban restaurant that, fortunately for my stomach, I was never able to find again. The place had a sawdust floor and stinking, ripening sausages and cheeses hung from ropes on the ceiling. Lunch cost ten cents each, which included a meat sandwich, soup, salad and coffee. I said, "Even in this depression year of 1935, I find this price hard to believe — it's also hard to eat."

My escorts then took me to the National Office of ARTA, where I met President Hoyt Haddock and editor Willard Bliss. That office was a storm of activity and excitement. The Union had a radio operators' strike going on against several of the shipping companies. I was immediately initiated to a picket line, even though it was not my strike or my doing.

I spent most of the time meeting with the New York Mackay operators and sometimes meeting with RCA employees. Broad Street is the communications center of the world. All of the men who manned the international radio and cable circuits terminating there were interested in me and what I was there for. I traveled out to the big transmitter and receiver stations on Long Island at Rocky Point, Riverhead, Brentwood, Southampton, and Hicksville and met with the men from those stations. I signed up many of them into the union.

ARTA was still an independent, unaffiliated union at this time so I didn't meet any outside union officials. I did meet Representative Marcantonio, the congressman from New York who was elected on all three political tickets, Republican, Democrat and American Labor Party. He was a human dynamo and stayed in Congress several terms. I was very impressed with him. I asked, "Mr. Marcantonio, would you be willing to address a union meeting of cable and radio operators?"

He surprised me by saying, "I'd love it!" The members loved it too.

I lived in the St. George Hotel in Brooklyn, just across the river from Manhattan and one subway stop from Broad Street. It was a nice older hotel with a heated indoor swimming pool, the walls and ceiling all mirrors. There was a coffee shop and cocktail lounge; it was handy for the communications people who wanted to see me privately. Many would call me and ask if they could have a beer or a cup of coffee with me. Their interest in the union was cautious and clandestine at first, especially the cable operators.

I Go All the Way   103

The crucial day arrived. Mr. Ellery W. Stone called Hoyt Haddock, president of ARTA, and said, "I'd like to meet Mr. Salisbury."

When Hoyt told me this, I said, "Hoyt, that's fine. Let's get the committee together."

Hoyt said, "No, he wants to meet with you alone."

"No! Never that way!" I said.

He suggested, "All right, I'll go with you." I thought that would be okay.

We then took the elevator to the top floor of the I.T.&T. skyscraper. We entered an outer office where Mr. Stone's secretary said, "Mr. Haddock and Mr. Salisbury, we are expecting you. Follow me." She escorted us into an office that seemed the size of a tennis court. Mr. Stone sat at a huge desk twice as big as a ping-pong table, shined to a fare-thee-well and with nothing, absolutely nothing, on it.

He was a large, handsome man, a sort of combination of Daddy Warbucks and Yul Brynner, and just as bald. It seemed that with each step towards him I became smaller. The carpet was like a cranberry marsh, and the same color. I think I was up to my ankles in it by the time I got to the chairs he indicated for us.

Mr. Stone said, "Mr. Salisbury, did you know that A. Y. Tuel's last act was to sign your leave? Right at this desk, he dropped the pen and dropped dead."

That was the first time I had heard this detail and for the moment it made me feel guilty among other negative things. After those remarks Mr. Stone got right down to the confrontation. He said, "Salisbury," now dropping the 'Mr.', "what do you want?"

I said, "You know what I want, Mr. Stone. I want a signed union agreement for the members of the union I represent."

Mr. Stone said, "No. I mean what do you want out of life personally?"

I replied, "Security for myself and family."

He said, "Well, Salisbury, we are going to appoint a new district manager for Chicago and we are going to make that appointment to someone from the West Coast without regard to seniority."

He went on to say, "I'll study your demands." I handed these to him in legal form. Mr. Stone then said coldly, "I'll reply in a few days." We shook hands and the meeting was over.

Haddock and I took the elevator down and Hoyt said, "Well, Oliver, you had your chance to be district manager in Chicago."

I was rather surprised that Hoyt had ever exposed me to that situation, but he was young and inexperienced, too. Further, it was his nature to be conciliatory—a course which he followed clear over to the other side of the table a few years later.

Several days after this we received Mr. Stone's offer to his employees. It granted some wage increases to certain skilled hard-to-replace employees which included my own classification, but it was a very divisive instrument, carefully designed to break the union wide open once and for all had we accepted it.

I telegraphed the offer to San Francisco, where they held a union meeting simultaneously with New York. San Francisco voted unanimously to strike, as did New York. The outlying stations were notified and followed suit. A strike was called.

That strike is now a matter of record in the archives of the National Labor Relations Board in San Francisco and New York, in the records of the Ninth Circuit Court of Appeals, San Francisco, and in the records of the U.S. Supreme Court. While my daughter was a law student at Boalt Hall, University of California, Berkeley, she studied the N.L.R.B. v. Mackay Radio Supreme Court case. The decision was famous, having established that strikers were still employees.

A short description of that abortive strike is pertinent at this point. The New York office left their jobs *en masse* and came to the union office. There they held a noisy strike meeting which broke up in a foot race to get back to the central office and take up the best jobs vacated. This broke the strike in New York Central Radio. The men out at the stations on Long Island stood together for several days until the Union called off the strike.

After getting the men back to work in New York, Mr. Stone recruited a planeload of strikebreakers from among the ranks of the foot racers and loaded them on a plane for San Francisco.

We were able to get wind of the Company's plan, and had a sizable delegation of pickets out at the Newark Airport to see them off. We got some support from the Air Line Pilots' Association, also in its infancy at the time. They delayed the plane, to the embarrassment of Mr. Stone and the strikebreakers. The pilot said, "I don't like the smell of my cargo."

Mr. Stone chose not to hear that remark, since to have replaced the pilot would have meant an expensive delay of an hour or two and perhaps even the failure of the plan he was to execute.

No sooner had the plane taken off than the Company's plan in San Francisco was executed. A supervisor contacted a union member and told him that everyone was being replaced by people from New York and that he should get the San Francisco personnel together in a certain hotel at 2 a.m. and advise them of this. The first ones to sign up to go back to work would be hired in that order. The men coming from New York and Chicago had been promised they could stay in San Francisco if they wished.

Late that evening a union defector went from home to home telling the men to be at the Sutter Hotel at 2 a.m. He had been a close friend and a staunch supporter of mine so most of the members accepted his statement. Some thought it was a strike settlement; some asked, "Does Salisbury know of this?" He lied and said, "Yes."

The hotel banquet hall was packed; everyone was there with few exceptions, not all of them from weakness or panic. The superintendent, Mr. Jorgensen, was there too, and he read off a list of 11 men who would not be taken back since they had been fired. My name was not on that list as I was officially on leave of absence and still in New York. There was another foot race.

When the "Flying Scabs," as they became known, arrived, all the jobs were filled. A couple of them decided they liked California and stayed, but the rest went back where they came from. Those strikebreakers who stayed on were later fired when the Union won its closed shop contract several years later.

For the moment, the Union was smashed and the 'piggy bank' in the national Union treasury was empty. I was still in New York City on a leave of absence that had two months yet to run. I knew what would happen when I did try to turn in my leave. I had received a blow-by-blow description of the disaster via amateur radio at a member's home in Southampton, Long Island. I stayed around New York for a few weeks trying to pick up the pieces.

During this period, Union president Hoyt Haddock and vice president Roy Pyle proceeded to give me a liberal education on just why the Company was willing to pay such a price to defeat us. The strength and determination of these men was contagious and I caught it.

While we had been destroyed by Mackay and Mr. Stone, our brave action seemed to have won friends and respect on the "Street," as Broad Street was referred to in the international communications industry. Organization in RCA, Press Wireless, Globe Wireless and the cable companies continued.

My friends in San Francisco had written that they were taking up a collection to buy me a ticket home, which they did. I was told upon my return that even some of the company supervisors had contributed. It seemed they all felt bad at allowing themselves to be panicked that way.

I came back across the country on a day coach with no berth. Sitting up for four nights and three days, I had a lot of time to think. I was very happy to be returning to Margie and Robby. She had written that she was looking for a cheap apartment in San Francisco and preparing to leave Mill Valley. My good friends were being very loyal and helpful to her. Most of my thoughts were of how to carry on the fight to reorganize the Union in Mackay Radio. I had great faith in the National Labor Relations Board's ability to get the men reinstated. In fact, I never really felt we had lost. I made up may mind to study labor history, economics and Marxism, and to seek association with experienced people.

Margie was in full support of me and the Union. A friend, Lon Rone, had filled her in on exactly what happened. She was furious at the Company's diabolical plot and the perfidy of my friend Dick Burtz.

Dick Burtz, the nightrider of that infamous night, called on me at my home with his wife shortly after I returned. I told him that under the circumstances I did not care to have him in my home but there was going to be a union meeting the following week where he was to be put on trial for his treachery. He said, "No one will be at the meeting."

I said, "Well, you and I can be there." He took the challenge and said he would be there. This was a tremendous break for the Union. We never had such a large attendance before. Everyone came to see the fight which Dick promised them. He boasted, "I'm going to mop the floor with Salisbury."

We had prepared formal charges in detail. Dick showed up in a leather jacket and tight-fitting leather gloves. He was a strong, stocky, athletic fellow. During the course of our past friendship we had wrestled and boxed in a gym together and probably were fairly evenly matched. I had height and a little reach on him. Best of all, I had the crowd.

I read the charges against him. He sat right up front, squarely in front of where I addressed the meeting. Behind me was a large chair that was the speaker's chair.

Dick could contain himself no longer; he was itching for the fight that he had steeled himself to. At one insignificant point in the reading of the charges he shouted, "That's a damned lie!" and charged out of his chair, head down like a football tackler. I fell back into the speaker's chair under the impact. He tried to beat me in the body, but I had a good grip on his head with my left arm and my right hand was free. I let him have it many times, full in the face, before the members broke it up. I never had a mark on me but he was a mess. I was not proud of that, but was satisfied with the way the whole thing had been handled.

Dick was excused from the meeting, found guilty as charged, and expelled. The members voted to reorganize their union group and resume paying dues. A few weeks subsequently Dick confessed his duplicity and asked to be permitted to make amends. He was fined and his expulsion reduced to a period of suspension. He later became a good union member and a worthy person.

I continued to work for the Union. The fellows kept up with the shop collections to help me and my family survive. When I attempted to turn in my leave the Company advised me, "You are fired because you have violated your leave by calling on employees of other companies, whereas your leave read: ''...good and welfare work among employees." Tricky lawyer's lingo, I thought. "Your calling on employees of other companies has embarrassed us," they said.

Before I arrived back in San Francisco from New York, the local Union had already filed unfair labor charges with the NLRB on behalf of the remaining five men whom the Company had refused to take back under one subterfuge or another. They were the outstanding leaders in the Union. I reported to Mr.

Wagonet of the NLRB and he said, "To include you as a defendant, Mr. Salisbury, will delay the case. A date has already been set by the trial examiner and because of your activity in New York your involvement would surely complicate the case and make it doubly expensive for the Board. The Board is anxious to make a test case that will go the U.S. Supreme Court if necessary."

I felt that he made his point and it was for the general good of the Union members. Mr. Wagonet promised, "I'll personally see to it that you get the same treatment as the others if we win the case." That was good enough for me. Since the Board was new and this was their first case in San Francisco, they were meticulous in the care with which they proceeded. Fortunately for me, even this informal discussion was taken down in shorthand by Mr. Wagonet's secretary, Mrs. Alice Rossiter — who two years later took Mr. Wagonet's place as Director.

There was a new day coming, but those stuffy lawyers didn't know it. We thought we did.

It seemed as if the hearings went on forever. The Examiner finally ruled in our favor, ordering the men reinstated with back pay and the Company to cease and desist interfering with our efforts to organize a union. The Company thereupon appealed to the Ninth Circuit Court of Appeals in San Francisco. This meant another long delay and more hardship to the locked-out men.

A group of radio operator union activists in San Francisco in the early days of their organization. Left to right: me, Ed Croft, Rudy Asplund, Roy Pyle and Bruce Risley. About 1938.

I am with a group of shipmates in front of the Tiger Balm Palace in Singapore. An extravagant showplace done in very poor taste. 1936.

I ham it up with shipmates in Fez caps. Alexandria, Egypt. 1936.

I stand in front of the new house on Chenery Street, in Glen Park, San Francisco. This house was purchased under one of the very first FHA loans made in that city. 1937.

CHAPTER THIRTEEN

A Trip Around The World

In the spring of 1936 the Ninth Circuit Court of Appeals in San Francisco reversed the National Labor Relations Board trial examiner's recommendation that the five members discharged in San Francisco after the strike be reinstated. The NLRB appealed to the U.S. Supreme Court.

This meant more delay. Industry and the media were taking the viewpoint that the Supreme Court would throw out the Wagner Act along with other New Deal legislation which they had so negatively and rapidly disposed of. The companies were taking this cue and were proceeding very much as if the law did not exist.

Even though the men in the Mackay shops were continuing the weekly sustenance collection for me, I was starving out and needed a job to keep out of further debt. I said to Margie, "I think I'll have to take a ship job until the Supreme Court makes its ruling."

She replied, "We sure need money. What else can you do?"

An unemployed ship's radio operator named Rudy Asplund agreed to take over my duties in the Union. He was single, had money saved, and could afford to do the union work for little pay. He did a very fine job for the next couple of years. The Marine Division of ARTA had by then, as a result of the great Pacific Coast maritime strike of 1934, won a closed shop contract with the Pacific Steamship Owners' Association with all radio operators hired through the ARTA hiring hall. The Union was able to place me aboard the S.S. President Coolidge as third radio officer. The President Coolidge was sister ship to the President Hoover, the blue ribbon liner of the Dollar S.S. Fleet. The Coolidge was a big new ship carrying a crew of 350 and some 700 passengers. Her run was Honolulu, Yokohama, Kobe, Shanghai, Hong Kong, Manila and return.

The past year had been a rough one for me. I said to Margie, "This is only a relief trip. You go up to the ranch and visit your folks. I'll be home before you know it. I'm going to look on this as a rest and I've always wanted to see the Orient."

Margie said, "You enjoy it!"

The radio room on the President Coolidge was a busy place and required good operators to handle it. We had a powerful transmitter, and because the ship had the reputation of being staffed with the best operators she served as a relay ship for the Company's other vessels and as a favor to many other American ships in the Oriental service. Her time in ports was short and her sailings were always at midnight. She was not a fun ship, she was a work ship. The officers' mess and quarters were on the top side and we were not permitted to associate with the passengers at any time. Captain Ahlin, as the saying goes, ran a tight ship. I was severely reprimanded for standing at the rail watching the farewell party as we pulled away from the pier in San Francisco. Captain Ahlin wanted the passengers to think the ship ran by itself under his masterful guidance, which appearance he pretty well maintained until he ran this beautiful ship into one of our own mines and sank it at Guadalcanal during World War II. (Fortunately, I was not on it.)

The second radio officer, Jack Green, and I were both active Union members and politically conscious. Jack said, "Let's visit the J.W.O.A. (Japanese Wireless Operators' Association) in Kobe."

"Sounds like an interesting project. Let's do it!" I said with enthusiasm.

We met the president of their union, Mr. K. Misomo, the editor, M. Nagayama, and Y. Ogara, organizer. Nagayama had been to college in the United States and spoke perfect English. We invited them to dinner as our guests and asked them to take us to an interesting place. They took us to an ancient baron's castle which had been converted into an inn. It was a beautiful spot overlooking the harbor and the city of Kobe. They unraveled a fascinating story of the history of their union and themselves. The president had spent a year in prison for his union organizing efforts and had lost his wife and son in a divorce action resulting from his activities. The J.W.O.A. was militant, and had established the finest conditions for wireless operators in any merchant marine service of any nation in the world at that time. Talking to them was an education in trade unionism. I never knew what happened to these fellows during the war with Japan though I have often been curious about what their role would have been.

In Kobe one of the junior deck officers invited me to join him ashore for a cocktail. He said he knew a small place where the crew and tourists didn't go that was quiet and friendly. It was inviting and I joined him. His description was justified. I met the barmaid, Meiji. She was cute as a doll in a little pongee cocktail dress that fit like a snake's skin. She spoke a very little bit of English. The owner was a pleasant middle-aged woman and her clients were doctors and medical students from a nearby college. She spoke fluent English. We spent a few hours there and I made friends with Meiji. According to seamen's legend, there were only prostitutes available to seamen in Japan. A sailor could never meet any other kind. I was curious about that and did not believe it. Meiji's caresses did not seem to be for sale.

When the ship stopped in Kobe on its return from Manila, I called on Meiji again with a small present I had brought from the ship. This made her very happy and she warmed to me. I asked her, "When you get off work can we go somewhere more intimate, wherever you suggest?"

Her employer explained to me that Japanese workers have a system of working long hours for several days with short rest periods which they take in the back of the place where they work, before being off for two or three days. Through her interpreter, Meiji said, "Next time you come to Kobe, if I will be off duty, I will go with you to an inn I know of." This sounded very exciting, but I never expected to see Kobe again, since I was only making a relief trip on the Coolidge. It was flattering to know she liked me well enough to say that.

When I returned to San Francisco I was reassigned to the President Polk, a combination passenger and freight ship in round-the-world service.

The country was still in the Depression. I felt very fortunate to be on a payroll again. My youthful ambition had always been to go around the world. Now that ambition was going to be real. I decided I would have every experience that presented itself. I would make out a sizable allotment for Margie and spend the rest on sightseeing and fun. I wanted to know about everything and to miss nothing. I would be out of this world' for nearly four months. I'll be a free soul, I said to myself.

Because the Polk handled cargo she spent several days in each port, taking three months and twenty-two days for the trip around the world. Well! Wouldn't you know? I did return to Kobe and I did go to see Meiji with presents again, little things like candy and playing cards. She said, "I expected you. The officer on the Coolidge told me you were on the President Polk. I will be off this evening and off for three days. I will go with you." This promised to be an exciting experience.

I met Meiji about six in the evening. She had changed to a low-cut party dress and was molded into it. Meiji was taller than most Japanese girls and quite beautiful. She wanted to have dinner and go to a dance where they had an 'American jazz' orchestra.

We took a taxi and changed taxis several times. Meiji's employer had explained to me the Japanese law forbade girls to date customers, fellow employees, or anyone they met in their place of business. If they were caught, she said, the penalty was placement in the Yoshiwara, a government-operated red-light district where they would be compelled to work off their fine as prostitutes. Rather severe, I thought and I hope that the postwar era has changed all those laws. Meiji must have liked me to take such chances.

We had a leisurely dinner, rather a light American-style sandwich and cakes in a quiet simple little restaurant where Meiji seemed to be known. After dinner we walked from the cafe to the dance. It was in an international part of the city. German bakeries, Italian wineshops, French pastry places, and other small businesses were operated by Europeans and Americans married to Japanese women. I guessed this from the appearances of the children and young people I saw. The Eurasian girls were very beautiful, with olive skin, dark hair, and slightly almond shaped eyes, and were generally taller and more slender than Japanese. I did not think the Eurasian men were as handsome as their girls were beautiful. The men tended to have smaller noses and features generally associated with Caucasians.

The dance hall was very much like a public dance hall I had been to in San Francisco called the Trianon. It was a place where people who love to dance went to dance to good music. Meiji was a good dancer; she introduced me to some of her friends and I danced with them. When I tried to dance with a lovely Eurasian girl, Meiji shook her head and tried to explain that one just didn't dance with those low-class girls of mixed blood. She tried to tell me about the pure race of Nipponese. The law or social custom required Eurasian girls to wear a lotus flower in their hair, so any girl with a lotus flower was taboo for me if I wanted to keep getting on with Meiji. We had a good time and enjoyed the dancing.

I felt I was living a "now" situation, giving little thought to home, future or even the ship. However, I was very much absorbed by my surroundings and the high degree of happiness of the young people impressed me. I freely joined in their fun.

After the dance we went through the routine of changing taxis again. Finally, when Meiji was satisfied we weren't followed, we headed out into the country towards Osaka. About 15 miles from the harbor, up on the side of a mountain, we came to a picturesque inn. It was landscaped Japanese-style—moat, ponds, swans, lily pads, terraces, and exotic shrubs.

We entered the inn as if we were expected or perhaps as if Meiji had been there before or at least had called, or both, which was most likely. We left our shoes on the steps, putting on slippers. These we left at an inner door, and from there on it was barefoot on the finely-woven straw mats. The couple running the inn bowed and greeted us. All arrangements took place in Japanese with Meiji, of course, doing the talking. We seemed to have this large and beautiful place to ourselves. I never saw anyone except the middle-aged couple who served us, and they were so discreet that they seemed almost invisible.

The sleeping-room was furnished Japanese style with a mattress on the floor. We changed into kimonos which the inn furnished us—a brilliantly-colored one for Meiji and a drab charcoal-colored cotton one for me.

I then saw Meiji in the nude as she changed to her kimono. She was really lovely, with tawny skin, well rounded limbs, and somewhat small breasts. Best of all, she was so clean and smelled so good.

Dinner was sukiyaki, served on a low hibachi. We sat on the floor cross-legged and drank sake, a Japanese rice wine with the potency of brandy. It was a lovely dinner. I have tried sukiyaki in San Francisco and Seattle as served for Americans, but it just doesn't come off the same. Something was lacking in the atmosphere—probably it was Meiji.

Meiji was an exciting lover, and I must say she knew how to make a man forget everything but her. We spent three days there, loving, eating, walking and soaking in the wooden hot tub built for two. Meiji played some kind of Japanese mandolin and sang little songs, none of which were appreciated by me. I never pretended to understand any music, let alone Meiji's. It's probably too bad I didn't.

The only interference with the serenity of the place was that about once a day a policeman would walk through, come up to the inn and study my shoes bearing the Florsheim label. They surely must have confused him in that pre-war Japan, which was so suspicious and hostile to all foreigners. We watched him through the latticework. It seemed to worry Meiji.

However, he always went away with his saber clanking at his side. Whatever the innkeeper told him seemed to satisfy him—or maybe what the innkeeper gave him—or maybe we weren't doing anything wrong. I like to think it was the latter. Meiji would clap her hands and say, "Okay! Okay!" as he disappeared off the grounds.

She had arranged for the taxi driver to pick us up at 5 o'clock in the afternoon of the third day. On that last day I worried a little about whether the taxi would show, since the ship was scheduled to sail at midnight. I expressed my concern by repeatedly pointing to my watch during that final hour. Meiji responded by saying "So" each time. I interpreted that as meaning, "Don't worry. He will be here."

I must admit to being a little bored by the end of the third day. Our very limited vocabularies had been exhausted and I knew the landscape and gardens by heart. I thought at the time, There has to be more than sex to hold two people together. They say, "The language of love is the same the world over"; however, I found it pretty constraining.

The price of the inn and our food and drinks came to $50. That was expensive in those times, but the three days were a cherished memory.

Meiji measured me for a sweater. I tried to discourage her, but she kept on knitting. I have never been back to Japan to claim it. I do hope she has had a happy life.

I am sure this experience has been repeated by others thousands of times since World War II, judging by the number of GI's that came home with Japanese brides; but in those pre-war days it was a rare affair, not often shared by an American.

The ship sailed at midnight for Shanghai. En route we had some trouble with the radio direction finder on the ship that we were not able to resolve. In Shanghai we called the Globe Wireless agent and asked for help. He was a fine fellow named Neal Brown, who held his job because he was an expert in radio, diplomacy, and—I suspect—foreign intrigue, the latter being an important commodity in Shanghai in that day. The Whangpoo River alongside the International Settlement was known as Battleship Row; the warships of all the world powers lay at anchor there, reminding me of great sleeping monsters.

After Neal Brown had solved the problem in our radio compass, I asked him, "What does a fellow like you do for entertainment in a place like this?"

He replied, "Would you like to come ashore with me and see?"

"Of course, I'd be delighted."

Neal had a seven-room apartment—three bedrooms, three baths—quite luxuriously staffed with a cook and two helpers. We dressed in business suits and had a nice dinner in his apartment. He then took me to see "Anthony Adverse," a movie that was playing in Shanghai even though it had not yet had its premiere in Hollywood. Neal held a reserved box at the movie house and the movie seemed to be quite an event, even there.

We arrived home about midnight and Neal explained that he had a 6 a.m. golf date. However, if I would like a party or a date with a girl, he would fix me up and I could be on my own. This sounded both interesting and intriguing. He called a White Russian girl who had been deserted by her American Navy husband and was looking for another. In the meantime she was not averse to some fun.

"Yes, I am willing to date your American friend," she replied in response to his query.

Neal told her, "Hop in a cab and come to my place." She did.

I was soon introduced to Celia. She spoke with a cute Russian accent, which sounded more French than Russian. I asked, "How do you happen to speak English with a French accent, though Neal says you are Russian?"

"Oh! I went to the convent school in the French Settlement, and the Sisters taught me English. They were, of course, French."

Celia was a pretty young woman of about 30 with jet black hair and eyes, a very fair skin, and just a bit on the buxom side. It was immediately obvious that she had a crush on my friend Neal, but was willing to go to any length to please him even if it meant sleeping with his friend as an accomodation.

We called a taxi and went out to the Delmonte Club on Bubbling Well Road, a big night club run by White Russians. Every other person she introduced me to was a prince or princess, all refugees brought out of Vladivostok in 1920 by U.S. Army transports.

We had a good time; it was expensive and exciting. We went back to Neal's apartment and Celia slept with me, but her heart was in the next room with Neal. That was not my most romantic experience. She wanted Neal to know that whatever she did was for him.

Neal Brown was taken prisoner by the Japanese at the outset of World War II and died shortly after the war from illness contracted in the POW camp in the Philippines. He was a great fellow, and certainly lived a very full life in his 35 or 40 years.

Celia told me a great deal of how the Russian refugees were treated in China. They were people without a country, badly treated by General Chiang. They could not go back to their own country because they were classified by the Soviets as counter-revolutionists, and they could not migrate to America except under a quota system with a long waiting list. To migrate to America they must have a sponsor, money and employment after they got there. These requirements eliminated most of them, but there was still a waiting list under the quota. They could marry an American and come in that way. Many of the women married American Navy men, but it was common practice for the Navy men to desert them when their Asiatic tour of of duty was up. Such a stranded woman would appear at Navy headquarters, only to find that there had never been a man there in the Navy by that name or that he had left for the States. In either case, she could do nothing. The stranded women would then try to survive by needlework and other crafts. The Russian men generally worked as longshoremen and at other heavy work.

There were crazy laws in the 1930's. If an American married a Chinese girl she first had to migrate to Australia, gain Australian citizenship and then come to America under the Australian quota. This was because of our "no Orientals" immigration law. However, an American could marry a Russian and bring her in as his wife without regard to the quota. A friend of mine did this; his wife came back with him, but it took about three years to get his mother-in-law through the quota. Quite different laws exist today.

We went on to the Philippines, stopping several days in Manila. I took the opportunity to see the sights: the old Catholic cathedral established there centuries ago, the museums and the Manila Hotel with its famous St. Miguel beer served in stone mugs. I did not have any interesting contacts with the people. We sailed from Manila for Singapore. I looked forward to seeing Singapore with great excitement. It has such a romantic sound to it. Singapore seems to pop up in every seafaring tale.

CHAPTER FOURTEEN

Strange Places New Experiences

Singapore was a British military bastion with the guns pointed the wrong way. They pointed seaward and in 1942 the Japanese Imperial invading armies came down the peninsula.

We were there several days. I did a little sightseeing, taking a car and chauffeur to Johore, an independent country connected to the mainland by a long causeway. The chauffeur told us a story about the ancient custom of human sacrifices that had been practiced in that part of the world. The custom had prevailed until it became illegal. Nevertheless, he told us, an old man had volunteered his head, and it was buried in the causeway to guard against evil spirits. I wonder what the old man's spirit thought of the Japanese Army marching across the causeway.

That night I went to the "New World," a sort of "midway" entertainment area. There was a public dance with a good orchestra and lovely Javanese girls to dance with if you bought their tickets. The tickets were cheap and I bought a pretty young girl's tickets for the whole evening. That way she could sit at a table with me. I had a nice time dancing with her, but got "left with the morning paper," as we used to say. Her father came to pick her up when the dance was over.

In Singapore we were tied up alongside a German freighter named the SS Kaiserhind, a big new ship that flew the Nazi flag. I had become acquainted with some of the young officers on the dock and was invited aboard for dinner. They had nice quarters, free beer and cheap liquor. I talked to them about Hitler. They were all well educated and all spoke English. They thought Hitler was great for the German people. Some generously showed me their photograph albums which depicted frolicking in nudist camps on their vacations and "plenty of sex," they said. One young engineer explained the system of how they were picked and appointed to the Merchant Marine Academy at about middle-school age: it was decided way in advance for them by the authorities whether they would be engineers or deck officers aboard ship. The wireless operator was a combination doctor-radio officer with very high status, as he was also some kind of Nazi political leader. He remained aloof, and the other officers seemed satisfied that he should. I gathered he wasn't popular.

Their chief objection to the system was that Hitler never let them draw pay outside of Germany. He wanted all earnings spent at home. They were on the same run that we were and it made for a long, boring voyage, with their only recreation being a walk ashore when the ship was in. This was the fall of 1936. Hitler had not yet started his rape of Europe, though he was militarily supporting Franco's war in Spain.

On an afternoon while we were still docked in Singapore, one of the young cadet officers named Gene Daley came to me and asked, "Sparks, will you help me out?"

I said, "Sure, anything to help a shipmate."

Gene pleaded, "See that cute little brown flower girl on the dock. I've made a date with her for tonight but she tells me I have to bring someone for her mother."

I took a second look and calculated the flower girl to be about 16 years old. Quick arithmetic indicated her mother might be 32 or so and possibly still comely. I did feel compassion for Gene's problem.

"Gene," I said, "you're asking quite a favor, but I did say anything to help a shipmate."

That evening we took bread, cheeses, cold cuts, beer and gifts from the ship's store and hailed a taxi on the dock. The flower girl had given Gene instructions for the taxi.

We rode a long way and ended up at a place on the edge of the jungle. They lived in a grass hut with a thatched roof. We were welcomed, especially the food and beer.

The mother was about thirty-five and somewhat on the plump side but she didn't appear to be too bad a deal. They had a hand-wound portable phonograph with worn-out American dance records. The music and the beer, supported by a bottle of bourbon I had brought, warmed the party up.

My friend Gene was a little guy but not in all proportions. He was also an exhibitionist, and as the party got going he doffed his clothes and began what you might call his version of a voodoo dance.

At this time the mother turned to me and said, "You take the girl. I'm afraid this young man will be too rough with her."

She then grabbed Gene and pushed him behind a bamboo screen. I heard a thud when they hit the mattress, but no protests. I don't know if she just liked her men young—after all, I was only 30—or whether she really was considering her daughter; but too, she could have been most impressed by Gene's exhibitionism.

The daughter did not seem to mind the swap. She was as eager and willing as I, and, like her mother, very cooperative.

I might say here that I really didn't go looking for these experiences; they seemed to come to me. I never was good at kicking a woman out of my bed if she came tumbling in. Though I was married, loved my wife and had every intention of being a good husband, I did feel that I was out in another world on these voyages and I wanted the experiences of a trip around the world to include as many of every nature as I could pack in. It was part of my philosophy of being a completely free man.

We had a doctor on this ship who supplied me with prophylactics. After I had been exposed I would go to him when I came back aboard and have one of his "specials," which were almost painful enough to make me give up sex. I never contracted V.D. because of these precautions. There would usually be a line-up of crew members in front of the doctor's office a few days after leaving ports. Well, I never had a guilty conscience, never told these stories before and have no regrets.

In Penang, Malay Straits Colony, we stopped to take on a cargo of tin. It was piled high on the dock looking like silver bars and worth almost as much. Penang was a dull, hot, British Crown Colony with the natives occupied by mining the tin under British supervision. It was a perfect example of a Crown Colony: all resources being taken out, nothing being put in. It is little wonder to me that Great Britain lost her empire.

The evening we were there I went to the bar in the hotel and to a dance we had been invited to by the British establishment. I must say, it was a dull affair and I found both the men and women very proper and stuffy—especially after the wild party in the grass shack at Singapore.

Walking back toward the ship around midnight, I heard a combination of telegraph and wireless signals. I remembered from my communication experience that Penang was a relay point for the whole area. I followed the sound up a stairway to its origin. There was a Chinese in charge and at that hour not many operators on duty. I introduced myself and this led to a very pleasant and enlightening visit. He explained the British Colonial system to me, not that I was not already aware of it. In those days they never let the natives advance to skilled work or bothered to educate them. The policy was to bring in Chinese for the skilled jobs, such as his. For police they brought in Sikhs from India and, of course, the officers of all companies and organizations were British. This chap was politically aware. He knew all about the C.I.O., in America, about F.D.R. He didn't have much hope for his own people because of their great weakness for gambling. (History has proved him wrong.) He may have been speaking for himself. My visit with him was educational, and I thoroughly enjoyed the opportunity to talk with an intelligent person on world problems, at least to get a different viewpoint.

We stopped at Colombo, Ceylon, for cargo and passengers. While at the dock I watched some of our sailors teasing a huge shark. I heard the bos'n shout, "Watch out, it's a man-eater!"

The sailors would put a large steak on a stevedore's hook tied to a rope and let it over the stern of the ship. This big shark would go "whop" and the steak was gone without the shark's getting hooked. I thought what quick work he would make of a man's foot.

Later in the day, Hugh Fitzgerald and Bill Scullen, who were the other two radio men, and the ship's doctor called to me and said, "Come join us in renting a car and chauffeur. We'll go out to the country club about 12 miles out, where we have guest privileges, and we can have a good swim in the surf."

"Wait up 'till I get my trunks," I answered.

We swam into the ocean. Hugh and Bill started out as if they were going to swim back to San Francisco. The doctor had gone to the clubhouse. After we were a quarter mile out and still going strong I yelled, "I'm turning back!" I realized that I was in too fast company, though until then I thought I was a good swimmer. Swimming back alone, I started to think about that shark back at the dock. I began to panic. I tired and floated on my back to rest, but when I turned over the tide had carried me out further, so I resumed a strong stroke designed to get me to the beach. I was tiring fast and saw a rock jutting out of the water ahead. I thought, I'll swim to it and rest and then it will be a breeze from there to the beach. When I got to the rock, which was about 30 feet in diameter, I saw that it was a coral reef and jagged like a pile of broken bottles. Worse, it was completely covered with small crabs about the size of a silver dollar.

I said, "Get over, crabs," as they rustled and rattled away from me. I took a good rest and then noticed that I was bleeding profusely from every point where the coral had scraped my body. I thought of the bloody stream that would follow me ashore and invite the sharks. Well, I had to do it. Believe me, I made good time swimming that distance to the beach.

When my friends returned they said, "My God! What happened to you?" I told them of my hysteria about the sharks. They laughed and said, "Don't you know the sharks don't come inside of where the surf is breaking a mile out there? There is a bar there that stops them."

I said, "Now you tell me!" I'm sure many a good swimmer has drowned just because he panicked. That nearly happened to me right there. Back aboard the ship the doctor treated my wounds and gave me shots, warning me that coral poisoning was very dangerous.

On the way back, at the chauffeur's suggestion, we stopped at a 'lace factory,' as he called it. Little girls, eight or ten years old, young women and very old women were sitting, crocheting beautiful white lace for a few copper coins a day. They would do this all their lives with perhaps a few days out each year to bear a child. I found it very oppressive and hoped that there would be a day when it would be abolished. I understand now that it has been.

Our next port of call was Bombay, India. It was hot, dirty and smelly, and I find very little pleasant to remember. I spent a day sightseeing with Hugh and Bill, who joined me again in hiring a car and chauffeur. The chauffeurs would also act as guides, giving you a running story as they drove whether you wanted them to or not—rather like the New York City cabbies. The things ours seemed to love to show us were the very height of morbidity, such as the perpetual fires of human bodies, the place where another religious sect hung the bodies of their dead for the crows to feed on and then excrete all over the city streets, the lepers, feeble, aged and dying wrecks waiting outside the gates of human fire so they could be tossed on the fire and that way get to heaven. The chauffeur said, "They come from all over India hoping to gasp their last breath at the Gate of Eternity." This was his interpretation and explanation. What I saw was real enough, and it did not inspire me to do any study or research on the matter. My hope is that those conditions no longer prevail.

I did have one interesting experience there. A snake charmer on the dock with his cobra and mongoose act played a tune on a reed instrument while the snake swayed and swiveled. After the fakir caught the attention of the passengers aboard the ship and had what he considered sufficient audience, he took the mongoose out of a bag. The mongoose instantly showed hostility and desire to attack the cobra. The fakir did not let the fight take place until he felt enough coins had been tossed to the dock at his feet. The mongoose then took its deadly stance, silent and motionless with head slightly lowered and twisted a little to the side. The cobra, unable to stand the suspense, struck, but the strike of the snake was too slow. The mongoose ducked and grabbed the snake by the throat and pinned him to the dock. The cobra wrapped his coils about the mongoose in what he hoped was a death coil, but to his frustration when he tightened the coil the mongoose relaxed and fell out of the coil, never releasing his bite on the snake's throat. The mongoose would have made quick and deadly work of the cobra, but the fakir intervened at this point, pulling them apart and putting the snake back in the bag. Apparently, a cobra costs a lot of money and the fakir was not about to let it be a battle to the finish unless a great deal more money was thrown to the dock than when I watched. It was a good show.

I went down on the dock with Hugh Fitzgerald, the chief radio officer, and we talked with the fakir about his vocation. He spoke good English and said that he was really a priest of some kind but did this to survive. He explained that he had psychic powers and proceeded to show us that he did.

He said, "Think of a number from 1 to 10, turn your back to me, and I will turn my back to you. Write the number on a bit of paper, fold it, hold it in your clenched hand, turn around and say okay. I will then turn around and tell you what number you have written down." I followed his instructions and he turned around and told me the number. He did this several times, with both of us.

The fakir said, "Think of the number of letters in your wife's first name." I did and he told me, "Your wife's name is Marjorie. Now your son's name." I had not told him that I had a son. He told me my son's name, "Robert."

He then turned to Hugh, "You will return to India many times, Tiger Eyes." He had taken an early dislike to Hugh. His description was accurate of Hugh's eyes, if not his soul. Turning to me, the fakir said, "You will never return to India."

The funny part about this was that "Tiger Eyes" was resigning at the end of this voyage, which would complete 11 trips around the world for him, and I was to take his place as Chief Radio. As it subsequently worked out, I went ashore to work for Globe Wireless in San Francisco; Hugh did return to Bombay, and I never have. This experience made a believer in ESP out of me.

Hugh was interested in electronics and radio phenomena and whiled away his off-duty time working with ham radio equipment. He had real curiosity and understanding on the subject. He had made a 'breadboard transmitter' (miniature radio transmitter mounted on a breadboard) and tuned in to a microwave frequency. Then he made a receiver that would receive the signal he was able to send from this miniature transmitter. Among his other talents, he could sail a boat. If he were in a port that had rental boats and good sailing he would rent one. On this day he wanted to test this transmitter. He had me listen for his code signals, which he would transmit from his breadboard transmitter aboard the sailboat. He took Bill Scullen with him. I readily picked up his signal from a half-mile away, but I noticed that when he sailed behind an anchored steamer the signal disappeared and then re-emerged as he came from behind it.

When Hugh and Bill came back aboard we discussed this. I had kept a log on it. It was obvious that this frequency had the quality of a light beam. We talked about possible potential uses of this knowledge. It was only a few years later that the Germans built their strategic radar station at Dieppe on the coast of France. I wouldn't be so brash as to say that Fitzgerald invented radar, but he certainly was one of the early experimenters with microwaves. It did at least help to pass an otherwise dull day in the harbor of Bombay.

Bombay was the half-way-around-the-world point from San Francisco; we now considered ourselves to be on the way home. I had mail from Margie, reporting that she and son Robby were well and wishing us speed on the last half of our voyage.

CHAPTER FIFTEEN

Long Lazy Days

We headed out across the Indian Ocean, about five days' travel on the President Polk. It seemed endless: nothing but hot, blue sky and water, not even a ship; and one didn't even hear a ship on the radio. It seemed as if that old, old part of the world was uninhabited.

We entered the Suez Canal after a short stop at the city of Suez. It was under British mandate still and seemed, like any other British colony of that time, so dull it literally droned with laziness. The only apparent reason for its being was the canal.

As we went through the canal I couldn't help but be excited by it because of its history and its vital importance to commerce. In 1936 I could still see the barbed wire entanglements and wrecked lorries and equipment left from World War I and the Turks' attempt to take it from the British.

One of the sailors aboard built a box kite and lofted it as we went through the canal. He sent it a quarter of a mile high, and it was a big kite. He said he was an Arab and this was his way of letting his family know he was still on that ship. If he were to do that today, there would soon be jet fighters up from both sides of the canal to shoot it down.

Long Lazy Days

As we entered the Mediterranean, the ship stopped at Port Said. Though it seemed much like Suez, Port Said was reputed to be the most evil city in the world at the time. That was not evident in the daytime, and I did not venture ashore at night. I assume this reputation was based on the availability of drugs of all nature.

Alexandria was more interesting. Being a big city, it was a good place to shop for souvenirs, and was historically most important. The merchant sailors called these ports the "gyppo ports," since they were good places to get mugged, short-changed, and, one way or another, get badly gypped. I was short-changed in the post office buying stamps for my brother's collection. It took me a minute or two to translate my change from rupees back to dollars and I had to step away from the window to do that. After I had figured it out I found I was short $5. A window said 'Inspector' in English. I stepped over to the Inspector and told him. He said, "Oh, the clerk is probably drunk; go back and ask him for it." I did. The clerk had it all counted out and laid aside in case I came back, or ready to go into his pocket if I didn't. I didn't expect to get gypped in the post office.

Naples, Italy, because of Pompeii and Vesuvius, was one of the more interesting stops on this voyage. Mussolini was waging war on Ethiopia at this time and the harbor was full of troopships arriving and departing like glorious warriors after splashing the blood of Ethiopians "like budding roses," as Mussolini's aviator son is alleged to have said in a burst of sanguinary enthusiasm. The streets were full of soldiers and I could see and feel the iron heel of fascism everywhere. I stood in line for two hours at the post office again trying to buy stamps for my brother's collection. The soldiers could break in at the head of the line and constantly did—the line never seemed to shorten.

We were in Naples two or three days. I spent two of them at Pompeii. My imagination surely worked overtime there. The graffiti in Roman lettering on the walls, the chariot ruts in the lava stone streets, the ruins of the fountains, shops, crumbling villas, the amphitheater, and on and on. Vesuvius was still belching smoke and flames as a warning to man not to rebuild on her slopes.

Visiting the ruins of Pompeii made the Bible and ancient history seem very real to me. A street sign, for instance, read,

"Romulus and Remus Street" in the original lettering. The Italians truly had a rich history, if not always an honorable one.

We stopped at Genoa, where some of the ship's officers had arranged for a special Italian-style dinner to be served in a home where they were acquainted. The dinner was good, but those countries just do not have the ingredients to put into their dishes. What the food lacked, though, they more than made up for in hospitality and atmosphere.

The young women in Italy were stunningly beautiful, but few at that time could speak a word of English. There was an overabundance of streetwalkers who knew a few words of English and were quick to display their health certificates and prostitutes' licenses issued by the Fascist government.

Marseilles, France, was our last foreign port of call before heading out across the Atlantic. France was exceptionally interesting at this time since the Popular Front government was in control and the labor unions were riding high in power and influence. The forty-hour, five-day week was the law and it applied to virtually everything except entertainment and pharmacies.

Hugh Fitzgerald invited me to go ashore with him to purchase some perfume. He was going with the barber off the ship to a factory where it was made. They contacted the owner on the phone and she arranged to meet us. She was a handsome-looking, blonde French woman who seemed to know the barber from previous transactions. She explained that under the 40-hour week law she could not even open her own factory after hours without being arrested. She took us up alleys into a building that led to a catwalk across the roofs to her building. We went in through a skylight and a ladder. It was all very clandestine and I hoped that she really did own the plant. The barber bought a gallon jug of Chanel Number Five and Hugh bought a quart. It was very cheap but worth a lot of money in New York. I asked Hugh how he would hide it. He told me he would put it in the radio transmitter and leave the filaments lit in the big tubes, thus scaring away the customs inspector. It didn't work that way, though. In New York, when the customs inspector came to the radio room, he said, "Chief, what part of the transmitter did you hide that perfume in?" as he peered around the brightly lit tubes. Hugh pulled it out, the perfume was confiscated, and he was fined $100. The barber didn't get caught. I asked him, "How come?"

He said, "I put it in a bay rum jug on the bar in the barber shop and the inspector never lifted the lid." Well you figure it out. My guess (and it is only a guess) is that the barber informed on Fitzgerald and collected the fee, equal to half the value of the perfume. The barber had been on that ship for ten years.

When we left Marseilles we traveled along the coast of Spain, close enough to shore so that we could hear the sound of the artillery duels between the Loyalist army and Franco's army. The Spanish Civil War was a hot subject aboard ship at that time. When I was on the President Coolidge, the Captain would come into the radio room every night when I was copying press and watch over my shoulder until I had received the Spanish Civil War news. He was pro-Franco, and would get very upset if the news was against his hero.

On the President Polk the second officer was not only pro-Franco but pro-Hitler. He used to come to the radio room when I was on watch and argue vociferously and vehemently with me for the Nazi position. Because I didn't agree with him I was automatically a communist in his book.

We headed out across the Atlantic for New York. The big Pacific Maritime strike of that year was still on. I had hoped to miss it since it had been called only a month after we sailed from San Francisco. We all had about three months' pay coming, less allotments and draws, and no one was anxious to be asked to strike the ship and lose all that pay. However, when we came into the Hudson River, there was a picket boat with instructions for us all to hit the dock on arrival. Five other President boats of the Dollar SS Company could be seen tied up at the docks or anchored out. The old struggle was on again; and it was December in New York.

After receiving instructions from the various maritime unions to strike the ship immediately upon tying up to the dock, some of us began to wonder if there wasn't a way to avoid losing the three months' pay we had coming. The Captain had notified us that if we left the ship we were breaking the Articles that we had signed in San Francisco and the penalty was the loss of all pay owed to us. It occurred to me that the Company and the Captain had also been guilty of breaking the Articles on several occasions in this long voyage and that their violations had preceded our anticipated violation. Captains like to call men who think this way "sea lawyers." Well, let 'em call, I thought, I'll be a sea lawyer.

We radio officers discussed this matter among ourselves. I said, "Let's have a meeting in the passengers' salon immediately after the ship is secured to the dock, that is, a meeting of the ship's delegates from each department: deck, stewards, engine, mates, engineers and radio."

At the meeting, I proposed, "Let me go ashore and see my union, the ARTA, and get to their lawyer with the problem of our pay." All departments approved and I was delegated to go ashore. The other ship's delegates instructed their members to sit tight until I returned.

I took Bill Scullen, the third radio officer, along. We advised the union pickets on the dock of our plan and asked them to bear with us for a couple of hours. My union sent me to a friendly admiralty lawyer who listened to our story and then said to us, "Go back aboard ship and reconvene the dapartment delegates. You will then ask the Captain for permission to read the Articles, which it is your legal right to do. Upon reading the Articles, you are to list the violations known by you to have been committed by the Captain and the Company."

We did this and I returned to the lawyer's office with a list of 23 separate violations, such as lowering the cargo booms and opening the hatches at sea on arrival days, lack of boat drills, and insufficient certified able seamen on watch. (It was the practice to take the A.B.'s off the watches at sea so they could be used at daytime work which required more skills than ordinary seamen had yet acquired.) The list was long, and fines were computed on the basis of the number of days at sea that each violation had been permitted to continue. Some of these violations had run on for three months, from the start of the voyage. Our lawyer also prepared to file formal charges with the New York City Board of Health because the water, electricity, steam and toilet facilities had been cut off aboard ship by our strike. Well, it all brought quick, positive action. There was a hearing before the U.S. Shipping Commissioner and substantiating evidence was presented by the ship's department delegates. The Commissioner ordered the Company to pay us all off in full including the three days that we had by now stayed aboard in port waiting for our pay, and in addition, ordered the Company to furnish us all with railroad tickets back to San Francisco.

This was a resounding victory. Although I never got any medals for it, I did stick a feather in my own imaginary war bonnet. After the President Polk crew was paid off, the unions filed similar charges against the Company for the other six vessels that were tied up. The crews and officers of these had left, forfeiting their pay. It is my understanding that eventually all of those crews were paid off, as we were, and that the Company was fined many thousands of dollars. However, I only know for a fact that we were paid.

This was about the tenth of December and the strike committee ruled that we had to do ten days' picket duty in New York before we would be released to the picket captain in San Francisco. I arrived home just in time for Christmas. I had brought Margie a pure silk Japanese kimono and it made a great Christmas present. I was back in this world, with my family, and very happy to be there.

I finished out the strike in San Francisco. After the strike was won I never went back to New York to rejoin the ship. I was offered a position ashore at Mussel Rock, down the Peninsula from San Francisco, by Globe Wireless, the radio company that controlled the radio on the Dollar S.S. Company ships. They had liked my work and wanted me at their coastal station.

CHAPTER SIXTEEN

Better Days

Margie had been out shopping when I received the happy call from the General Manager of Globe Wireless, offering me a job ashore.

When she came in I was having a Scotch and soda and grinning broadly as she walked up to me. "I never saw you drink alone before! What's the matter? And why the big grin?"

"How would you like having me home for a change? Home to stay?"

"I guess I could stand it, if you didn't spend too much time around the house. What's up? Don't tease me."

"All right! Mr. Pelmulder of Globe called while you were out and offered me a job at Mussel Rock. I must have a car to accept the job."

"That does it! How are you going to buy a car with the little money you brought home? It's taken all of your allotment for us to live, while you were away."

I could contain myself no longer, "Look what came in the mail today!" I pulled out a bank check for $250 and waved it at her.

"Where in all the world did that come from?" Margie screamed.

"It was in my Aunt Gertrude's will that each of her nephews would get $250 as a token of her love for us. Remember? We received a copy about a year ago. I noticed her estate went to her daughter as we all expected and I never bothered to read the rest of it."

"Well! What in the world rubbed off on you today? You smell like a rose, your whiskey breath notwithstanding."

I ignored the sarcasm. "I've already checked the paper. We can get a brand new Plymouth sedan for $200 down. I called Mr. Pelmulder and accepted the job. He's calling the Plymouth dealer to arrange my credit. Leave Robby and the dog with the landlady and we'll go down to Van Ness Avenue and pick out the car." I hadn't seen Margie so happy since we were married.

As we rode down to the auto dealer I continued to pour out my elation at the turn of events. "Margie, you know all I've wanted was to work under a union contract where I'd be paid a fair wage. That'd give us the money and the time to enjoy our children and each other."

"That's quite an order. Are you sure that's all you want?"

"What else? I'll tell you what let's do. If we get delivery on the car this afternoon, we'll go back and get Robby and the dog and go up the Russian River to your folks' cabin for the weekend."

"Wonderful idea!" She clapped her hands and said, "I'll call the folks and tell them we want the cabin. We'll have a real honeymoon, forget all this trouble we've been through and only talk of the future."

"That's great! We'll do it!" and I kissed her as we got off the street car, "but how'd we explain a two-and-a-half-year-old son on a honeymoon?"

"Hey! not so eager." She pulled away as I gave her a hug and reached for another kiss.

My new job was located off the Skyline Boulevard above Spring Valley Lakes, down the Peninsula from San Francisco. Globe Wireless had direct radio circuits to New York, Honolulu, Manila, and Shanghai as well as to the ships. These were manually operated International Morse code circuits, not automated or semi-automated as was taking place in other companies. Globe had gathered a fine group of highly skilled operators and paid well.

It was a 30-mile drive to the station, but the Company had plans for moving the operation into the Robert Dollar Building on California Street in San Francisco. I made the long drive for about a year until the move took place.

After the first day on the job I said to Margie, "I'll never go back to full time union activity. I'll try now to give you the stability you're entitled to."

Margie had found being a wife to a radical, left-wing union officer distressing, which was understandable, given her background as the daughter of a prosperous Sonoma County fruit rancher. She was proud and had never asked her family for help, nor had I ever asked anyone. If we bought a box of apples or a bag of walnuts from her folks we paid $1 for it. This was a principle at all times observed.

Nineteen-thirty-eight was a year of great growth, progress and solidifying of gains in our union and in the labor movement in general. The Wagner Act had been upheld by the U.S. Supreme Court in the Greyhound Bus case and again later that year in our very own Mackay Radio dispute, the second test of the Wagner Act before the Supreme Court.

This Mackay decision resulted in reinstatement with three years' back pay for the discharged members in San Francisco and New York.

For reasons I have described I was not included in the U.S. Supreme Court decision; but I had been promised by Mr. Wagonet, Regional Director of the National Labor Relations Board, that he would personally see that I received the same treatment as the others if the case was upheld in the courts even if he had to file charges all over again. I had accepted his promise in good faith and in the interest of helping the others get on with the case. The Supreme Court ruled in our case, "Strikers are still employees and cannot be discriminated against for their union activities." This ruling is studied in many law schools throughout the country today.

When the back pay for the others came through and reinstatement was effected, I went to the NLRB and asked that the promise to me be kept. It was now three years later and Mr. Wagonet was long gone, having accepted a Roosevelt appointment as head of the Securities and Exchange Commission. Fortunately for me,

Alice Rossiter, Mr. Wagonet's former secretary, had been promoted to Regional Director of the NLRB. I reminded her of Mr. Wagonet's promise.

She said, "Why, Mr. Salisbury, I don't remember that."

I said, "But, Mrs. Rossiter, you were present at the discussions with Mr. Wagonet and took verbatim shorthand notes on our conversation."

"If I did, I still have them." She looked up her notes, and to my joy and her surprise found they verified Mr. Wagonet's promise. "I will see what I can do," she said.

Several weeks later Mrs. Rossiter phoned me and said, "Mr. Salisbury, will you come to my office?"

On my arrival there she said, "I have a certified check for you from Mackay Radio for $3,500, which represents back pay less what you have been able to earn in the union work, on the ships and at Globe during this period." My eyes bugged and my heart pounded as she laid the check in front of me. I had never expected to see that much money all at one time on a check written out to me.

"Mr. Salisbury, there is a joker. You will have to sign this." She handed me a letter written on the Mackay Radio lawyer's stationery which said: "I accept this check as full settlement of my claim and I will never accept employment in Mackay Radio again even if it is offered."

I had not planned to return to Mackay, since I liked my job at Globe Wireless; but in the communications industry mergers were constantly taking place. (Years later, Mackay absorbed Globe.) Besides, the very indignity and principle of the thing incensed me. I pushed the check and letter back and said, "Mrs. Rossiter, you know I'll never sign that. I want the same treatment as the others."

I was surprised and disappointed that she would even offer me such a deal. Though I didn't say so, I felt she was new in her position, and such a highly responsible job as she held was in those days a new thing for a woman, so I forgave her. Fully three months later, she called me back and offered the same check again, with a letter offering full reinstatement as the others had received.

Mrs. Rossiter said, "Mr. Salisbury, I congratulate you for your courage."

Margie and I bought a new small house in San Francisco's Chenery Park, a little dell nestled back at the foot of Twin Peaks. It was a stucco house and only $3,800 full price. We had one of the first FHA loans in the city of San Francisco. I said to Margie, "Franklin Roosevelt is a mighty great man."

"I fully agree," she said.

I tried hard to tone down my political feelings and become a good stable husband and father, but I was a born rebel and it was beginning to show. I continued to be politically active, attending lectures by the socialist leader Norman Thomas, the communist Earl Browder, and any other militants who appeared on the scene. I was active in my union, serving as shop chairman, as delegate to the San Francisco Industrial Union Council, and in any other way I could find time to help. I wanted others to win the happiness we now had.

Margie did not quarrel with me about this activity and made an honest effort to participate, but it was all against the grain for her. She said, "I have two loyalties: to you, and to my father. It pulls me two ways. It's hard to handle."

A couple of years passed while I worked at Globe and tried to be a domestic type and an activist all in one person.

Then Rudy Asplund, who had taken my place as administrative secretary of the Radio and Cables Local of the union, decided he wanted to return to the sea. He was a bachelor, liked the sea life, and didn't like the nitpicking on the part of some of the members. He had a low boiling point. Rudy had done a good job during a trying time and we were all grateful to him.

Who was to take his place? The Executive Committee of the Union came to me and said, "We feel that with a full-time secretary in the office to handle the books and paperwork, you could administer the office on a part-time basis after your day's work at Globe. We want you and need you."

The Union's office was on California Street, not far from the Globe Wireless office. It looked feasible. I accepted, conditional on Margie's approval. I explained to her, "This is only part-time. I'll get my pay from Globe and some pay from the Union, too."

"All right, but you know, with that arrangement I'll never see you. You'll be at work or at the Union."

This went along very well for a while until the winter of 1939–1940, when things came to a head in Press Wireless. This company was owned by several of the nation's largest newspapers and the wire services. It was an international radio communications service designed to save these newspapers and news agencies cable and radio tolls.

After weeks of fruitless negotiations, the members' patience became exhausted and they voted to strike. The Press Wireless operators presented their problem to the Local's membership meeting of all the members in RCA, Mackay Radio and Globe Wireless, which were then under contract with us. The entire membership voted full support, financial and otherwise. We also obtained sanction from the San Francisco Industrial Union Council/CIO. Press Wireless' central operation was located in the San Francisco Chronicle building. The Chronicle was a stockholder.

Since I was Administrative Secretary of the Radio and Cables Local of ARTA (now renamed the American Communications Association/CIO), the strike was my responsibility. The night it was called we put out pickets in front of the Chronicle building, forgetting that nearly everyone who worked in that building was a member of some union or other. When the printers showed up for the night shift they wouldn't pass the picket line, even though they were AFL and we CIO and there was rivalry between these two parent bodies at that time. The men manning the presses inside stayed on duty while their reliefs contacted Mr. Christie, president of the Allied Printing Trades Council. Mr. Christie then attempted to contact me.

After setting up the pickets at the Chronicle I had gone out to South San Francisco and Daly City, where the transmitters and receivers were located, to set up pickets there. A strike is like a battle; if you are the commander, you move fast and fearlessly if you are to win. It was about four o'clock in the morning when Mr. Christie finally reached me. He had left word at the main picket line for me to come to his headquarters. This I did, as there seemed to be much more excitement going on than I had anticipated.

Mr. Christie was furious at me for having called a strike in the building without first notifying him. I said, "Mr. Christie, I am sorry, but I didn't think; I am only a babe in the woods on these matters."

He commented, "I like your attitude. What is the strike all about?" I related the situation.

"We sympathize and will do all we possibly can to help. What do you want from us?"

I explained, "It is not our intention to shut down the San Francisco Chronicle, but we do feel we should keep pickets there since that is where the men work and they can't very well picket in the hall."

"Suppose you picket only the front entrance and my men will use the back entrance. If you want to stop them you should contact me before putting pickets at both entrances. I wish to be kept posted at all times on your progress." This was excellent union spirit and was a big break for us, one we had not expected.

At this time the American Newspaper Guild was in its infancy, going through its growing pains as we were. They also agreed to use the back entrance. I had kept close liaison with them as they were also CIO involved in communications, and they were dealing with white collar and blue collar workers, as we were. Their officers were invited to our strike meetings and the Newspaper Guild gave us fine support, financially and morally. We seemed to get very fair treatment in the various San Francisco newspapers, even the Chronicle.

Because of the publicity in the papers and the nature of the service, our strike received attention and support way out of proportion to the number of people involved.

Our members in Globe, RCA, Mackay Radio and the Commercial Pacific Cable companies refused to handle any press dispatches over the international circuits, so we maintained a 'hot press' embargo for several days, finally modifying the embargo to include only diverted traffic from Press Wireless.

One day a Newspaper Guild member came in and reported that Naval Radio Communications was preparing to handle press across the Pacific under the terms of an old rate structure set up in the early days of wireless, before World War I. The reporter excitedly told us, "Copy has already actually been filed with the Navy!"

The 12th Naval District Commandant was located in the Federal Building a few blocks from the Chronicle. I went there with a committee and asked to see the Admiral. His aide, a captain, said, "Mr. Salisbury, what is the nature of your business?"

I stated, "The Navy is being used to break strike, and it is my belief, if they are aware of the role they are playing, they will not want to be involved."

In a few minutes the Captain came back and said, "The Admiral will see you, Mr. Salisbury, but without the committee."

The committee members said, "Go in, Oliver, see what you can do."

I had never been exposed to high ranking Navy protocol before and I was awed. The Admiral's aide was a captain; two more captains stood on either side of the Admiral with arms folded in front, faces forward like pages or palace guards. There was a lot of gold braid showing in that room.

The Admiral said, "Mr. Salisbury, be seated." He proceeded to very skillfully put me at ease, saying, "In my day a requirement for graduation from the Naval Academy was proficiency in the International Morse code and I can still read it whenever I hear the signals."

I said, "Admiral, it will be nice to talk with someone who understands our skills." I explained our problem. He seemed sympathetic, and issued an order through his aide to cease handling press dispatches until further notice, as it appeared the Navy was being asked to serve as a strikebreaking agency.

He turned to me and added, "I will seek further advice from the Chief of Naval Operations in Washington. I suggest that you have your Eastern representative call on him too."

This was done. After a day or two we were advised that the matter had been referred to the President of the United States. He had issued an order as Commander-in-Chief to this effect: "News is like any other essential commodity. If commercial facilities fail, the Navy in this case will supply." Needless to say we were bitterly disappointed in the President.

A few days later a Navy radio operator, a petty officer, came to our picket line and told us, "Don't worry about the Navy handling press. It is being done with less than enthusiasm. We have plenty of our own fleet work and the amount that we can handle will never break your strike."

The Navy personnel were very friendly in this situation. Many of our members were retired Navy chiefs. The Navy and the Army Signal Corps were nearly the only sources of men sufficiently skilled to handle the jobs our union was beginning to control. These servicemen looked forward to employment under our union contracts at such time as they would separate from the services.

I liked the Admiral and his men. I said to Margie, "I'm glad our Navy is in the hands of men like them."

We knew we were winning the strike because Mr. Marvin Cooke, Press Wireless superintendent, would go into his office in the Chronicle building and write a letter to the president of his company every day reporting on the strike. He was very discouraged by our solidarity and the support that our strike was getting.

How did we know the superintendent wrote such letters? The pickets knew when the janitor cleaned that section of the Chronicle building, and a smart picket would snatch that nice clean carbon out of the garbage every day and hold it up to a mirror and read it. We had our intelligence sources too.

After 60 days, spanning Thanksgiving, Christmas, and New Year's, Mr. Pierson, president of Press Wireless, recognizing pressure from his customers and stockholders and the fact that we had not had a single defector, decided to settle the strike. We won a closed shop, hiring through the union and the best wages in the industry. It was a whopping, well-earned victory for the employees involved, for our union, and for labor in general.

With the many ramifications, it was exciting. I had taken a leave of absence from Globe Wireless. A provision in our labor contracts allowed for a certain number of 'Union leaves' at the Union's request. I didn't draw any salary during this period, since the strikers were not getting any wages or strike benefits. Margie was very unhappy with this strike since I only came home to change clothes and not very often for that. This added coals to the smoldering fire of resentment that she was building up during these years.

By now the Union was strong enough to pay a radio operator's salary for a full-time officer. The members prevailed upon me to consider it again. I pleaded with Margie to release me from my pledge. She grudgingly acquiesced. I became full-time Administrative Secretary of the Radio and Cables Local.

Once full-time again, I was called upon by other unions in other industries to speak at strike rallies. I also visited labor's martyrs in San Quentin, of whom there were several, Tom Mooney being the most famous.

As a delegate to the San Francisco Industrial Union Council/CIO, I found that I was not a very good speaker, so I enrolled for a course in public speaking. The man who ran that school was training "Toastmasters." He furnished the students with anti-labor speeches that they could deliver before fraternal organizations, women's clubs or wherever. However, he did teach us how to speak and tell stories, using a tape recorder. If you are a poor speaker and don't realize it, you should listen to yourself on tape. It will make you wonder how your own mother could ever bear to listen to you.

I thought these were exciting, rewarding, useful years in my life. But they were not without cost.

CHAPTER SEVENTEEN

I Go To The Left
The Cost Of It All

I thought that I had a good understanding of what freedom was all about. To me it meant free right of association, free press, freedom of assembly, freedom of speech and the many other fine things written into our Constitution and the Bill of Rights.

I started to read labor history: the Tom Mooney case, the Haymarket Massacre, the Centralia Massacre, the imprisonment of Eugene Debs, the execution of Sacco and Vanzetti and on and on. I became an avid reader of social writings. I asked myself, Why did our government infringe upon the liberty of all these people, in view of our constitution?

There were militant speakers on special occasions at the CIO Industrial Union Council, speakers from Mexico, from Great Britain and other places in the world, most of them socialists or communists. What they said sounded like common sense to me.

My reading material became heavier: H. G. Wells, Hendrik Van Loon, Karl Marx, John Strachey, Sidney and Beatrice Webb, Norman Thomas, Earl Browder, William Z. Foster.

I also read books by the most contemporary writers of world politics: Eric Sevareid, Pierre Van Paassen, Vincent Sheehan, William Durant and other writers who were pointedly calling attention to what Hitler was doing in Germany and to other places where fascist dictators were seizing power—Spain, Italy, and Japan.

When I wasn't at union meetings or attending lectures, I was home absorbed in my reading—that was if Margie was home. If she was away, I couldn't stand the quiet of the house and would go out looking for a friend who would talk politics.

Margie complained, "Raising Robby is making me nervous, driving me crazy. I would like to get a job and hire a live-in woman to take care of him and do the cooking and housework. What do you think?"

I said, "We can use the money. There's nothing wrong with your idea if we can get the right woman."

"I've been to our doctor and he recommends that we do this. He says he knows a Welsh woman who happens to be available. She is a real 'English nanny' and will be wonderful with the boy and in the home."

We were able to hire Mrs. Evans at a wage less than Margie could expect to earn. Mrs. Evans said, "I think I'll enjoy working for you. Your home is small and new, the work will be easy and the boy and I'll have a jolly time."

Margie quickly obtained a well-paying job as secretary to a produce broker. Being the daughter of a fruit rancher gave her a good background for the job. She liked the work and the arrangement seemed to be working well. I said, "This makes me feel better about leaving you alone so much."

"Well, that isn't exactly why I'm doing it," she quipped.

Every Friday afternoon Margie would take the bus north to Sonoma County and spend the weekend on the ranch. She would take Robby with her, giving Mrs. Evans Saturdays and Sundays off.

I was always busy with a weekly meeting on Friday nights but would generally be alone Saturday evenings, feeling a bit sorry for myself but not knowing just what to do about it. It did not occur to me to seek the company of other women, though there were opportunities as a lot of young women were members of my union. I usually ended up in a bar somewhere drinking with my cronies. In an effort to understand economics, I attended Sunday sessions in a Marxist class in Berkeley taught by a professor from the University of California.

One Sunday night Margie returned from her folks in the country. I met her at the Greyhound bus station. She announced: "I've made up my mind to get a divorce. My father and mother have agreed to raise Robby. You know how he loves it up there."

I was dumbfounded. At a loss as to what to say, I stammered, "I know Robby will like that. He loves the ranch—but how long have you been thinking like that?"

"Two years," and she offered nothing further.

"That makes it a bit late for me to do anything about it now, doesn't it?" I was furious that she would live with me two years, hating me all the time. Since she offered no explanation, I jumped to that conclusion.

Margie was a moody girl and not inclined to complain verbally. I had been so busy that I had not really been aware of her unhappiness. I had been doing what I wanted to do—as it seemed, at the cost of my marriage.

I was unhappy about it but did not see what could be done. I felt that she had been wrong in not making me more aware of her feelings. I resented this deeply, so I did nothing to stop her. My lifelong habit of stubborn independence came to the surface, as did my temper.

Our son, who was then seven years old, loved the idea of living on the ranch with his grandparents and cousins. He didn't realize we were divorced for some time.

The very next day Margie filed divorce papers, going to her father's lawyer. The lawyer drafted a property settlement, providing that the home be sold and the proceeds divided equally, Margie to get the furniture, and the car to be mine. The few hundred dollars we had were divided. I was to pay the major part of Robby's support. I did not contest the divorce.

The divorce was granted on grounds of incompatibility. Margie's lawyer charged: "He stays out all night, is a carouser, doesn't love his son and is so involved with the CIO that he ignores his wife in the home. This is causing her a loss of health and generally creating unhappiness."

Mrs. Evans was called to the stand as a friendly witness for Margie. When the lawyer asked her to verify that this was the pattern of my conduct as a husband and father, Mrs. Evans, being a very honest person, said, "Why, I never knew Mr. Salisbury to be like that or do any of those things."

The lawyer immediately asked for a recess, which the judge granted. The attorney said to Mrs. Evans, "Mrs. Evans, you came here to help the Salisburys, didn't you? Well, then you say 'yes' when I ask you on the stand did you see those things."

When the court resumed, the counselor pursued a different tactic, exaggerating my participation in union activities and giving the judge a list of my radical reading material. He struck the right chord with the judge. Margie had been very reasonable in the amount of money she had asked for child support and had asked for no alimony. The judge perked up in his seat and said, "A man like that should pay more than double the amount counsel has asked for!"

The attorney said, "Your Honor, I thought so too, but Mr. Salisbury only earns $200 a month and I think my client is asking all the defendant can afford to pay."

"Well, let him pay ten dollars a month more than you ask. That won't hurt him!" the judge snapped as he settled back in his seat.

Mrs. Evans would have done better letting me stand as a scoundrel and a rounder who stayed out all night. That was something the judge might have had more sympathy for. Since I did not contest the divorce, I was not present at the trial; but Mrs. Evans reported the trial verbatim to me and accurately, I believe.

After the divorce, with no home responsibilities, I threw myself deeper and deeper into union work. To relax I would end up at a North Beach night club, sometimes with friends and more often alone. There was a lot of action there and it was a good place to forget the struggle and tensions that made up my day. I was in excellent health and could really take the punishment of hard work and late hours. I had an apartment and thoroughly enjoyed my bachelorhood.

One night a well dressed, prosperous looking woman sent me a note while I was sitting at the bar, asking me to join her at her table for a drink. She was alone, and I did. She said, "You are wasting your talent, young man. I have been watching you operate here for several nights." She handed me her business card which showed that she owned an "Escort Service." She went on, "I will pay you $50 an evening and expenses if you will come to work for me. Wealthy women living at the St. Francis and Mark Hopkins and other leading hotels call me every night for escorts. You can do the same as you are now doing and get paid for it. The work involves being strictly an escort. If you go further and get in trouble, I will fire you."

I was insulted by the whole proposition, and told her so; but it made me take a good look at myself. Being a gigolo wasn't my bag, and I didn't like anyone thinking it could be.

I was invited to many very nice and exciting parties during this period. My friends in the Newspaper Guild seemed to have all kinds of contacts in society, and to have radicals to your cocktail party was an 'in' thing to do at that time.

In spite of all this, I really was a homebody. I felt I would prefer to be married. A friend in a bar said, "Oliver, it looks like you can't live with 'em and you can't live without 'em."

"That's a help! And I've heard that one before. You know, what I need is a good union gal, a Marxist, who will understand what I'm trying to do."

The friend said, "There's plenty of 'em around. Keep your guard up and your pants buttoned."

"Smart ass! You're no help to a lonely guy."

"You call your life lonely?"

It seems that I was destined for greater work. In March, 1940, I was nominated to the office of International Vice President in Charge of the Radio and Cable Division of our union, with offices in New York City. The election was to take place by secret referendum during the following summer.

In April, I was sent to the Union's National Convention in Chicago, along with four other delegates from San Francisco. The convention was held in the famous old La Salle Hotel, a Chicago landmark for many years, but recently demolished. It was a big convention. Our International Union now had 15,000 members, holding nationwide contracts with Postal Telegraph Company, considerable organization in Western Union, contracts with the international communication companies and with most of the shipping companies on the East, West, and Gulf Coasts. Our name was now changed to the American Communications Association/CIO.

I had met Geraldine Shandros, secretary to the Union's president, several times on my trips to New York. She was a tall, pretty, young woman with light brown curly hair, blue eyes, a ready smile, quick wit, and a good figure. I was enormously attracted to her. She was in charge of details of the convention and had a nice suite of rooms commensurate with her responsibilities, courtesy of the hotel management.

Gerry, as she was called, approached me during the evening session of the convention and said, "Oliver, would you like to come to Room 1112 after the convention recesses? It will be a chance for you to meet some important people in our union."

I said, "I'll be delighted." I had heard that Gerry was single and unattached. I thought, what a break.

It was near midnight when the convention broke up and recessed until morning. I went to Room 1112, knocked, and Gerry let me in. She said, "It was so late the others begged off, but come in and have a drink anyway." Gerry was already in a kimono. Well, I didn't have to see flashing lights to recognize a welcome sign.

This began an affair that lasted through the six days of the convention and ended up in my second marriage a year or so later.

After the convention Gerry and I took a trip into the Illinois countryside to test our love in a more quiet atmosphere while my convention buddies spent the day and night seeing the sights of Chicago.

Since I had been nominated to the office of Vice President and would be on a national ballot that summer, we talked about our future together in New York if I was elected. Gerry said, "I'll fly out to San Francisco this summer on my vacation, and if you are elected and drive your car back, I'll ride back with you."

This gave me additional incentive to get elected. Some friends were anxious to put on a campaign for me in the big New York local. I gave them the green light.

I was elected, and that August Gerry kept her promise and flew out to San Francisco. We took a trip to Seattle, saw my mother and took care of my union business up and down the coast. We then drove to New York via Chicago, visiting her mother on the way.

We drove into New York City on a hot, humid Sunday afternoon in late August, tired from the long drive across the country. We went directly to Gerry's apartment, which she had furnished very attractively in an ultramodern decor. The apartment was clean and comfortable and freshly painted. The Third Avenue L rumbled and roared close by. Gerry said, "Home at last. You're welcome to share it."

"That'll be exciting," I said.

We lived together for a year, then decided to legalize the arrangement and get married. Gerry was an exciting girl. She had been a member of Martha Graham's dance workshop and had been on a WPA (Work Projects Administration) arts program. She knew many actors, actresses, dancers and artists. I found her exotic and lovable and her friends warm and interesting. Knowing her and being married to her was surely a pleasant part of my life's education.

Gerry had broken her leg in a hit-and-run bicycle accident which ended her ambition to be a professional dancer. This had happened before I met her. The ankle had healed crooked to the eye but she had no limp or handicap.

She was a brilliant secretary to the president of the union and a fine organizer of union affairs. We were both so active in our careers that we seemed only to have time to pass each other going and coming.

One Sunday morning, I said, "Gerry, I think our arrangement here is hell-bent for destruction. The only thing we're getting out of it is sex. There should be more."

"More what? More sex! I'll scream." She laughed and said, "What are you talking about?" Gerry had a fine sense of humor.

"More responsibility, more planning. What is our future?"

"If you're talking about marriage, let's go! I know the way to City Hall, I'll call my friends Lillian and Ron for witnesses."

It wasn't what I had been thinking of when I started the conversation but it seemed like a respectable idea. I said, "O.K., let's go!"

After all, I thought, she had all the things I wanted in a wife: compatibility, understanding and sympathy for my objectives, physical appeal, passion, culture and many other attributes that should make a marriage work. She loved me and I certainly felt I was in love with her.

Chapter Eighteen

I Hit The Big Apple

My first days in New York were spent getting acquainted with the officers and the staff in the International Office of the Union. Evenings were spent socializing with the rank and file members who had supported my election and who, for that reason, showed a certain possessiveness of me. I had met many of these people at the Chicago convention, but knowing them on their own stomping grounds was different. There were a lot of fine, hard-working, compassionate men and women among them and I got along with them smoothly.

This was the fall of 1940 and the military draft had just become law. Legally I was a single man, having been divorced in California and not yet married to Gerry; I was classified 1A, even though I was 34 years old. At the outset I was able to get several occupational deferments on the request of Joe Selly, president of the Union. As time went on the draft board advised me that they could not defer me on that basis any further. I was then in the middle of negotiations with RCA Communications, and the company supported my request for a further extension of my deferment, to which the draft board agreed. I headed the Negotiating Committee for the Union and we were making good progress, although the negotiations dragged on for many months. The company wanted to bring the talks to a peaceful conclusion and so did we. We had had too many strikes.

The RCA negotiations ran into the Globe Wireless contract renewal, and I was again deferred. Globe's head office was in San Francisco. Pearl Harbor took place while I was there. Like other young men, I wanted to rush up and enlist, but I called the President of the Union long distance. He convinced me of the importance of finishing the jobs that I had started and of their importance to the war effort.

While I was in San Francisco I went to see my son Robby, now eight years old. His mother let him come down to the city and spend the weekend with me. We were in a roadhouse having a nice dinner when we heard the news of Pearl Harbor on the radio. The next day I took Robby into Roos Brothers and bought him a little soldier suit with a Sam Brown belt. He made quite a hit walking up Market Street with soldiers and sailors saluting him. After that day I did not see him again until many years later, when he returned from the Korean War as a sergeant in the Marine Corps. He missed having a father and I missed being a father to him. A big price to pay for my activities.

The constant pressure from the draft board, which had begun soon after my arrival in New York City in 1940, was an annoyance. I had no intention of going into a peacetime army, but I began to feel that someone besides the Army wanted me in the Army. I was also called in by the Internal Revenue Service on some small item which they said they could not allow. The amount and the item were ridiculous and I began to feel harassed. I wondered if someone was sicking these agencies on me just for that purpose.

We launched an ambitious organizing campaign in the Western Union Cable Company. I did this the hard way—by standing out in front of the cable office on Broad Street and handing out leaflets to the men and women as they came and went to work. Many were friendly and stopped to talk with me. Some had heard of me through friends in the other companies. It wasn't long before I was able to get a group of them together and really discuss their problems. They were in an organization called the Western Union Cable Employees' Association, which had at one time a history of being an out-and-out company-controlled and company-dominated union. In fact, the very concept of a company-controlled union originated with the Western Union Telegraph Company during World War I.

The Wagner Act made company-dominated unions illegal and the company had revamped their association a little to allow free elections of officers in order to comply with the law. To the credit of the Western Union Cable employees, they had elected honest members to become their representatives, people who were pledged to support a really independent union. I worked closely with them. This association called a meeting and asked for a written ballot on the matter of affiliating with the American Communications Association/CIO. The vote to affiliate carried, but the Company then called for a National Labor Relations Board-conducted ballot before they would recognize us as the bargaining agent.

This was a fine victory since the cable department of Western Union had always been considered the elite in the industry. They had at one time been the highest paid and most skilled of all communication workers. Since the advent of our union this had ceased to be true. The NLRB vote was a resounding majority for our union.

Originally all cable operators were trained in England, where the only submarine cables were spun, up until World War II. As Great Britain spun her web of cables around the world she sent her own trained operators out to distant places to operate them. The British operators were home-lovers; they asked for and got individual contracts which provided for a fortnight home every year plus travel time. This vacation time could be accumulated. As time went on those employed in America and Canada married local girls and no longer cared about the visit home, but they continued to receive four weeks' vacation with pay in lieu of the trip home. When local apprentices became available to take the place of retiring British operators, the cable companies abolished the long vacation and other more favorable working conditions that cable operators had enjoyed. However, they could not abolish the memory of them. Restoration of these privileges became one of the first demands that international communication workers wanted inserted into their union contracts. We had been able to win this concession from the other companies even where it had never existed and that was a big incentive in the organizing of Western Union Cables. I believe our union introduced the four weeks' vacation into American labor union agreements.

During the RCA Communications negotiations the closed shop had become a big issue. RCA was the largest single employer of international communication workers in the country. They were the richest and, in my opinion, the most competent, too. I had worked for them several years in San Francisco.

To bargain with the union, RCA employed very talented executives who were experienced in labor negotiations as well as other highly expert technical heads of departments. These talks lasted for months, meeting several afternoons each week.

It was my first experience as head of a negotiating committee with RCA, although it was not their first labor agreement with us. As the negotiations dragged on we called in the Labor Department's Conciliation Service to help bring them to a conclusion.

When the contract was finally signed it was a book-length document. Many new concepts of what belonged in a labor agreement came to be in that contract. One provision in particular was new: a 'maintenance of membership' provision. It provided that if an employee joined the union he must remain a member. He could also elect to have his dues checked off, that is, withheld from his paycheck like his taxes. Our agreement with the Company provided that all of our membership in RCA had to be re-signed into the Union on a form approved by the Company. The form ended up with everything but a skull and crossbones on it.

I believed that the Company felt this would be the most divisive issue ever presented to a union membership. If so, they underestimated us. We were in a union that believed in the education of our membership. We set out a program to teach the members: "Why a closed or union shop?" We held meetings after meetings, all over the country, just on this one issue. I believe we were the first union to negotiate such a clause in a labor contract. Many of the older, purist unions thought and said we were crazy to sign such an agreement.

We then went after those who had never joined the union but

I Hit the Big Apple 153

were receiving the benefits and we got nearly all of them in, too. One group like this consisted of about 75 graduate radio engineers and technicians employed at the huge Rocky Point, Long Island, transmitters—one of the largest stations of its type in the world, if not the largest.

Only a handful of these engineers had to this time joined the union even though they had been receiving wage increases, longer vacations, and other benefits resulting from our bargaining with the company. They were hand-picked graduate engineers, many from MIT (Massachusetts Institute of Technology) and other fine engineering schools. They were not disposed towards becoming members of the CIO.

Their biggest gripe was that many of them received lower salaries than the radio operators and technicians, even though in addition to their degrees thay also had to hold FCC (Federal Communications Commission) radio operator's licenses. Sometimes skills are more precious than academic degrees and they were a victim of that twist of economics.

With the aid of a handful of our members at Rocky Point we were able to get a meeting called to be held in the Rocky Point school auditorium. I was invited to speak at the meeting, as was Harold Taylor, shop chairman of the Broad Street RCA Central Radio. The meeting was so well attended it was almost frightening. I think everyone employed at Rocky Point, including the riggers and laborers, was present. The fellow elected from the floor to chair the meeting was himself not a union member. This was an organizing meeting and it was not unusual under those circumstances for a non-union person to chair the meeting. Of course Harold and I were very happy to have such a turnout.

The chairman said, "Mr. Salisbury, if you can answer to our satisfaction the charges and questions that we will put to you, probably the majority of us will join your union and sign 'maintenance of membership' clauses. Most of the charges and questions that I will ask will be based on matters appearing in Westbrook Pegler's column, with which you must be familiar."

I said, "I am a consistent and hostile reader of Westbrook Pegler. To know what the anti-labor forces in the country are saying, his column is the quickest and easiest source." I proceeded to field all the questions that this highly educated group could throw at me in addition to the ones that the chairman had written down for me.

Westbrook Pegler was a widely syndicated newspaper columnist of those times; anti-union, anti-Roosevelt, he saw a Red under every bed. His talent was to be as provocative as he could get away with; he was finally fired by the Hearst papers, but years later.

The men gave me enthusiastic applause after I had answered the last questions. The chairman said, "We can set up a table over to one side to accept applications and fees while the meeting goes on to local matters of working conditions in our station."

That night every single person present joined the union. It gave us almost complete organization under a maintenance of membership agreement with a check-off of union dues for our entire national bargaining unit in the RCA Communications. It set up a long period of stable collective bargaining with that company.

I do not mean, in telling this story, that I did not have lots of strong and able help in bringing these successes about; and a lot of hard work had preceded me. Many of these workers went on up through the ranks over the years and became company executives and might not like to be reminded of their youthful militancy, though most would be pensioned by this time. For that reason I have not mentioned more names.

These negotiations and the subsequent approval of the maintenance of membership and dues check-off clauses should prove to anyone that when workers thoroughly understand the closed shop, they want it. It was always the anti-laborites' position that only the union bosses wanted that provision, and only to protect their own interests. Our union was always strong on education of its members and this was an example of how we carried it out.

The struggles were not all victories. We carried on an energetic organizing drive in the Eastern Division of Press Wireless employees at Little Neck, Hicksville, Long Island and New York City. About 50 or 60 employees were involved. We already had the San Francisco and Hawaii stations under contract resulting from the strike out there. The company had recognized an employees' association for the New York group. We tried to get a national collective bargaining unit set up as we had in all the other companies, but for some odd reason the

NLRB in New York ruled in this case in favor of the local unit. We had a large percentage of members signed up but despite hard work and person-to-person contacts on the part of the organizing committee, we lost the election by a slim margin. It was a big disappointment and one that we were never able to overcome in that company.

This was a very busy period. The events I have been describing were constantly overlapping each other and sometimes piling up into crisis situations. It was as if there were not enough hours in the days or days in the week.

Chapter Nineteen

I Go Into The War

With the outbreak of war, the problems and demands increased. The Army Signal Corps asked my help in recruiting experienced technicians for a crash radar engineers' program they were developing at Knoxville, Tennessee. I did find and recommend several very good men whom they accepted. Many of our rank and file members held commissions in the military reserve and as they were quickly called to active service, it left vacancies in our union working committees, grievance machinery, shop chairmen, shop stewards and so on. The Red Cross and other agencies called on us for speakers to help encourage blood donors, and many other opportunities to help the war effort presented themselves.

I was involved in legislative work in Washington with congressmen and bureau heads. I appeared before the House Committee on Merchant Marine and Fisheries headed by Chairman Bland. I presented a brief urging that the coastal radio stations continue to be maintained by the private companies and their present personnel during the war. The Navy had announced

I Go Into the War

intention of closing them down or taking them over and replacing the men with Navy personnel—they said for "security reasons." The Navy seemed to look upon our union as an arm of Joe Stalin. You would have thought we were at war with Russia rather than Hitler's Germany.

A Navy spokesman had the audacity to say, "The Union only wants to keep those stations manned by their members so they can continue to collect dues from them."

I addressed Chairman Bland's committee and said, "The Navy does not have competent personnel to staff the coastal stations and I am prepared to prove that."

Chairman Bland said, "That's a serious charge, Mr. Salisbury. For the next 30 days let the Navy keep a log on all distress messages received from vessels sunk by enemy action throughout the world and let the commercial coastal stations on both coasts do the same. At the end of this period we will meet again and compare results." I had no doubt of what the results would be. Our country's commercial coastal radio stations were manned by the most highly skilled and experienced men, many holding high ranking commissions in the Navy and Army Reserve Corps. Their equipment was designed for communications with ships of all classes and nationalities. Navy men were trained for fleet procedures which were entirely different. Navy staffing policies never left a man on the job long enough for him to really gain the experience he should posess.

At the end of the 30 days we met with Chairman Bland again and presented station logs showing 143 enemy sinkings. The Navy had a list of only 70. Our logs showed many ships sunk about which the Navy had no knowledge from any other source. We had the cooperation of the various companies' management in gathering the material and our data was technically correct.

Chairman Bland said, "I'll see what can be done about this!"

About this time, and perhaps because of those hearings, President Roosevelt set up a Board of War Communications, with representatives from the Navy, Army, the major communications companies and labor. The purpose of the Board was to determine the use of and the coordination of the nation's communication facilities to their greatest efficiency on behalf of the war effort.

On the recommendation of Joe Selly, president of my union, I was appointed by Philip Murray, president of the CIO, to be his representative on the Board of War Communications.

We met in Washington. The Board consisted of the Chief Signal Officer of the U.S. Army, the Chief of Naval Communications, and vice presidents of AT&T, IT&T, RCA Communications, Radio Marine Corporation (RCA), Mackay Radio and Tropical Radio (United Fruit Co.) and the CIO, which I represented. The AF of L communications union was present but I do not recall their making any contribution or participation, so, in effect, I represented labor.

Our appointments called for security clearances. I was given such a clearance. Our first meeting was in Washington. One of the first problems we were handed was the matter I have just related, pertaining to the manning of the coastal radio stations. Chairman Bland had asked for the Board of War Communications' recommendation on the matter. A subcommittee was set up to make such a report. I was named to the committee, along with the Radio Marine Corporation, Mackay Radio and Tropical Radio vice presidents.

Since I had done all the work in preparation for appearing before the House Committee on Merchant Marine and Fisheries, I was right up on my data. The subcommittee met in New York City. I had prepared a written report; the others liked it and moved it be submitted to the Board as the committee's report. This recommendation called for "continuance of the Coastal Radio Stations under current management and staffing."

The final resolution was that the Coast Guard, now under wartime Navy jurisdiction, would take over the operation of the stations with their present commercial personnel. The men would be brought into the Coast Guard at ranks befitting their skills and with a waiver of any physical examination. The men at the stations were happy with this solution. My presentation did not enhance my personal popularity with the U.S. Navy brass. Historians would be hard pressed to find any category of men that served their country better than these men. It was through one of these stations that communications with the underground resisters in the Philippines was established, around which the great naval battle of Leyte Gulf was plotted. The big station at Amagansett, L.I., also made contact with Tito's partisan camp, helping the Allies to supply him with needed equipment and personnel.

During this very period the Navy came out with a so-called

list of suspected subversive commercial radio operators whom they considered to be untrustworthy to sail as radio operators on board American vessels.

I was number one on the list. Two of the men named were radio officers who had already given their lives for our country, having been on ships sunk at sea in the early days of the war. I considered it an honor to be number one as I knew who had made up the list and that I was in very good company.

The list was reported to be the work of an Admiral Hooper, who, we were told, was a liaison man for the communication and shipping companies with the Navy Department and with the Congress. He had been after our union and its members from the very outset, and with the full support of those interests. Westbrook Pegler was the Admiral's oracle. According to Hoyt Haddock, president of the union, Admiral Hooper at one time tried to get the FCC to require radio operators to submit a list of their reading material before they could be signed on a ship. He was hot to have us fingerprinted long before the war. The names appearing on the list were in exact relation to their degree of activity in our union.

When I was seated on the Board of War Communications, other members of the Board joked about my being cleared to sit with them but blacklisted from sailing on even a dingy freighter as radio operator.

A sidelight: many years earlier, when I had been a cable operator on the WAMCATS (Washington Alaska Military Cable and Telegraph System) out in Seattle, Washington, Colonel Dawson Olmstead was the officer in charge of that system. It was rather a unique outfit within the U.S. Army Signal Corps, operating the communications system to and in Alaska. We wore civilian clothes and drew living allowances and lived where we chose and with whom we chose. Colonel Olmstead was new to the system, just having come from the War College in Washington, D.C., and he tried to accept things pretty much as he found them, but he could never forget that he was a Colonel in the U.S. Army, and did not want anyone else to forget it either.

I came on duty in the Seattle cable office one evening about six o'clock and a new order was posted on the bulletin board. "Though you are not required to wear uniforms, you are ordered to wear clean shirts!"

I read it, not feeling it was aimed at me, let out a loud youthful guffaw, and said, "Tough shit! I just put on my last clean shirt today." I was unaware that Colonel Olmstead was standing behind me.

The Colonel said in his sternest military voice, "Private Salisbury, if you want to lecture, hire a hall!" No doubt, more effective than any other kind of discipline he could have meted out.

Well, I was now sitting across from General Olmstead at the Board of War Communications' long mahogany table. General Olmstead, Chief Signal Officer of the U.S. Army, wartime, had shown not the slightest recognition of me, as might be expected. I could not and did not resist; I wrote on my CIO business card, "I now have a hall," and passed it across the table to him.

The General had a sense of humor. He laughed heartily and said, "I remember."

The Navy blacklist was sent out to all employers of radio operators, not only the communication companies but the shipping comanies as well, and released to the newspapers and the wire services. The men on the list were the last to hear, and of course, those who had died at sea never knew that our Navy considered them subversive as they made the supreme sacrifice.

The Navy set up an appeal apparatus. Our union decided to appeal my case since I was number one and handy, being there in New York City. We asked that a date be set for my appeal. It took weeks before the day in court arrived. It was a real kangaroo court proceeding. Five Navy commanders made up the panel. The chairman of the Navy panel simply stated: "The Navy has reason to suspect you of being subversive and therefore denies you the right to sail as a radio operator on an American vessel. What can you tell us to make us believe otherwise?"

I did have counsel with me, but he was not allowed to speak. Well, that question struck me as about as asinine as if they had said, "Mr. Salisbury, we think you are an ugly person, what can you say to make us believe otherwise?"

So, I recited my birth, my military discharge with special commendation, my father's military service, my grandfather's Civil War service and my genealogy going back to the Mayflower—not just to the Mayflower but to Captain Wm. A.

Pierce, captain of the Mayflower in 1629 (according to the University of Chicago Genealogical Library). I recited the number of times I had been to the blood bank. Then I asked, "What else would you like to know?"

Commander Valentine asked, "What is your position on the Spanish Civil War?"

I replied, "My sympathy was with the duly elected Popular Front government. I think Franco is a fascist, since that is where he is drawing his support from."

"What about your position on the Russo-Finnish War?"

"I think it is a trap by Mannerheim to draw us into the war against Russia and on the side of Hitler."

There were no further questions and no comment or ever any word from that panel. All I ever did hear was that one of the officers, who was a Navy lawyer, met a lawyer friend of mine by chance, and said he had heard a funny case: "A man that appeared to be a true-blue American, but yet in actuality was a dyed-in-the-wool Communist...." and he related the story of the hearing.

The ACA/CIO never bothered to have any more of those hearings, since it was obvious what we could expect from them, which was nothing but further abuse. The New York Daily News picked up the story about the descendant of the captain of the Mayflower being declared subversive and ran it on the front page.

We then attacked the problem from another angle. Joe Selly, president of the ACA, sent a message to all business agents of our Marine Division locals asking them to send telegrams to the President of the United States each day stating the number of ships tied up in each of their ports waiting for assignment of a radio operator. There was, in truth, such a shortage of licensed radio operators that it was common for a total of 40 or 50 ships a day in all the ports of this country to be loaded, staffed and ready to sail, but with no radio operator. Each day Joe Selly would send the President a telegram stating, "We have 70 experienced radio operators, all good union men, waiting to take out those ships that are tied up for lack of a radio operator."

It was only a few days before Joe Selly received a telephone call from Frank Knox, Secretary of the Navy. Mr. Knox said, "The President wants me to have a talk with you. Can you come to Washington?"

Of course Joe knew what that was all about. Joe told me, "When I entered the Secretary's office, Mr Knox said, 'Mr. Selly, the President wants me to extend the olive branch to you.' He had a dossier ten inches thick on his desk in front of him and he proceeded, 'Now, on this fellow Salisbury, there has obviously been a terrible mistake made.'"

Joe said, "I replied, 'You bet there has been, and on 69 others too.' Not being one to overlook an opening, I pressed for and got the complete abolition of the list. I also got his assurances that we would not have any further trouble with Admiral Hooper."

We read shortly after of Admiral Hooper's retirement. Westbrook Pegler was furious about the treatment of the Admiral and what he called the favoritism shown us, and continued to remark about the incident in his column as late as the McCarthy period.

The Navy Department sent out notices clearing us all, but it seemed to take a long time for the clearances to reach the same level the original list had. I kept running into it all during the war. One captain told me he had been warned about me and to watch me.

While all this was happening, my marriage of less than a year to Gerry was deteriorating. We were both so involved with our own careers that we seldom seemed to have time for each other. She seemed to go her way and I went mine. We certainly had an "open marriage," though that phrase had not yet been coined.

My work brought me in contact with Norma, a startlingly beautiful brunette, loaned to our union by the big United Electrical Workers' Union to be office manager of the Western Union Organizing Committee. This was an elaborate, well financed committee supported by the CIO parent organization and aimed at winning an NLRB election among New York City Western Union employees.

Norma was handling a hectic job in a masterful and orderly way. This, plus her beauty, attracted my attention. We had a couple of coffee breaks together and several after-work cocktails. Norma seemed disenchanted with her husband and she said, "I'm making plans to leave him."

Gerry and I went to the Union's convention in Atlanta that April. It was to last a week. I was called home by an emergency meeting of the Board of War Communications, to be held in New

York City. When that meeting was over it was too late to go back to Atlanta. I took the opportunity to make a date with Norma. I fell deeply in love with her. We went away for a weekend together and that was it.

I moved out on Gerry and Norma moved out on her husband. We were married as soon as it became legally possible. This took a year or two because Norma's husband insisted on a Jewish divorce conducted by a rabbi as well as a legal divorce in the courts.

Some people were naturally critical of us, but all I can say in defense is that I am sure Norma would not have stayed married to her husband, from what she had told me, and I do not believe that I would have stayed married to Gerry, since I was really looking for a more stable kind of marriage than Gerry was inclined to have or want and I don't think I was in love with her. Custom might require that we feel guilty, but we never have felt so.

Norma and I have been happily married now for more than 37 years and have raised a fine son and daughter, and in our minds that seems to justify the action taken back in early 1942. We were not Bohemian but we certainly were non-conformist and we did exercise a great deal of freedom of thought and action. There was a big war on, things were topsy-turvy, and who is to say today that we did wrong? Gerry remarried happily, as did Norma's ex-husband. There were no children involved.

A friend provided Norma and me with a place to live. It was a room in a penthouse owned by a bachelor, a composer. Living there was an unusual experience in itself. Our bachelor friend would hold late-night parties with Broadway show people that he was writing music for. We heard musical operettas before they were played on Broadway and some that were never played.

This was now the spring and summer of 1942. It seemed that we were constantly attending "going-away parties" for our friends on their way to war, some who never came back. Friends from San Francisco and Seattle were frequently stopping in to see me on their way to the war theaters.

I was deeply involved with negotiating a labor contract with the Western Union Cable Company at this time. During a lull in these negotiations Norma and I took a week off and spent it on the beach at Hampton Bays, Long Island. While we were there a Nazi U-boat landed two saboteurs. When they hit the beach they went north and bumped into a Coast Guard patrol and were arrested. They were later shot as spies on the orders of President Harry Truman. If they had turned south instead of north, the first thing they would have come to was the cabin where Norma and I were staying. We were awfully glad about that word "if."

The Western Union Cable Company negotiations dragged through the summer. Finally, the agreement was signed in the last week of August. It was a fine labor agreement and was won without a strike. One of my proudest possessions is a large glossy picture of the president of Western Union Cable and myself with the Union committee and the Company officials standing behind us while we were signing the contract. I felt that everything pertaining to the organizing, the negotiations and its consummation was done right. I had been working with a very intelligent membership and an excellent cool committee, and the Company's representatives were reasonable men.

I then went to the draft board with a clear conscience; my union work was done. I said, "I'm here to serve my country."

The chairman said, "We've been expecting you. We think you should go into the Merchant Marine as a radio operator as that is your training. You have 15 days to get on a ship."

This allowed Norma and me time to take another honeymoon. We went to the famous Green Mansions in the Adirondack Mountains near Lake George and spent a wonderful 14 days. The management made a big cake in the form of a liberty ship for my "going-away party."

I had resigned as vice president of the ACA/CIO and a very able person by the name of Harold Taylor took over. I began a new life.

CHAPTER TWENTY

The SS Charles Carroll

It was September 1942. The going-away parties had been held. I was assigned to a ship, which I joined in Philadelphia. Norma, her sister Betty, and her brother-in-law Natie went to the train with me. The parting was the usual hugs, kisses, tears and handkerchief-waving as the train pulled away.

On arriving at the dock in Philadelphia where the ship was tied up, and after passing all security guards, I saw hundreds of General Sherman tanks, all with Russian markings on them. I knew immediately my destination would be Murmansk, the northern port of the U.S.S.R., because they were loading the tanks on the SS Charles Carroll, my assigned ship.

The Charles Carroll was Liberty Ship Hull No. 2, the second one of these famous wartime ships to be launched. This was not her maiden voyage since she had already been out to India and back. In two or three days all of those tanks had disappeared into the holds of that vessel and two huge railroad locomotives were loaded and lashed to her deck. This ship's capacity to hold tremendous cargoes of bulky nature and our country's ability to produce them rapidly in great numbers made the liberty ship a heavy winning factor in World War II.

I met Captain George Evanson, an old timer at sea though only about 50 years of age, and also a veteran commander of a Navy minesweeper in the North Sea in World War I. He greeted me and, like most old-time skippers, had had good reason to appreciate his radio officer. He said, "Sparks, I'm happy to have a veteran radio operator rather than a kid just out of school for this trip."

"It sounds ominous," I said.

As the newly-assigned officers and crew came aboard, it developed that most of them were survivors of the sinking of the SS Express. To make matters worse, when the armed guard (Navy gun crew) came aboard they had also been reassigned from the ill-fated SS Express, which had been sunk by a Nazi U-boat off the west coast of Africa. These men were on their first reassignment after that experience. They had been 21 days in a crowded lifeboat and then spent 30 days camped in the West African jungle, eating only birds, leaves, and fruit.

It was my luck, at first exciting, and then boring, to have to listen to that story of the sinking of the Express over and over again.

We sailed out through Chesapeake Bay on a dark night to rendezvous with a convoy headed for Murmansk, with our cargo of General Sherman tanks for the Eastern Front. Sometime during the next day I heard, "dit daa daa dity daa dit daa daa" crackle out from a coastal radio station in Morse signals—the Charles Carroll's secret wartime call letters, followed by a ciphered message. I hadn't expected to earn my keep quite so quickly. Decoded, the ciphered message to the captain read, "Your orders are cancelled report in to the Army Dock at the Port of Boston for further orders." Wartime procedure forbade breaking radio silence to acknowledge receipt of the message. You were just supposed to be on watch at that time and be alert enough to intercept it. Not to receive such a message could put your ship in the wrong place at the wrong time. Plenty of stories where just that kind of thing did happen were recited to us at the Radio Officers Convoy Procedure briefings as examples of the costs of our failures.

When we docked in Boston they started taking off the Russian tanks. We were to learn later that all convoys to Murmansk not already underway had been cancelled. The Nazis were annihilating them as they came into the North Sea. The German pocket battleship, Tirpitz, was on the loose and raising havoc.

I was permitted to rejoin Norma in New York for a few days. When I came back to the apartment my brother-in-law, Natie, was there and the girls were out shopping. When Natie heard them coming down the hall he said, "Let's have some fun with the girls. Get in the closet!" Natie said to Norma after she entered. "What do you think Oliver is doing?" He added, "How did you hook that guy?"

Norma answered, "You want to know how I hooked him? Well, I'll tell you...." Natie, wisely, quickly opened the closet door so I never have learned how I was "hooked." However, I've always rather felt like Charlie the Tuna—"Happy to be hooked." Of course the girls were shocked to see me; Natie's prank was successful.

A few days later we sailed again. We had been reloaded with 10,000 hundred-gallon barrels of hi-octane (aviation) gasoline for Great Britain. This was for the beginning of the heavy bombardment of the German industrial cities.

Our convoy was not long in getting into action. We lost a ship the first night on the Atlantic. That loss was a result of one ship ramming another. One sank and the ramming ship had to turn back. The air crackled with the SOS and rescue operations. Of course, I didn't see any of it but heard it all in the radio room. It was a very black and foreboding night that set me up for what was to come.

In the first year of the war there was only one radio operator to a merchant ship. We scheduled hours like two on and four off spread over 12 hours; and then the commodore ship, which carried several operators, could signal with flags or signal lamp for radio operators to get on watch and stand by, and they often did this. We were a slow, six-knot convoy consisting of 44 merchant ships plus four Canadian corvettes as escort. We zigzagged and took a route taking us far north into winter weather though it was only early October. The days aboard ship were humdrum, but radio waves were exciting. I spent a lot of time in the radio room even when not scheduled to be there. The Nazis were at the height of their submarine warfare and we had not yet learned how to cope with the Wolf Pack attacks.

I heard the SSS followed by the ship's call letters (SSS was the submarine sighting or enemy action signal followed by the call letters of the ship) from a vessel in the convoy a day or two ahead of us getting torpedoed and sunk. All day long isolated attacks were taking place, and it was nothing to hear 15 or 20 ships sunk in a single evening. Ship's officers and crew members were constantly sticking their heads in the radio room door and asking, "What's going on, Sparks?"

I think they could tell by the expression of my face that I wasn't listening to an "Amos and Andy" comedy on the radio. I was very careful not to put out any information that could create hysteria or panic, and only passed on information to the Captain that was directed to him. One night I logged 23 sinkings from one single convoy going into Murmansk. I was glad our original orders had been changed, because that was just about where we would have been. The enemy was attacking with bombers, submarines, fighter planes and the pocket battleship Tirpitz. I learned later that my friend Red Stalworth lost his life in that battle.

That was the last convoy trying to make it into Murmansk until the Allies were able to get the Nazis on the run a couple of years later.

Five or six days out, just at dusk, the Canadian escort corvette pulled alongside with a megaphone and called out, "We are surrounded by at least six U-boats and are expecting a Wolf Pack attack as it gets dark. Be prepared!" I thought they were very cool about the announcement, like hunters expecting a duck flight, except that we were the ducks.

All hands were alerted and at battle stations. I was glad that the War Shipping Administration had seen fit to armor-plate the radio room. They had found in submarine warfare that if the enemy chose to do battle from the surface, as they sometimes did, the first shell would be aimed at the radio room so the presence of the submarine could not be announced to other ships. The armor plate was psychologically comforting to me.

As surely as it was scheduled, shortly after dusk the first ship was torpedoed. The snappy SSS followed by our convoy call letters and the ship's letters crackled out so loud I knew it was one

The SS Charles Carroll   169

of ours even before he gave his identifying signal. The poor fellow never finished his message before I heard a big explosion which was his ship blowing to smithereens from the cargo of hi-octane gasoline. That night several more fine ships and their heroic crews went the same way. There were no survivors. It was all the four little Canadian corvettes could do to try to protect the ships that were still afloat. To stop to pick up survivors would only have cost more ships and their precious cargoes.

There was a very large Norwegian whaling vessel in our convoy. She looked like 20,000 gross tons and perhaps 600 feet long. The Nazis were hot after her. They put a hole in her the first night and another the second night, but she bravely kept her position in the convoy. The third night they disabled her so that she could not maintain her position, but during the next day we could see her struggling unescorted several miles behind. That evening, just at dusk, with black smoke belching from her stacks she rejoined the convoy. Sailors on the decks of all ships cheered. I made a light "dit" on the radio telegraph key; others in the convoy followed with dits from every ship except, I am sure, the Commodore's. He must have been furious, but what the hell good was radio silence when you were surrounded by enemy submarines? It had to make that operator on duty aboard the whaler feel good, just as the sailors' cheers from on deck conveyed the crews' congratulations.

The fourth night of the attack the dogged Wolf Pack came in and finished her off. She was still in sight, the sailors said, when I heard her "——torpedoed and sinking" message.

A year or so later I rode the train from Halifax to Montreal and sat with a member of the Norwegian Consulate from New York, who was in charge of the North American interests of the Norwegian Merchant Marine. Norway was then Nazi-occupied. I told him this story and he said it confirmed to him that the Germans had intelligence on the nature of the cargo of that ship since he said it was a very strategic cargo. He did not even then tell me what it was.

The Consul confirmed that there were no survivors from that brave ship and her crew. He said, "Radio messages indicated the captain and chief radio officer had elected to go down with the ship in keeping with maritime tradition, rather than take to lifeboats, which they wouldn't know would never be picked up anyway."

I said, "It was a battle of skills and, I must say, your Norwegian crew made a magnificent effort to deliver that strategic cargo, whatever it was. It's too bad they lost." The Consul and I both sat silent a few minutes thinking of those men. When we resumed conversation it was about the beautiful scenery along the St. Lawrence River where the train was traveling.

On the fifth night of this Wolf Pack attack we were in a tremendous North Atlantic blizzard. I was going on watch at midnight and having coffee in the mess room with the second mate, Cecil Davies, who was also going on watch. I said, "Cecil, no one could be mean enough to sink a ship on a night like this." I was hoping for a night of respite from the continuing attacks of the Pack. The mate gave me a skeptical look, gulped his red-hot coffee and left for the bridge. He had been through it before on the SS Express and knew that the enemy could be just that mean.

One minute later I turned on the radio receiver in the radio room just in time to hear the SSS crackle out from a ship in our convoy, and the following boom of the ship's explosion. We were running in 30-foot seas with high wind and blinding snow and cold, but it seems the submarines snuggling under the waves are not affected by the surface weather. At least they were able to sink several more ships that miserable night.

At dawn I heard a tragic drama in code on the radio. It was a lifeboat sending a message to one of our escort corvettes. I copied it into my radio log, "We are 41 men. High seas and bitter cold in immediate danger of swamping can you attempt rescue? Signed The Captain."

The corvette's radio operator sent out, "Now we see you. Now we don't." I put that in the log too.

The lifeboat's radio operator said, "We see you 30 degrees to your port at one hundred yards."

This exchange of 'Now we see you, now we don't' went on for 10 or 15 minutes.

The corvette's operator said, "You disappear in a deep trough and then reappear somewhere else. We see you as you crest a wave."

The lifeboat's operator answered, "I know, but it's hard to keep from swamping."

After about 30 minutes of this the commander of the corvette sent a message to the captain of the lifeboat saying, "I am sorry, we must abandon you and return to the convoy."

The captain of the lifeboat replied with a short message, which his radio operator had difficulty transmitting, saying, "I understand. Thanks for a hard try."

I said aloud to myself, "How cool!" In that bitter cold and with those seas they didn't survive the day out. I never heard their signals again. I put my head on the table and wept. The Navy lieutenant came in and said, "What's the matter, Sparks? Get a 'Dear John' letter?"

I said, "Read it, Lester. It's all there in the log." I ignored his bad humor.

This was a hard crossing, and we weren't done yet. We had been through six days and six nights of this Wolf Pack attack, had lost 14 ships and their crews—in the neighborhood of 1,000 men with no survivors. Needless to say, everyone was jumpy. I was on duty in the radio room in the afternoon when a tremendous "Boom!!" was felt and heard. I said aloud, "This is it! We've been torpedoed!" I counted to five, waiting for the ship to explode.

Then I heard machine gun fire and the phone from the bridge rang. Adrenalin took over. It was the Captain on the phone. "Send an SSS—there is a submarine in the center of the convoy!"

I said, "Yes sir!" and sat back down and sent the message. Quickly a radio message snapped back, "Cease fire, you are firing at our towing spar." I rang the bridge; no answer. (They were handling the ship from the flying bridge.) I ran topside, where the gunnery officer, Lieutenant JG Hubert Lester Evans, was screaming into his phones, "Fire one! Fire two!" He was really raking the water with shell fire. With his headset on he could not hear me and shoved me away. I grabbed him and held him and jerked off his headset, yelling in his ear, "Cease fire!" He was hysterical with excitement at this point and one of the mates helped me hold him until we got through to him. I'll give him credit, his gun crew was accurate; the towing spar went floating by, shot to pieces.

We had been traveling in heavy fog. To avoid collision, some ships put out a towing spar which makes a wake or spray about 200 feet astern of the ship's propeller, thus alerting the ship behind to his location. One of the Navy armed guard, unfamiliar with this procedure, thought it was a periscope and sounded the alarm. In these situations the word is 'act first and check out later,' since later may never come.

When we got in to Liverpool we learned that we had sprayed the deck of the ship ahead with machine gun fire and the steward had broken his arm getting below deck. Fortunately, we did not hit them with the five-inch cannon which had caused the big boom that made me think we had been torpedoed. That was the first time the five-inch cannon had been fired on the trip. I found from this experience and later ones that false alarms can be more frightening than the real experience.

We finally got an old four-stack destroyer down from Greenland that drove off the Wolf Pack after six days and nights of attacks. Thanks to President Roosevelt for his foresight in giving these old World War I destroyers to the British even before we were in the war, an action he was much criticized for. Had it not been for that destroyer, no doubt the deadly Wolf Pack would have completely destroyed us and I wouldn't be writing this story 36 years later.

We came into the Mersey River and to Merseyside Docks, Liverpool, England, just 21 days out of Boston—a long three weeks, a gruesome three weeks. I was amused at the conversations in the mess room. All agreed that we must all go to church in a body and give thanks to God for our safe arrival. This was as we relaxed at the sight of land. However, I noted when we were safely tied up at the dock and the men started going ashore not a word was said about thanking God or going to church, but a great many questions were being asked of the bobby on the dock about the nearest tavern, the nearest cocktail lounge, the nearest brothel, or "Where is the action?"

A theologian probably would not agree, but I am not sure those are not just exactly the places the Lord himself would have directed us to, that is if He really had anything to do with the war.

What we needed after that Atlantic crossing was cheerfulness, friendliness and the soft touch of a woman. A psychiatrist might say we were ready to crawl back into the security of the womb. Certainly, the warmth of the womb was the biggest thing on our minds and I was no exception, though I like to think of myself as more discriminating than some of the younger men.

We still had to go back across.

CHAPTER TWENTY ONE

The Land Of My Ancestors

This was my first visit to the United Kingdom and England. I felt really good: no language problem, no cultural problem, and historically, I related to it. In all probability my family is descended from the Salisburys of North Wales, so prominent in English history. I have never thought of myself as an Englishman, though, and resented being called a Limey or a bull-headed Englishman by my friends when I was young and boys hurled ethnic epithets as taunts. I've always thought of being as American as one can be, though my genealogy is pure WASPish; I bore a deep resentment against the British for their part in the American Revolution and the War of 1812. I had never liked their colonial policies from what I saw and read. I did admire their guts in standing up to Hitler, though a bit belatedly. You might say I was a little confused as to what my attitude should be towards these people. I decided to get out and get acquainted with them.

Before I had a chance to make up my mind on this score, a British security officer came to the ship in Liverpool and said that the King and Queen would like to visit our ship that afternoon. "They are in Liverpool and want to see the dauntless Liberty Ship that is expected to win the war of transportation for the Allies. The officers and crew can muster on the dock if they wish, and the King and Queen will shake hands with the officers. If you don't feel like it, you don't have to be there. You can dress as you are."

I thought about it and said to Captain Evanson, "What do I want to shake hands with the King and Queen for?"

Cap said, "Suit yourself, Sparks," looking at me rather quizzically.

The ship's radio antenna had been damaged in the storm and I had planned to repair it that afternoon so I would be free to leave the ship for a few days. When the King and Queen arrived that's where I was, and I watched the handshaking and informal greetings from topside. No security officer bothered me and no one paid any attention to me.

The confidence and calmness with which the British do things is admirable. In retrospect, I know that I made an immature judgment in not being down there on the dock to shake hands with the King and Queen. I regret my conduct on that occasion. **As Dr. Overstreet wrote in his book** *The Mature Mind,* "It takes some of us longer to grow up than others." I realized later that it was really a very warm and generous act on the part of the King and Queen.

A day or two after arrival in Liverpool I experienced a happy coincidence; I was still thinking about my labor union back in the States and decided to call on the British Cable and Wireless Operators' Association. I looked them up in the phone book and walked into their office where the business agent was sitting at a desk reading a small newspaper or magazine over a cup of tea. I introduced myself. He said, "Strange, I was just sitting here looking at your picture and reading the story about your successful consummation of negotiations with the Western Union Cable Company."

I hadn't even seen the article myself. We were both overwhelmed with pleasure. He was a very busy man despite the fact that I caught him reading a paper during his tea break. The

British will stop in the middle of a battle to have their tea if it is "time for tea." I joined him for the tea while we visited. I said, "It's sure a small world. Here I come all the way to England, and the second day here see the King and Queen and the third day find an important person studying my picture and reading about me."

It appeared we would be about two months unloading and loading (unbelievable today, but true). I decided to see some of England. Jack Ackerson, our poet/purser on the ship and one of the finest minds it has ever been my good fortune to know, suggested we visit the Roman Wall at Chester. Jack was a historian, among other things. He could tell you the cause of every war, the results of the battle, the outcome of the wars and their impact on history. This made him a very good travel companion. His knowledge of history made things like the Roman Wall come alive.

After Jack and I came back to the ship I decided to take a trip by myself to London. I was not really a loner by nature, but no one else on the ship had the free time that I did. I wanted to see the sights in London Town.

On the train I sat beside a very pretty young woman who was a British morale officer for His Majesty's Armed Forces. Her duties were to go aboard battleships, to garrisons and wherever military men were gathered and tell them about their allies. Her specialty was Russia. She was born there under the Czar, had been a ballerina, had visited the Soviet Union recently and spoke that language. I found her very interesting. She said, "I'm going to be very busy in London but I'll be back in Liverpool in a week and I'd be happy if you looked me up at my hotel." Her name was Anna.

I proceeded to see the sights of London. The damage from the Blitz was tremendous. The city was blacked out like a drunkard's mind. A stranger like myself had better be in his hotel before it got dark. On the street at night, I really couldn't see my hand in front of my face. There were few Luftwaffe raids at this time, since the Allies had seized the initiative, thanks to the hi-octane gasoline we were delivering. There were gas balloons all over the city. People were saying, "If it were not for the balloons the British Isles would sink."

I found it very depressing, wasn't able to get good food and could not get warm to save me. I asked a waitress in a cafe what I could have to eat. She said, "SPAM! You ought to know what that is." Truth was that I didn't. Spam had not been introduced in America up to the time I left. Well, I had some, and it didn't taste any better than the little waitress made it sound.

I was always mystified by how the British could spot me as an American, and they always did. I was not in uniform. Some asked me, "How does it happen you speak the King's English?" (If Miss Oberton, my grammar school principal, had heard that she would have shouted "Hallelujah!" She flunked me in eighth grade grammar.) I didn't know my English was that proper, but they were meeting and listening to Southerners, Texans, Bostonians, Brooklynites and Americans from all over the States. This question always pleased me, especially if we were in a bar with shipmates who were mostly Bostonians and New Yorkers and were always razzing me about my Western lingo.

I visited the main landmarks: Buckingham Palace (the gates and change of Guard), St. Paul's Cathedral and Westminster Abbey. I was most impressed with the architecture and the age of St. Paul's. I found myself standing over General Cornwallis's grave inside the Cathedral garden. I said aloud to myself, "What should a good Yankee do when he finds himself standing over General Cornwallis's grave? What would Tom Paine do?" I got the answer. I spit on it. Perhaps we should forgive the dead after 165 years, but then there are a lot of graves of fine young men at Valley Forge and elsewhere who didn't get to live their lives out because of him.

I tried to visit the tombs of the Kings and Queens in the vaults underneath Westminster Abbey, but the guard said, "Sorry, but the Jerries dropped a bomb among them and scattered the bones helter-skelter, and now King Henry VIII is sleeping with Anne Boleyn again. We'll get 'em sorted out again after the war."

I said, "Yes, I'm sure that will be the first important job." I did like the guard's joke.

London was cold, foggy and drab as a result of the severe bomb damage from the Blitz. After several days I decided to take the train back to Liverpool to get warm and get some good food in me.

Once warm, well fed, and becoming bored, I decided to look up the pretty British morale officer, as she had suggested to me

The Land of My Ancestors

on the train to London. This venture promised some escape from the anxieties I still felt after our trip over and from my anticipation that the return would be no better. I found that Anna was back and glad to see me. Although she was busy with her official duties we had a few dates. She was warm and understanding and gave me the comfort that I needed. Anna had a week's holiday coming; she had leased a cottage in the Lake Country at Grasmere near Windermere and invited me to join her there. This was a few hours from Liverpool by train. I left word with my friend, the purser, where I would be, just in case the Captain received orders to move the ship to another port.

I joined Anna at her cottage and we had a wonderful relaxing time there, hiking the hills and the countryside, visiting 500-year-old houses built of shale with thatched roofs. Her cottage was 300 years old. Anna had saved her meat and liquor stamps so she was able to be a generous and perfect hostess. I would say that as a "morale officer" she did a fine job for me. After I left I never heard of her again. "C'est la guerre." I have thought of her loving generosity many times since.

Judging by the cargo we were loading, the ship appeared to be preparing to join an invasion on the continent of North Africa. One day a great number of ships pulled out while we were still loading. Of course, I knew from that we would not be in on the initial assault. A week later we finished loading and pulled out into the Mersey River to join a convoy headed for Scotland. We sailed from Gourock, Scotland on Thanksgiving Day, 1942.

CHAPTER TWENTY TWO

We Join The North African Campaign

The steward had told me when leaving New York that if we were not home by Thanksgiving at least we would have a turkey dinner; he had bought 75 turkeys which were in the ship's freezer. On Thanksgiving, when roast beef was served, I asked the steward, "Where's the turkey?"

He glared at me, saying, "What turkey?"

I asked a few questions of men who stood gangway watches and they told me they had seen the turkeys go off the ship in Liverpool carried by soldiers and an American Army captain, who had loaded them into an unmarked private lorry. The sailors, members of the ship's Armed Guard, added, "We think those turkeys were on the way to the black market."

The steward later bragged to me, when he was drunk, "I've made $10,000 on this trip and I don't mean in wages." He eventually sold off so much of our food and supplies that we had to go on British rations, which consisted mostly of Brussels sprouts and fatty sausages.

We Join the North African Campaign

The crew was furious, and the sailors' union delegate told the steward, "Steward, if you don't get some good American food on board when we get to North Africa, you will never arrive at the ship's next port. We'll feed you to the fish." The steward believed they meant it and I think they did, too.

He took no chances; in Oran he mysteriously was able to arrange truckload after truckload of hams, chickens and goodies from an Army warehouse, and so the fare aboard improved at the expense of some Army officers' mess. The steward's $10,000 profit no doubt shrunk, and some Army quartermaster had a fat wallet.

We were the supply ship for the 1st U.S. Rangers who took the Port of Arzew in North Africa. We arrived there about 15 days after the actual invasion. The Rangers had taken some casualties, largely from a machine gun in a church belfry, which, as the soldiers told me, the officers wouldn't allow them to destroy by cannon.

There was a makeshift hospital at Arzew where the 48th Medical Corps attached to the Rangers was taking care of the sick and wounded. I spent a good deal of my leisure time visiting these men in the hospital. The rest of the time I spent in a tavern drinking new beer and green wine with the off-duty Rangers (the Germans had taken all the good beer and wine with them when they evacuated). The Rangers were a great bunch of men. A few of them gave me their names and addresses of wives and sweethearts in the States for me to carry their greetings to. I never did deliver those greetings. We didn't get back until after the Anzio Beach landing where the 1st U.S. Rangers took such heavy casualties, and I was afraid I might be carrying greetings from the dead.

We were the only ship tied up at the dock in Arzew when a British destroyer, again one of the old "four-stacker" gifts of President Roosevelt, was torpedoed while patrolling the Harbor of Arzew and, in fact, again protecting us. The torpedo went right through the engine room, in one side and out the other. I then understood why the sailors had nicknamed those destroyers "tin cans." Somehow this disabled vessel managed to make it to the dock and tied up to our side. There were dead men in the engine room, wounded men all over the ship's deck and disorder and destruction everywhere.

The commander of the torpedoed British destroyer came aboard and asked Captain Evanson for permission to let his men sleep in the companionways and asked for food and hot coffee. Cap, cruelly, I thought, told them there were U.S. Naval facilities a half mile up the road from the dock and he should seek help there rather than from us.

Cap noticed my look of bewilderment at his action. He said, "Sparks, if I let those people aboard we'll never get them off and there'll be investigations, hearings and never-ending red tape which I don't want to be involved in." I thought he was severe at the time, but now I believe he knew what he was doing. You had to respect his experience. After all, this was not his first war.

Captain Evanson was very good about letting the officers get whiskey out of bond in England. We could buy a case of Scotch whiskey, the best, for about $1.20 a fifth. We were also allowed a few cases of beer, which I kept in the battery room where it was always cool. Cap said, "As long as you don't abuse the privilege I'll continue to allow it each time we're in the U.K."

One of the Army doctors from the 48th Medical Corps was aboard and saw us drinking Scotch and soda and joined in. The next day he came back with a message saying, "If any of you are willing, there are several nurses at the hospital who will sleep with the owner of a fifth of Scotch. Some of them are feeling the strain of combat fatigue, from the landing."

One of the ship's deck officers took the doctor up on the proposition and went forth with fifth in hand. He reported later that the nurse recipient of the fifth drank it straight down and passed out, leaving him with an experience similar to sleeping with a corpse.

I became friends with a Ranger M.P. while drinking in a popular tavern. He suggested we stick around after the curfew and have the French barmaid cook up a good dinner with some wine. I asked, "How in hell will you get all these soldiers out of here at 9 o'clock curfew?"

The M.P. said, "Watch me." He locked and bolted the front door, went back and moved the "Gents" sign to the rear exit, which had a snap lock, and then moved the "Exit" sign to the gents' room. About 50 men disappeared in the next 30 minutes. A few belligerently pounded on the bolted front door but most quickly realized they had been had. I said, "Corporal, that's the

We Join the North African Campaign

best non-violent police action I ever saw."

After we had discharged our cargo at Arzew, which took about two weeks, we moved west a few miles to Oran. This was a big military base for the Allies. There had been considerable resistance from Admiral Darlan of the Vichy French at the time of the invasion. We lost some ships and took some casualties. The Vichy French had scuttled their ships, both naval and merchant, and the Allied port authorities were busy pumping them out and refloating them. We went in there to wait for a convoy we hoped would take us to Gibraltar and home. While there we learned that our ship had been transferred to His Majesty's Sea Transport and that we were now under British orders. We didn't know just what this meant, but it didn't sound like going home orders. What it did prove to mean was that we were to be on a shuttle service between the United Kingdom and North Africa.

There was a French cargo vessel named the SS Chateau Pavie refloated near us that the Vichy French had scuttled. Her original officers were on board. The sinking of the vessel had ruined her food supplies, but her wine and brandy were in good condition. The Frenchmen would willingly trade wine or brandy for bread or whatever.

Christmas eve some of the officers on the Charles Carroll suggested a Christmas party on the Chateau Pavie.

"Of course, a party," the Frenchmen said, "you bring the food, we'll furnish the drinks."

The French vessel lay about 200 feet away from where we were anchored. Our work boat was at the foot of the Jacob's ladder. The captain of the Charles Carroll and the Navy lieutenant had gone ashore and probably would not have been invited anyway as their authority might have inhibited things. It was a crazy party. The French spoke no English and only a few of our men spoke some high school French. We could all sing the Marseillaise and we sang it many times, louder and louder as the drinks took hold.

The French captain, Captain Saint, would stand up as though he was going to make a profound statesmanlike speech, and say in English, "I was at Dieppe!" End of speech. Those were his only English words. Dieppe had been a British commando raid on a German radar station and I understand the French captain had played a part.

When we started back to our ship everyone was so drunk from the wine that they were sottish and limp like a Salvador Dali painting. I was the only one who could lift an oar and there was only one oar. There were 17 men in that small boat and it took me 15 minutes to paddle 200 feet. There was a heavy scum of crude oil from the scuttled ships and the men started falling out of the boat and being dragged back in, oil, crud and all. Getting them up the Jacob's ladder was another task which was finally accomplished with many dunkings in the filthy, oily water. It could have been a scene out of an old buccaneer pirate movie.

Once back aboard, showered and clothes changed, the chief engineer told me he had a fifth of Scotch in his room if I'd like to join him, which I did.

Chief had not only a fifth, but several of them. His idea of serious drinking was to sit down at a table with his feet up on it and pour out Scotch by the water glass full, drink and say nothing.

We were busy doing just that. Sometimes I'd ask, "Chief, how's your wife in Marseilles?"

"I hope she's not collaborating with the Boche."

Then I said, "How's your wife in New York?"

"I hope she's not collaborating with the cop on the block."

"Chief," I said, "are you sure that's the right word?" The Chief had been on a regular New York-to-Marseilles run in peacetime, and kept a wife in both places. The arrangement seemed to have worked all right for him until the war interfered. He didn't talk very much even with this kind of provocation from me.

There was a big "BOOM!" followed by another big "BOOM!" I said, "Chief, your engine just went out through the smoke stack."

He mumbled, "If it did, it's too late to do anything now." He didn't even bother to take his feet off the table or lift his head up, just poured another drink.

In a minute or so I heard a hell of a racket and went out of the room to see. The whole sky over Oran was lit up like daylight and air raid alarm sirens were blasting away. Someone on board was hollering, "Who fired the PAC's?" The PAC's were little cannons loaded with parachute rockets to be fired in the convoy

We Join the North African Campaign

in case of attack at night by planes so the ships could see to scatter. The parachutes also dangled cables which would snarl a plane if it came in for a low-level attack.

We learned later that all liberty and Christmas leaves were cancelled and Oran was put on a steady alert as a result of this prank.

It seems President Roosevelt and Winston Churchill were at Casablanca not far away. The military thought there had been a security leak and this was a Nazi air raid. Casablanca was put on alert and all Christmas leaves there were cancelled as well.

We never did know who fired the PAC's. As far as I know to this day only the guilty party knows and he was probably too drunk to remember. We were to sail for Gibraltar the next morning, and at the arranged time we lifted anchor and pulled out. Some Naval officers ashore were shouting through a megaphone, "Did you fire the PAC's?"

The captain kept replying, "What'd you say?" as the anchor winch kept on grinding and the ship got under way. He was a wise captain and certainly knew how to avoid entanglements.

CHAPTER TWENTY THREE

Second North African Shuttle

We docked at Bristol, England, and took on another load for North Africa. Since we were caught in this shuttle service for the duration we had all given up ever going home again before war's end, if ever.

I lost interest in sightseeing and spent most of my time in the Old Mauretania Bar in Bristol, drinking whatever was available. Sometimes in the afternoons I would go to a tea dance which the Bristol ladies put on. In the evenings I'd go to a movie if I could find one I hadn't seen.

The ship began to have crew problems—guys cracking up, being sent home, getting married when they were already married, being hospitalized, fathers coming to the captain looking for violators of their daughters, and all kinds of casualties that happen to men under stress. We had experienced a fire on board; we had been rammed by another ship. This kind of thing seemed to be a constant occurrence. It was now 1943 and the Allies still hadn't landed on the continent.

Heading back to North Africa and crossing the Bay of Biscay, I was listening to Axis Sally on my radio. I never repeated what I heard her say, no matter what, but I was a sucker for listening to her. It never occurred to me to believe her but she played American music and had a nice sexy voice like an American girl (which it turned out she was), so I listened.

We had a German plane flying over us at a great height beyond the reach of our guns, obviously a scout plane. Like a buzzard, it made us nervous since we never knew when the Luftwaffe bombers would appear. It was up there every day.

I heard Axis Sally say, "Your convoy of 23 ships crossing the Bay of Biscay is scheduled for annihilation tomorrow!" I went out on deck and counted the ships and there were just 23 of us. Don't think she didn't make me anxious, but I never repeated her story to anyone on board. I felt the Commodore's ship would be monitoring her too, and if he had thought it meant anything he would have acted, I trustfully hoped and presumed. The threatened attack never came.

Before we left Bristol the Chief Officer, John Pershing McKenna, a fine young man from Boston with an unusual fascination for horses, found I was originally from Montana and asked if I had owned a saddle horse. I said yes. He asked me to tell him about it. He kept coming to the radio room and saying, "Sparks, tell me about the horse."

So I did, and when I ran out of stories I began making them up. He was intrigued by anything Western. I told him the story of the D'Autrinot brothers holding up the mail train at Siskiyou Pass in California. The mate said, "Any story with names like that in it has got to be a made-up yarn. I'm not going to let you tell me any more stories." The sad part of that was the story was true, word for word.

One day, still in Bristol, he came into the officer's mess and said, "Sparks, I've got it all set, we can go this afternoon."

I looked surprised and said, "What's all set and where can we go?"

"Go horseback riding, what else?"

Everyone in the mess room looked at me expecting me to welch, which was exactly what I wanted to do but decided there must be a better place to "chicken out" than in the mess room. I said, "O.K. fine, let's go."

We got out to the riding academy and there were a couple of real nags saddled and waiting for us. They were obviously refugees from a soap factory—pitiful. We mounted and couldn't get them out of a slow walk. Mac, the mate, was very disappointed. Well, I thought, I got out of that one easy.

Next trip to North Africa, coming into the port of Mostaganem, Algeria, Mac called me to the bridge, handed me his big binoculars and said, "What do you make of that?"

I looked and could see lots of horses, paddocks and barns. I said, "It looks like an army barracks to me."

"Barracks hell! It's stables, lots of 'em. That means horses."

"You are probably right," I said, but I failed to share his enthusiasm.

A few days later as we were discharging our cargo of huge Army tanks, the Chief Officer came into the mess room again. "Sparks, I've fixed it. There's a French Army stud farm here with 250 Arabian stallions, horny and waiting to be sent out to spring mare farms. They're aware that it's spring and they haven't been ridden for months. The French Commandant has invited us to come out and ride."

I said, "Great," as though a death sentence had just been pronounced.

The following letter written to Norma at that time tells the story of that ride. (This letter was printed in the Milwaukee Journal in March 1943, submitted by my sister Maxine Salisbury Stoelting, to whom I had sent a copy.)

Somewhere in Northwest Africa
February 23, 1943

Hello My Darling:

Yesterday I had a little excitement that the censor may permit me to write about.

I am beginning to think that if you are going to worry you should worry less about me when I am at sea than when ashore.

I wrote you from England about my experience in horseback riding and about the Chief Mate and his weakness for horses. He made friends here with a French Cavalry officer who invited him to come out to a

French Army stud farm for a ride. It is a farm where they raise blooded Arabian stallions for breeding purposes and in considerable numbers. They have nothing but stallions on the place.

Of course, the Mate accepted the invitation; in fact, I think he wangled it out of the French officer. He also, while he was at it, arranged for a friend to accompany him. In view of my Western reputation the Mate chose me as the victim. These Arabian stallions have bad reputations for their ability to unseat the rider.

So, yesterday we went out to this farm by special invitation of the French Lieutenant (the only way one could get such a treat). The stables were beautiful, built of adobe with red tile roofs and spacious box stalls, like only the cavalry provides for its animals. The yards and stables were immaculate and it would only be exaggerating slightly to say that one could have dropped a bon-bon on the ground and picked it up and eaten it without revulsion.

To go back a bit, I accompanied him with the intention of only looking at the stallions and watching him ride. Just to increase my timidity, while we were looking over the stables a couple of studs broke loose and had a good fight before the stablemen parted them. By this time I had lost all desire to get any nearer to them than the nearest strong fence.

The Lieutenant appeared about then and instructed his men to pick out a couple of calm ones. The Mate, without batting an eye, followed along. By this time I realized that I was roped in or I could never again mention being from Montana. The "calm" ones were a couple of beautiful dapple-gray stallions, four years old. "Just colts!" the Lieutenant said. They appeared a little too enthusiastic about being saddled to suit me, giving the impression of an extreme desire for exercise.

While they were saddling them a French officer and a very pretty 15-year-old girl came along. The girl was in riding habit and asked the Mate, who spoke French, if he was an experienced rider. The Mate answered, "Well, I have ridden once before."

She asked, "How about your friend?"

The Mate answered, "Oh! he's an old cowboy from Montana." She then suggested to the Mate that he take her horse since it was gentle. She thought she could hold the one that had been saddled for him since she had a scissor bit bridle.

Mac asked her, "How's my friend's?"

She replied, "Oh! he is very fast!" All this conversation between the Mate and the girl took place in French and, as you know, I don't parle that well. By the time Mac had translated and repeated the conversation to me the girl was gone and the stable boy was indicating that I should mount.

By this time the scene was set for what appeared to be an impending massacre. The Lieutenant had mounted a gorgeous looking animal that was rearing and prancing all over the place—I thought he had just picked a tough one to impress us.

The Lieutenant instructed the stablemen to hold the horses' heads while the Mate and I mounted. The second it was released the Mate's animal reared and plunged around the corner of the barn and out of sight. Mine tried to follow, but I held its head up tightly while it reared and walked around on its hind legs pawing the air, jumped around a bit more, pranced a little and then settled down and stood still. I had won the first round. Much to my amazement I was still in the saddle—and thankful at that, as the yard was cobblestone.

The Mate came back around the corner, still seated, but with a stableman leading his horse. I suggested that perhaps we had better call it off. As I wrote before, he is very fond of horses and knows so little about them that he has no fear. He looked happy as a kid with a new toy sitting on that horse.

I have had a saddle horse run away with me in Montana and have been thrown so high in the air that the wind was knocked out of me when I hit the road. I've not forgotten it yet, though it is more than 20 years past. I was also aware that at that time I weighed around 125 pounds as against my 192 of today, and that I was fit and in condition which I certainly am not now. I also possess a little higher evaluation of my life and limbs. However, my friend the Mate was only concerned with his love for horses and he is only 24 years old and in fit physical condition.

The Lieutenant then started walking and prancing his horse towards the runways. We followed as our stallions appeared to be calming down. I also had the benefit of a slight increase in confidence, having won the first skirmish. The Lieutenant suggested that we turn into the training paddock which was about 100 yards long and 55 yards wide and calm our horses down before going out and running them on the desert hills. He warned that the horses loved to jump and if we were not used to jumping to keep the horses away from the jumps.

No sooner had Mac completed translating these warnings than my horse spotted the jumps and spurted for them. I was able to turn him before he reached the first jump, that is, I turned him into the outer track and went into a lightning-like gallop 'round and 'round the paddock. It took me 30 minutes to stop him. As he slowed he expressed his resentment of my trying to hold him by raising both front feet arched high in the air and throwing his head from side to side. The Arabian horses do not buck like a Western mustang but seem to rely more on speed and maneuverability to dislodge their rider. I don't think this stallion really wanted me off his back, he just wanted more action than I was able and willing to give him.

I finally got him to stop and slid off. A stableman took him from me. I was wet and limp as a rag. The Arab stableman said, "Fatigue, beaucoup, beaucoup." It was a great understatement.

The Lieutenant said, "I can see you have ridden before but you are out of condition." Another understatement, but generous of him. The roofs of the stables were lined with French Arab cavalry men watching what they thought was going to be an international disaster.

The Mate's horse was a bit calmer and he held it up,

never permitting it into a gallop. He was so intent, that he never saw much of what was going on with my horse and the Lieutenant's. The Lieutenant jumped the barriers with his stallion and raced it full speed around the arena. The way he rode was something to marvel at and remember.

To further agitate my anxiety a trainer brought in a big beautiful bay Arab stud to exercise it. He had it on the end of a long rope. The horse was running around the trainer so fast and trying to break loose and come after us that it was a little hard to tell whether the horse was swinging the man around in the circle or the man swinging the horse. It, too, finally calmed down, much to my relief.

The Lieutenant asked us if we were ready to go out and run the hills. The Mate said yes. By this time, although I had managed so far so good I had become fully aware of the speed and deviltry of a young Arabian stallion, and felt that it was crazy for us to go out. However I was prepared to leave it up to the Lieutenant's judgment and fate as to whether we should. The Lieutenant talked the Mate out of it, explaining that he was afraid we could not hold them. The Lieutenant, no doubt, felt responsible for our welfare as well as that of the two valuable animals.

One must remember that we were riding a French saddle which was a flat pancake affair, whereas I had learned to ride on a Western saddle.

Mac continued to ride for another ten minutes before dismounting. He admittedly was as thankful as I to get on the ground and that we did not go out for the run. These animals were faster and more spirited than anything I ever saw in Montana. Do you get a picture of me on a dapple gray plunging around like that?

Don't get worried that I will be demanding you take up horseback riding. I was contented with what riding I had done when I left Montana and I'm more than satisfied now.

The Lieutenant asked the Mate if he would like to ride again. Mac explained that he thought he would be busy until we leave, but if we ever come here again he would appreciate the invitation. The Mate need never fear any riding-academy nags from now on. He did very well, but has a tendency to sit his horse like a jockey which is the only way he ever saw a horse ridden. He loves it, though, and his passion for horses has increased to where I believe he would take an Arab colt back on the ship for a pet if it were permitted.

Now that it's over I feel it was worthwhile and I'm also very happy that I'm not writing this from a hospital cot. I've just read this over and find it is a factual account of a fine afternoon. A proper way to spend a great horse-lover's birthday (George Washington's).

I love you very much, darling.
>Yours until the sea horses get me,
>All my love,
>Oliver

Oliver M. Salisbury
Radio Officer
k143 Care CPO London, England

We sailed for a return trip to the United Kingdom about the middle of March, though not without event; we were to follow the SS Nathaniel Green out of the breakwater at Mostaganem, but she was torpedoed by a German submarine right outside the gates and sat on the bottom with her decks above water. We had to wait for tugs to push the hull aside for us to pass. This delayed our departure a couple of weeks.

Finally we made it to Gibraltar, with orders to join a homebound convoy; but on the day of departure our Chief Engineer reported we had lost our fresh water somehow, and the homebound convoy sailed without us. A few hours later he found the water in another storage tank. We then lay in Gibraltar Harbor for 30 days waiting for a convoy which was homebound via Scotland. While waiting it out at "Gib" several merchant ships were sunk around us by Italian one-man submarines. Depth bombs were dropped every three minutes around the clock as a defense to that sneaky little weapon.

Crossing the Bay of Biscay, Scotland-bound, we received radio orders to split off from the main convoy and come into the

English Channel on the word that the Channel was clear of the enemy. Well into the Channel we received a flash message for the small convoy to disperse because enemy torpedo boats were streaming out from the French coast to intercept us. While making the turnaround, two ships ran aground and were lost. We ended up out in the Atlantic unescorted. The Captain then headed for Scotland via North Ireland. After running in dense fog for several days, Captain Evanson asked me to break radio silence and get a radio bearing. We had been seeing too many shore birds and too much flotsam on the water.

I called the Belfast Radio; they took a radio compass bearing on us and reported: "According to our calculations you are 100 yards inside of Ireland." We waited for the fog to lift. When it did, there were big rocks protruding from the sea all around us. We heaved a bit of lead finding our way back to deep water.

Coming into the Clyde, the harbor to Glasgow, we passed a British aircraft carrier. While I was still watching her through binoculars she hit a mine and her munition chambers exploded, sending a spiral of smoke a mile high. I heard in port that night that the only survivors were those on deck who had been blown into the water and pilots who were in the air at the time. We never heard any confirmation of this, or what ship she was. All I knew for sure was what I saw. This was the way of war. Those closest to it knew the least about it.

We finally sailed for home but developed steering problems in a storm off Greenland and had to return to Scotland unescorted. Though we reported by radio that we were returning, it took us five days to get back. The Admiralty told us they had reported us missing and presumed lost.

Again we sailed from Scotland for home. We had a baby flat top (small carrier) for an escort and thought that was great. However, we hit a North Atlantic storm and the flat top had to turn back, leaving us with three Canadian corvettes for protection. A lone submarine made a daylight attack and sank four ships. We ran far north to escape the submarine and ran into heavy ice floes and icebergs, finally having to turn around and come out through the ice exactly where we went in. The submarine was there waiting for us and sank another ship. I think the corvettes got the submarine that time; they appeared to have it in a depth-bomb triangle and were still dropping depth bombs as darkness descended.

At last! In the middle of May we dropped anchor in the Hudson River. The pilot informed us that there was no berth for us until Monday morning. It was then only Friday night. Captain Evanson and I were able to go ashore with the pilot boat. I really felt sorry for the rest who had to spend the weekend looking at New York's skyline from the deck of a ship after nine long hectic months away.

CHAPTER TWENTY FOUR

The Poor SS John A. Poor

We took a trip to Wisconsin to give Norma a chance to meet my family for the first time. The family was having a reunion at my sister's home in Kiel, my mother now residing there.

Norma and I returned to New York City at the end of May, 1943, and a heat wave latched on like it was for all summer. To escape the heat, I accepted an assignment to a new merchant ship nearing completion in the New England Ship Yards at Portland, Maine. As chief radio officer I would have no duties while the ship was in the yards, but I would be on a payroll in a fairly cool climate. The name of the ship was the SS John A. Poor. All seamen are a bit superstitious and, though I have never liked to admit it, I was really no exception. That name, John A. Poor, "bugged" me. I tried the initials J.A.P. We were at war with Japan. That set of initials was about as bad as "Poor." I meant no disrespect to John A. Poor, a nineteenth century railroad builder and financial scion whom the ship was named after. Well, it was a new ship, and what's in a name?

Norma joined me at Old Orchard, Maine, a lovely beach resort near Portland. I got sunburned and looked and felt like a burst baked potato. I was in such terrible pain that Norma couldn't even sleep with me. She got mad at me for being so careless and remarked, "What a way to spend a second honeymoon!"

I asked Captain Uppitt if I could go back to N.Y.C. and have him mail my checks. He said, "Well, there isn't anything for you to do, but I do think you should at least show up once a week to get your pay check." Not an unreasonable suggestion, I admitted. The ship was near launching date and wartime secrecy made it prudent that key men not be hired on the day before sailing because that gave away vital information.

The first ill omen and misfortune took place aboard the John A. Poor soon after I signed on. An inexperienced fireman blew up the ship's boilers the very first time they were fired. That meant another month to six weeks in the shipyards. The company was paying my hotel bill and meals since none were provided as yet on the ship. It wasn't a bad summer. I made many trips to New York to see Norma, always managing to be in Portland on pay day.

Near the end of July the ship was ready to launch. We took on a cargo of logs for a British pulp mill, that being the only cargo available at Portland. We were ordered to proceed to Boston to join a convoy. Interestingly enough, we tied up alongside "Old Ironsides," of John Paul Jones-Revolutionary War fame. I took that as a good omen.

On sailing day all radio officers were briefed as to the convoy communication plan and other details. The Navy commander briefing us was a real jerk. He started his briefing by addressing us as draft dodgers and threatened us with induction into the infantry if we didn't perform our duties properly. He told us the submarine menace had been beaten by the Navy and not to be thinking of ourselves as heroes. I had just come back from nine months in the war zones, having seen 14 out of 44 ships in my convoy blown sky high around me and not a single survivor, but that's another story. I wanted to walk out on this S.O.B. but restrained my temper for once, later to wish that I hadn't. I'd been offered a commission in the Army Signal Corps and could have spent the war at a desk in Washington. There were 125 ships in this convoy and I am sure there were many other veteran radio men like me, but the bravest ones were those going out for the first time to—they knew not what.

It was the luck of the John A. Poor that she be equipped with a Rube Goldberg contraption designated as the Mark 29 by the Navy. Very hush-hush at the time, this was an anti-torpedo device to prevent a ship's being sunk by that weapon. As it worked out, the prevention was worse than the disease. The device constituted a paravane, or a huge bowlike arm, that stretched across the prow of the ship out about 50 feet on either side. This paravane was fairly rigid; from each arm two rubber hoses about the size of fire hoses floated back the length of the ship like streamers, one about 25 feet out from the ship's hull and the other about 50 feet out. Each streamer contained 700 pounds of T.N.T. At the end of each streamer was a sealed hydrophone device which was electronically connected with a listening post aboard ship in a little room set aside for the Navy operators of this apparatus.

The Navy men showed me how it worked. They had been trained to recognize the 'swish' of a torpedo disturbing the normal static noises of the ocean picked up by the hydrophones. They had a phonograph record of this noise and played it frequently to keep their ears alert to that wicked sound. If and when they heard such a sound they were to throw a switch that would charge the electronic system of this equipment. The noise of the torpedo swish increases in volume as it comes closer and closer to the ship, finally reaching its crescendo just as the torpedo passes over the T.N.T.-loaded rubber hoselike streamer. The crescendo would trigger the explosion which would blow the warhead (explosive nose) off the torpedo causing it to clank harmlessly against the hull of the ship. Theoretically, it sounded good. Operationally, it wasn't so good.

If the Mark 29 gave me any false sense of security, that was quickly lost when they assigned us to "Coffin Corner"—the name given by seamen to the outside rear corner of a convoy most exposed and generally the first ship lost to enemy action. The Navy really wanted to test this device, it seemed. The chief officer had been trained on how to rig the Mark 29 and get it into the water once the convoy was underway.

The Poor SS John A. Poor

To add another foreboding sign, Captain John Uppitt was an exiled Lithuanian gentleman, we suspected no less than a Count. His only previous American experience had been as a yacht's master in Miami. There was no question of his training. He was familiar with all the electronic devices and gadget aids to navigation. The Captain and the radio officers were specifically briefed not to use the radio compass, the depth finder or the foghorn. These devices emit a signal for a few miles that can be detected by an alert radio operator, making him aware of a convoy or at least a ship in his vicinity. By this time many German U-boats were equipped with radar but we were not to take that for granted.

The first night out of Boston a dense fog settled over the huge convoy. The U-boat warfare, which forced shipping into convoys, cost us many merchant ships, as collisions were frequent. However, alert ship's officers could minimize this danger and the experienced ones did. Our yacht's master felt the weather conditions justified blowing the foghorn every three minutes. What this did to my sleep was awful, never mind my sense of security. On top of this he turned on the depth finder, which sends an electronic beam to the ocean floor and back indicating the depth of the ocean. Then he turned on the radio compass.

At the risk of being insubordinate, I reminded Captain Uppitt of the briefing warning against use of this equipment, particularly in these waters. The Captain said he thought navigational conditions justified his making these exceptions, especially since he had now lost the convoy. I could say no more.

My quarters were about 50 feet aft of the radio room. I had a nice room to myself equipped with a huge gong over my pillow to wake me up in case of emergency. I was the only radio man on the ship. After my conversation with the captain I had gone to bed, since I had a rigid schedule to observe and you never knew when sleep would be at a premium. At 4 a.m. I was awakened, which is too mild a word for that bit of action. I'm sure the tremendous explosion, the cracking and popping of the oak cabinets in my room, the splintering of my mirror, and the deafening sound of that gong over my pillow had the effect of raising me two feet off my bed. It all seemed like one terrible thing. I thought, "This is it!" Then the adrenalin took over and I started to function. The ship was in complete darkness.

I made it to the radio room just as the lights came on from an emergency ship's source. The procedure in this situation was to await word from the bridge. The captain is supposed to immediately give the radio officer the ship's position and a message describing the situation to send out in International Morse code on the distress stand-by frequency. I sat silently awaiting my instructions which I expected momentarily. The operator of the Mark 29 sat in a room the other side of the wall from the radio room. He hollered "Here comes another one!" and turned the volume up so that I could hear the swish, swish, swish, of the torpedo propellers coming toward the ship and becoming louder and louder and louder. I felt like a duck on the water. Then "BOOM"—another explosion and the ship's lights went out again. With independent power from a bank of emergency batteries off the radio room, I got a light on again. The ship was still underway.

Time passed; it was getting light, perhaps now 6 a.m. I did finally get the ship's position from the bridge, but the captain was reluctant to send a message as yet. He said, "It might have been a mine." He held this opinion in spite of the Navy operator having heard the torpedo swish and in spite of our briefing instructions calling for a message whenever mined or torpedoed, as you might not get a later chance.

Captain Uppitt's son was the officers' messboy, and he had disappeared during this battle with the submarine. He was frantically looking for his son, who we learned later had been hiding in a linen closet, scared stiff. The Chief Officer, Ed Gavin, who was on the bridge, realized that with two explosions we were now bare on one side of the ship. With excellent thinking he ordered the ship to make a horseshoe turn in the direction the torpedoes were coming from in order to expose the other side of the ship, which still had two good streamers. He estimated the submarine was 700 yards off, that being the ideal distance to attack a slow-moving ship in good weather. As we made the turn we caught the third torpedo. One must have been able to see daylight under that big liberty ship as it was lifted right out of the water. The two remaining streamers were dragging right alongside the ship as we made the turn. They exploded all right, but being so close to the ship, were about as disastrous as the torpedo itself would have been. One of the boilers in the engine room exploded simultaneously, apparently from the concussion. I was thrown across the radio room, hitting the radiator hard with my back. Equipment was down all around me and again it was black. I pulled myself to my feet, switched the emergency lights on and got the emergency transmitter operating. Then the bridge rang the 'abandon ship' bells. No one gave me a final message to send, though the captain had given me a message after the second torpedo which stated "We are under attack" and gave our position. According to the battle procedure, when the 'abandon ship' bell is rung a cadet from the bridge was supposed to come to the radio room with orders from the captain to leave the ship, and the cadet then was to help carry the portable lifeboat radio, which weighed 60 pounds and was cumbersome, to the designated lifeboat. I had heard stories from other radio officers about getting left on the ship and having to jump into flaming water and other wild stories. The advice from those veterans was, "Don't trust 'em, they'll forget you." That's just what happened. I called the bridge on the voice tube and on the phone and no answer, all was quiet. The Navy men in the next room had left, too. I was alone on the top side of the ship. I dragged that bulky 60-pound radio along the deck and down the steps. I wasn't going to be without it. I got to my lifeboat station as they were lowering the boats. The second mate said, "Let Sparks get in the lifeboat with his radio and lower the boat with him in it!" It sounded good and I got in. They were lowering the boat when someone yelled "TORPEDO!!" I looked out and there was a spray breaking the surface and coming straight for my lifeboat. Everyone dropped their lines except the bos'n. He put a hitch around the davit holding the bow of the lifeboat up while the stern fell free, leaving the boat perpendicular in the air and me hanging onto a seat with both hands waiting for the torpedo to strike. The precious lifeboat radio, of course, went into the drink. The bos'n then realized the "torpedo" was only a playful porpoise and got some men to wind the boat up again. About that time the captain came around cancelling the abandon ship order and informing us there was no hole in the ship. The damage had come from the Mark 29 and the explosion of one of the boilers. We were then lying on the water like a dead duck. I went back to the radio room and took it on myself to send a message. I sent the specified, "SSS SSS SSS" which meant submarine attack rather than the conventional "SOS." I sent out, "We have been torpedoed," and gave our position.

One book of wartime instructions, named "Bams," tells the radio officer that in a situation where he feels the officers on the bridge are so involved that they cannot give him instructions and where he is reasonably sure of what has happened, he should take the responsibility himself of sending a message. This is what I did. There was another book of instructions which said, "Under no circumstances should the radio officer ever send a message without specific instructions from the captain." This was in the "Camsi" book. If my action was right, no harm was done; if my action had been wrong, I would be in all kinds of trouble. The authorities could pick the book that suited them.

Events proved me right. About fifteen minutes after my last self-authored message, the chief officer saw the conning tower of a submarine through a brief opening in the fog. The gunnery officer, on his first trip to sea after 90 days of training, could not see the submarine even with the chief officer pointing at it. Chief Officer Gavin said, "Direct your fire in the direction I'm pointing!" which Lieutenant Stacey did. We were well armed, having two five-inch cannon and eight twenty-millimeter cannon plus several thirty-caliber machine guns. Stacey's gun crew raked that fog for five minutes with everything we had. About five minutes later we saw flares in the fog. Foolishly, the captain answered them with flares. If the submarine had still been there that would have been a cute trick to get us to expose our exact position. Forty-eight hours later, when we were able to talk by megaphone with the destroyer that came to our aid, we found that they had taken a German officer and three sailors prisoner from a rubber lifeboat. Apparently, the men that were in the conning tower escaped.

There were a couple of human interest stories during this battle. When I was putting the radio into the lifeboat the Captain came up with a long box, like those that precious jewels are kept in, and put it in the lifeboat. When the porpoise showed up that box went into the North Atlantic along with my lifeboat radio. I noted the look of sad disappointment on his face. It may have been the crown jewels of Lithuania, or more likely it was navigational instruments; the captain never confided to me what was in that box.

During the boiler explosion the third engineer on duty was knocked across the engine room and showered with bursting and falling asbestos. As he emerged silently from the engine room looking hideously white, with blood seeping through the dust and shreds of asbestos sticking to him and with a limp, broken arm dangling at his side, he provoked the chief officer to comment: "My God! You look like you just stepped out of a grave!" This was exactly the way he looked and probably felt. The remark drew loud laughter from all of us, even under the circumstances.

At this point Chief Engineer O'Connor came up to the Captain and asked for rubber boots from the ship's store so his men could examine the engine room, there being a couple of feet of water in it from the burst boiler. Captain Uppitt said, "Who's going to pay for those boots?" I suppose that could be charged up to hysteria. There is never tragedy without some humor.

When the battle was over, things seemed awesomely quiet. We were 125 miles east of Halifax, Nova Scotia, the sea was as calm as a lake, and the fog lifted, showing the whole North Atlantic, horizon to horizon. Our only company was a U.S. destroyer which was circling us in a one-mile-diameter circle. The destroyer came up close and spoke to us with a megaphone. They said they had captured German seamen from a rubber lifeboat, thus confirming our sinking of the submarine. I always felt that I deserved the Merchant Marine Medal for having suckered the submarine to the surface. If I had not changed the Captain's message to read "We have been torpedoed," the submarine never would have surfaced. Also, if the chief officer had not with "seaman's eyes" penetrated the fog and seen the outline of the sub's conning tower, the submarine would never have been sunk. However, the chief officer and I were later to hear of the Navy's awarding a citation to the Captain and the gunnery officer for having sunk an enemy submarine. Neither winced as they accepted, we were told, but the chief officer and I both chuckled when we heard of the awards. Let them be heroes. We were happy to be alive and we were not anxious to get in a quarrel over medals. Besides, I didn't want some 'brass' saying, "Why did you change the Captain's message?"

The Navy sent out a tiny tug from Halifax that couldn't budge us. We lay like a dead duck on the water for six days before they got a tug out there big enough to move us. The North Atlantic was full of German submarines, and despite the protection of the single destroyer circling us we were still badly exposed. There was no power on the ship for several days. I had noted a little brass kerosene lamp mounted over the desk in the radio room. It was a cute little lamp that would surely be a collector's item today. On seeing it I thought it was a useless thing and wondered how much money some war contractor must have made out of equipping the Merchant Marine ships with that. Well, I learned to appreciate that little lamp; it was all the light I had for several days. I wanted to preserve my emergency batteries for communications if needed. The chief engineer finally got one boiler working so we had some power to help the big tug that was towing us. He never was able to restore the ship's power to the radio room.

During the long tow into Halifax the Captain sighted our big 40-man life raft that someone had released during the battle. He ordered the Navy signal man to signal the tug with his lamp to let go the tow and retrieve the life raft. The captain of the tug paid no attention to him. It would have been ridiculous to let go of a 10,000-ton ship to retrieve a life raft that might have cost $1500.

After the last torpedo it had been my duty to help the Captain and the Chief Engineer prepare a detailed amplifying report describing the damage to the ship, its present condition and what was needed for repair. This was necessarily a long message, and I had to reduce it to naval cipher before transmitting it in code to Yarmouth Radio in Nova Scotia. It was a tedious job and I felt that I had earned my "war bonus" when I got through. This was the message that brought the tugs out.

This battle took place on the 28th of July, 1943. It was warm summer weather and the sea was calm. To have abandoned ship and made the coast, 125 miles away, would have been much easier than staying on that ship. We had a motorized lifeboat and could have tied the four lifeboats in tandem and made shore in 10 or 12 hours with ease.

The dreary tension of waiting for tugs, of just waiting, was a dull and torturous experience. When the circling destroyer was on the port side the crew would move to that side and when it was on the starboard side they would move to starboard, feeling that a submarine lying out there would release its torpedo when

The Poor SS John A. Poor

the destroyer was on the far side of its circle. The crew were jumpy, and who could blame them? I stood a 24-hour vigil in the radio room for six days. If I slept at all it was just a wink and a doze. I was so trained in telegraphy that a station calling my letters would alert me just as if someone had called my name. On the ship's radio I could hear convoys being attacked and tankers being sunk along our coasts. Oftentimes the radio operator never got to finish his crisp "SSS SSS SSS——." From where I sat, the war still didn't seem to be going too well.

We finally were pulled into the shipyards in Halifax. I made an effort to get the radio service company to send a man down to repair the ship's radio equipment, which had suffered considerable damage during the explosions. Their men were so busy that they couldn't get a man around, and the rules were that the ship's radio officer was not supposed to make repairs. The radio service companies were able to charge extra for repairs and it was in their contracts that they were the only ones that could do it. However, I knew I couldn't get leave of the ship until the radio had been inspected, so I spent a couple of days making the repairs and finally got the Canadian radio inspector to make his inspection and give the ship a clean bill of health as far as its radio was concerned.

Being free of duties, I asked Captain Uppitt if I could go to New York City and see Norma. He said, "No, but you can go anywhere around here that you wish. We will be in drydock two months. Just keep in touch."

I was the only man among the ship's officers that had not made out an allotment to a wife. Norma was working so I had not bothered to make one out for her. As soon as the ship was in a safe port we went off the war bonus and on to base pay. Most of the men's allotments absorbed their full base pay. The captain took a hard-nosed position that there would be no draws in Halifax except for me. I could draw my full pay if I wanted. When a bunch of men go through what these men did and finally hit port, they expect to do some beer drinking and relaxing. The men were furious at the "no draws" order. Dissension began to brew both among the crew and among the officers. I felt I wasn't involved; I would get away from the ship until the dispute worked itself out.

I called Norma on a censored telephone, which allowed me to

say, "Meet me at the Mount Royal Hotel in Montreal, Quebec." She didn't know what had happened and I wasn't allowed to answer but she readily agreed to meet me in Montreal.

I had never looked at the map. Montreal is a long way from Halifax. All day, all night, and all the next day the train wound along the St. Lawrence River. It was peaceful travel after what I had been experiencing. I was in a high fever at the prospects of seeing Norma again so soon.

Norma was there when I got in—what a welcome sight. We spent a couple of days in Montreal enjoying the fine restaurants, night clubs and points of interest. We then decided to go to Quebec, but found all public transportation was sealed off to Quebec and no reservations could be made. We later learned that Winston Churchill and Franklin D. Roosevelt were there for one of their secret wartime meetings. President Roosevelt showed up in North Africa while I was there, too. I was beginning to think he was following me around.

When we couldn't go to Quebec we made a reservation at a mountain resort in the Laurentian Mountains of the Province of Quebec. It was quiet, peaceful and secluded. The food was not great but the bed was good. We borrowed fishing poles for trout fishing and spent seven very relaxed days. I had been gone from the ship two weeks and Norma was due back at her job in New York City. So this third honeymoon had to come to an end.

I traveled back to Halifax and arrived aboard ship just in time to become involved in the trouble that had been two weeks brewing.

The deck and engine officers were having a meeting on the ship. They had drafted a resolution calling for the removal of the Captain on grounds of incompetency. Since I was the only one besides the purser with a typewriter, they asked me to type it up for them. The purser was timid and wouldn't cooperate, but he did report every word to the Captain. I typed the resolution and all ship's officers except the purser signed it. It was delivered to the American Consul, the U.S. Navy, the War Shipping Administration and the steamship agent managing the ship. The resolution set forth a good many of the things I have described here plus many other incidents and items that the others were more aware of.

Next morning Captain Uppitt came to my room and said,

"Mr. Salisbury, I understand there was a meeting of the officers aboard ship last night. Will you tell me what happened?"

I said, "Captain, yes, I was at the meeting. Our union contracts permit such meetings, but I was not instructed to tell you what happened and am not about to."

The Captain said, "Mr. Salisbury, I was warned in Boston that I might have trouble with you."

I asked him if his informer also told him that I carried a personal security clearance from the Secretary of the Navy, no less.

Later in that day the chief officer and I were called into the Captain's office and told we were fired and to go to the American Consul for our discharges and pay. The chief officer, Ed Gavin, and I talked it over between us and decided what we wanted most was to be off that ship. We would be assigned another one in New York and would have a chance to file charges against the Captain with our unions. Later in the day we met Captain Uppitt in the American Consul's office and arranged for our pay and discharges. I asked the Captain if he was satisfied with my work.

He said, "Mr. Salisbury, you are a very competent radio officer-and handled your duties well, but your conduct is improper and I want you off the ship."

Ed Gavin and I were very happy to leave. They provided transportation by train to New York and that's a long train ride too. When the train slowed down coming into the station at Boston a group of Navy S.P.'s and a commander hopped aboard. They came through the train paging "Mr. Salisbury." Of course, I spoke up. Ed and I had been playing cards and socializing with the people all the way down and because we were in uniform were treated as war heroes, though we did not tell our story. Needless to say, it was embarrassing to be summoned by the S.P.'s. We were told to come with the Navy detail to Naval Intelligence Headquarters. There the Navy illegally confiscated our papers, which they said would be returned in New York. One Navy commander who was interested in the Mark 29 questioned Mr. Gavin at length. I could see as the story unraveled that there was some recognition of an inkling of miscarriage of justice. We were told to proceed to 90 Church Street, Naval Headquarters in New York, and report there at 9 a.m. the next morning.

We reported there, as instructed, the next morning. It seemed the Navy had set up a Trial Hearing Unit for the purpose of trying merchant seamen who are, in fact, civilians. Trials could be held for incompetency, violation of laws and, it seems, for whatever reason the Navy wanted to impose.

When we reported, a Navy lieutenant, who said he was a lawyer, advised us that he would ask us questions and a court stenographer would record our answers. After we had told our stories they would decide what to do with us. He started off with me, the authorities having already assumed that I was the ringleader. He said, "Mr. Salisbury, after all the trouble you have been in I would think you would go aboard ship and keep your mouth shut."

I answered, "Lieutenant, just because the Navy persists in making mistakes does not mean that I should surrender my rights as a citizen." He let me tell my story which I did about as I have done here. He then put Mr. Gavin on the stand. Gavin corroborated all that I had said and had much to add about the Captain's absence from the bridge during the battle. Gavin himself held captain's papers, but had wished to make one wartime trip as a mate before accepting command. It was his first wartime ship, though he had sailed for many years prior to the war including World War I. In my opinion he was a very competent ship's officer and a fine man.

When the questioning was completed the Naval lieutenant said, "You men have not said one word to indict the Captain and everything you have said is against yourselves. I will let you know what we are going to do with you, if you will report back here at 1 o'clock after you have had your lunch." It sounded like they were going to put us in the Tombs and throw the key away.

As it turned out, it was our good fortune that a Navy captain sat in as an observer of this hearing. As we took the elevator down to lunch he asked us, "Where are you going to lunch? I think there is about to be a grave miscarriage of justice here. I am going to see what I can do about it." He explained that he was from San Francisco and was being trained to set up a similar hearing unit out there but had no authority in this particular trial. During lunch he appeared again and sat down with us, asked a few questions and excused himself.

At 1 o'clock we reported back at the hearing chambers. The lieutenant handed us our papers and said, "The case is dismissed." He did not apologize but had the embarrassed look of someone who had been severely reprimanded. The chief yeoman who had been the court reporter winked at me as if to congratulate us and there was a little humor in the wink. This wink and the Navy captain's friendly act reminded me that there are good men in the Navy and that all of them don't settle "at their highest level of incompetence," though I had met quite a few who did.

During wartime it is easy for justice to miscarry. The third engineer on the John A. Poor subsequently looked me up in New York and told his story. The John A. Poor made another effort to cross the Atlantic after completing repairs and again lost the convoy and had to return to St. John's, Newfoundland. This third engineer had his belly full and asked to be paid off, which Captain Uppitt agreed to do. When he got to New York he was arrested by the F.B.I. as a draft dodger. He spent twenty days in the Tombs (N.Y.C.'s famous prison) before his lawyer could get him released. The charge was based on his alleged failure to notify the draft board that he had moved. It seemed he lived with his mother and she had moved while he was out at sea. They admitted their mistake and let him out.

The sequel and finale to the John A. Poor story is that she made it to England on her third try. She made another voyage out to India and was sunk by the Japanese in the Indian Ocean.

The men off the John A. Poor continued to look me up in N.Y. for several years after this and there were many more ridiculous stories to tell.

I shipped out of Chester, Pennsylvania, a few days after the Navy hearing on a big new tanker, the SS Front Royal, and Ed Gavin shipped out as captain of a new liberty ship headed for the Middle East.

CHAPTER TWENTY FIVE

The SS Front Royal

Having rested up from the SS John A. Poor experience, I was ready for reassignment to another ship. This time I was sent to Chester, Pa. to join a big new tanker coming out of the shipyards named the SS Front Royal. There were three of these tankers built at Chester: the Front Royal, the Chickamauga, and the Shiloh, all named after Civil War battles. These tankers were fast for those times—22 knots cruising speed—and designed to travel alone out of convoy. I was pleased with the ship and my assignment. The radio equipment was the latest, and my quarters were large and roomy with a private toilet and shower and a bed instead of a bunk. Tankers paid a little more than the dry cargo ships, and they fed us better because they were in and out of port often and could keep fresh food aboard. With these attractions they didn't have trouble getting crews to take them out, even though they were more dangerous due to the nature of their cargoes.

I quickly learned the unattractive part. They loaded and

The SS Front Royal

unloaded and turned around in twelve hours. You were always at sea. My thought that I would have more time with Norma was a delusion.

The master of the Front Royal was Captain Magnon, a veteran of both wars and a man who should have written his life history. His life had been a very exciting, if not always an orderly, one. As an officer in the Czar's Navy, he had jumped overboard and swum ashore at Alexandria, Egypt, when the Bolshevik Revolution took place and the crew mutinied and took over the ship. After doing time in a British prison—they thought him to be a German spy—he ended up with a commission in the American Navy in World War I. Years later he became master of one of the Great White Ships in the Pacific. Just prior to becoming master of the Front Royal he had lost a ship to the enemy off the Azores and had spent about four months in a Portugal internees' compound. He was the most competent captain I ever sailed with in that he had complete knowledge of all activities on the ship—that is, when he was sober. He was seldom sober at sea. The mates and steward would start working on him about 24 hours out of port so he could bring the ship into port and not get in trouble with the authorities.

My room joined his. That is, I was on the other side of a wall from him. He would start drinking whiskey as soon as we had put the pilot off and were safely underway. He brought whiskey aboard by the case and never had the good fortune to run out. After a few hours of heavy drinking in his room he would start banging around. The Captain never came out of his room during these periods and apparently never ate anything, but would continue until he became delirious or some kind of stupefied condition close to it. He would start crashing around in his room and by the noise you would think there was a bull moose in there. He would throw the empty bottles against the bulkhead, knock over furniture, break mirrors and it was just unbelievable how much noise one man could make in that room and over how long a time. After about 48 hours of that he would pass out and sleep it off. He wouldn't allow anyone to come near him or come into his room during this performance. After he slept for about 24 hours he would ring for the steward and the resuscitation procedure would commence. If one could overlook that problem he was a great guy. I understand from my successor on that ship that he was later removed from the ship while at sea by the Navy and by force.

On the day that the ship came out of the yards at Chester we proceeded to Little Creek, Virginia, a big naval base, to await sailing orders. The Navy sent out word that they would pick up the Captain and the chief radio officer, meaning me, and take us ashore for briefing. (I then had Navy enlisted men as assistant radio operators.) When the Navy shore boat arrived, the petty officer in charge said the order to pick up the radio officer was cancelled and his instructions would be handed to the Captain.

I was all ready to go ashore and Captain Magnon said, "Come along, Sparks, you are all dressed for shore, we'll go have some drinks after the briefing." So I went along. When we arrived at the Navy base we were escorted by the S.P.'s to the briefing room. There was no chance for me to slip off to the PX's or a canteen to wait for the Captain. Cap said, "They won't know the difference, just go along and sit through the briefing." That was what I did. I sat through the very boring briefing, which I understood little of since it had to do with navigation and ship movement and procedures. Happily it was a short briefing, as we were only going to Port Arthur, Texas.

Just as the briefing ended a Navy officer came in excitedly and announced the Italian surrender. This was the first break in the Axis Front and was great news. The officer invited us all to join them in a celebration in the Officers' Club. Of course, I was supposed to be a "captain" or I wouldn't have been there. A Navy commander asked me my name, became my host, and introduced me around as "Captain Salisbury." I would have given anything to be anywhere else at that time. I tried to get away by telling a Navy officer I was visiting with that I had a letter to mail. He generously volunteered to mail it for me when the party was over. To make matters worse, my letter was a postcard to Norma and because I didn't have any other stamp I had put on an air mail stamp, though it was only going from Virginia to New York and would go straight mail anyway. As if to make it still worse, I had put the stamp on upside down by accident. The officer looked at the card and stamp quizzically but said nothing and put it in his pocket. Norma got the card o.k. After all of the problems I had experienced with the Navy all I needed was to get caught crashing a captain's convoy briefing, posing as a captain and then mailing a postcard with an upside down stamp which could easily have indicated some mysterious intelligence. Being a "captain for a day" was not a lot of fun, but I was awfully glad about the surrender of Fascist Italy.

We made our maiden voyage to Port Arthur, Texas and return to Rahway, New Jersey without incident other than what the Captain provided with his drinking. We were in twelve hours and turned around and went back to Port Arthur. We were loading hi-octane gasoline and traveling out of convoy. The newspapers and radio were saying the submarine warfare had been whipped. From my experience this was anything but true, at least up to the fall of 1943.

On this trip a Navy blimp appeared overhead and signaled us to participate in some anti-aircraft practice. They would tow a sleeve (a target) for us to shoot down, if we could. The gun crew was unable to bring the target down after firing many rounds of ammunition from the 20-millimeter cannon, of which we had eight mounted in gun turrets. The Captain was going through his resuscitation period preparatory to arriving at Port Arthur. He was annoyed by the racket from the firing of the 20-millimeters; he came out of his room in his droopy underdrawers, mounted the nearest gun turret, took the 20-millimeter cannon from the sailor, swung it around and with a couple of bursts brought the target down in shreds. He grumbled something in Russian and returned to his cabin.

The Captain had already demonstrated to me that he could read the Morse code coming in on my radio, and at a fair speed. The ship was driven by electric turbines and it was the chief engineer's first experience with them, though he had been trained in a school on how to handle them. However, when he had problems, he would bring them to the Captain and they would sit down and figure them out. There was nothing on that ship that the Captain couldn't do or didn't thoroughly understand. It was just tragic that he couldn't have been put ashore and treated for his alcoholism. This would have happened had he been a Navy or Army officer, but there was no such consideration given to merchant seamen. We had our Merchant Marine hospitals and you had to be physically sick to get into them. Alcoholism was not recognized as a sickness. The treatment for that was jail.

After leaving Port Arthur for Rahway we found we had a

Navy sailor aboard who had the symptoms of acute appendicitis. The Captain asked me to radio Miami to have a small boat out at the Miami Buoy at 4 a.m. to take the man off where he could be hospitalized. I sent the message and received the acknowledgement from New Orleans Naval Radio, but there was no boat at the buoy at 4 a.m. We had to circle and circle outside the buoy until we could get the shore station to acknowledge our signal lamp. They then sent a boat out there and took the man off. With all the commotion we created out there and with our breaking radio silence and using the signal lamp, it is just luck that we didn't get torpedoed right there; daily and nightly sinkings of our ships along the coast were so common one could hardly turn on the ship's radio receiver on the distress band without hearing the desperate "SSS" calls.

We were no sooner underway again after putting the stricken sailor off than I heard our sister ship the Chickamauga, traveling just a few hours ahead of us, sending out an "SSS" message and saying that a submarine was firing on them. I presumed the Chickamauga got away.

Captain Magnon said we were following the same course which had been charted by the Navy for the Chickamauga. He shifted our course so as not to engage the same submarine. By this period of the submarine warfare, the Nazis had given up the "Wolf Pack" technique as a result of many convoys having "baby flat tops," a small aircraft carrier, as part of their escort. What now appeared to be the strategy of Admiral Donetz of the German submarine fleet was to station submarines along the commonly used convoy and shipping routes and pick off stragglers, that is ships that couldn't maintain their position in the convoy for one reason or another or ships like us traveling alone. This also made pretty ripe pickings for the submarine commanders, as we had found out on the SS John A. Poor.

Within an hour or two after leaving Miami Buoy we were attacked by a submarine. I suspect they had heard our radio signals and were waiting out there for us. The SS Front Royal was equipped with a different type of anti-torpedo device from the "Rube Goldberg" deal that was on the John A. Poor. The vessel had hydrophones planted on the exterior of the hull on both sides of the ship. When a torpedo was fired at us on the port side a siren would sound on the bridge and in the radio room or the starboard side, which ever. A red flashing light would signal

The SS Front Royal

which direction the torpedo was coming from. On a fast ship the officer on the bridge could order "hard to port" or "hard to starboard" and swerve the ship enough to dodge the oncoming torpedo. This was more than exciting for me sitting in the radio room listening to the "whirp, whirp, whirp" of the siren and watching the flashing red light, holding my breath to see if the mate would make the correct swerve at the correct time. This was what was happening and a torpedo was darting through the water headed right for us. With the siren going and the lights flashing, holding my breath is just what I did until the torpedo passed us and the starboard light started flashing indicating we had successfully dodged it. We were loaded to the gunwales with hi-octane gasoline and would have exploded and burned had we been hit.

The submarine launched another torpedo and the same excitement was repeated, though it was easier to dodge since the Captain had ordered full speed from the engine room and we were already further away. The Captain was still on the bridge and, as a result of the radio messages telling of the attack on the Chickamauga, he had not resumed his drinking.

The Captain cautioned me to stand a very alert radio watch since we could expect to be intercepted again that night. Not that I needed warning—I wanted to live too. Submarines were, of course, in radio communication with each other.

About two o'clock in the morning another ship put a huge searchlight on us, scanning us from bow to stern. The ship with the searchlight signaled us with a lamp, "Stop or we will fire." The signal he used was the international signal with that meaning. If it had been one of our naval vessels it would have used the secret wartime signal with the same meaning. The Captain was on the bridge and instantly perceived this. He also noted that the angle of the searchlight indicated it came from a submarine or a very small surface craft. Instead of stopping he ordered full speed ahead. He also ordered me to send an "SSS" and our position, which I did. When we arrived at Rahway, N.J. the Navy came aboard to find out what it was all about. They said there had been no U.S. Navy vessel at that location, so the Captain's instant deduction had been correct. The submarine was aware of our ability to dodge a torpedo when we were underway. Had Captain Magnon heeded his message to stop, we would have received a torpedo full blast midship and I wouldn't be writing this story.

DOLLAR STEAMSHIP LINES Inc. Ltd.
S.S. "PRESIDENT POLK"

Date: Oct 29 – 36   Voyage: 40

I hereby certify that the bearer of this pass, O. M. Salisbury, is a member of my steamer now in the Port of Bombay.

This certificate enables the holder to land during the stay of the ship in port subject to the following conditions:

Nº 14126   From DEC 2, 1936
Date   To

STRIKE PICKET CARD
of the
STRIKING MEMBERS
of
INTERNATIONAL SEAMEN'S UNION

O. M. Salisbury	A RTA Loc #3	819
Name	Union	Book No.

5' 11"	30	200	Fair	Brown	Br.
Height	Age	Weight	Complexion	Hair	Eyes

Thomas J. Cerio — Chief Dispatcher
A. B. Anderson — Chairman Strike Com.

Seaman's Signature

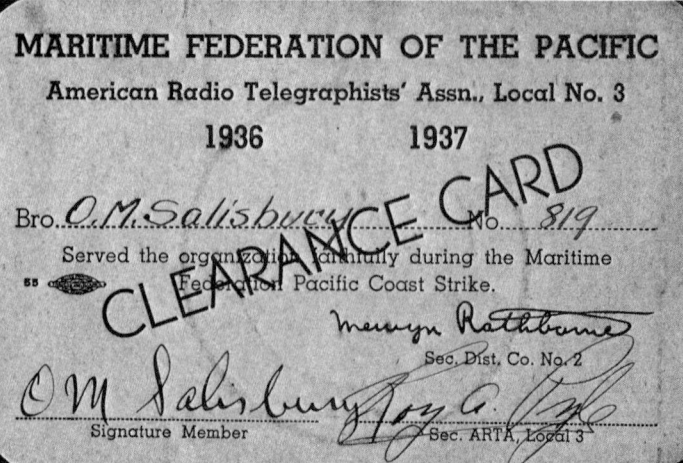

MARITIME FEDERATION OF THE PACIFIC
American Radio Telegraphists' Assn., Local No. 3
1936   1937

CLEARANCE CARD

Bro. O. M. Salisbury   No. 819

Served the organization faithfully during the Maritime Federation Pacific Coast Strike.

Mervyn Rathbone
Sec. Dist. Co. No. 2

O. M. Salisbury
Signature Member

Roy G. ___
Sec. ARTA, Local 3

SAN FRANCISCO CALL-BULLETIN—Thursday, July 11, 1940

Labor News

S. F. Radio Union Aide Given National Job

O. M. Salisbury, secretary of San Francisco Local 9 of the American Communications Association for the past two years, was notified today of his election as international vice president of the radio and cable division of the union.

He will take office August 1. His headquarters will be in New York city.

The election was held as a nationwide referendum.

Before becoming an officer of Local 9, Salisbury was a radio operator for Globe Wireless here.

Richard P. Clifford has been named acting secretary of the San Francisco union to replace Salisbury. A special election to fill the position will be held in September.

Clipping from San Francisco Call-Bulletin. Herb Caen wrote the labor column in those days and interviewed me for that nice sendoff. 1940.

American Radio Telegraphists Association, Inc.
20 IRVING PLACE, NEW YORK CITY.

819 This is to Certify that 1934

Oliver M. Salisbury is an Active Member, in good standing, with dues paid as indicated on other side.

Hoyt S. Haddock
President

Sitting down with Mr. Kimball, Vice President of Western Union Cable Company, to sign the first labor agreement with that company. I was International Vice President in charge of the Radio and Cables Division of ACA/CIO and resigned that office to go into the Maritime Service immediately after this signing. This was the picture I found the secretary of the British Wireless and Cable Operators Association looking at when I dropped in to pay my respects in Liverpool, England. October 1942.

BOwling Green 9-3006   263

OLIVER M. SALISBURY

Vice President, Radio and Cables Dept.
AMERICAN COMMUNICATIONS ASSN., CIO

10 Bridge St.
New York

A rough crossing for a North Atlantic convoy. 1942.

HALIFAX SHIPYARDS LIMITED.
CREW PASS

Date **JUL 31 1943**

S.S. **S/S JOHN A. POOR**

NAME *Oliver M. Salisbury*

Signature of Master.

There was no rest for crews in these seas. North Atlantic convoy service. 1942.

Norma and me on the roof garden of the Mount Royal Hotel, Montreal, Quebec after the torpedoing of the SS John A. Poor off Halifax. August 1943.

Portrait of me in the uniform of a Lt. j.g., United States Maritime Service. Ribbons are the European Theatre. 1943.

Lovely picture of Norma at that time. 1943.

A welcome word from Norma.

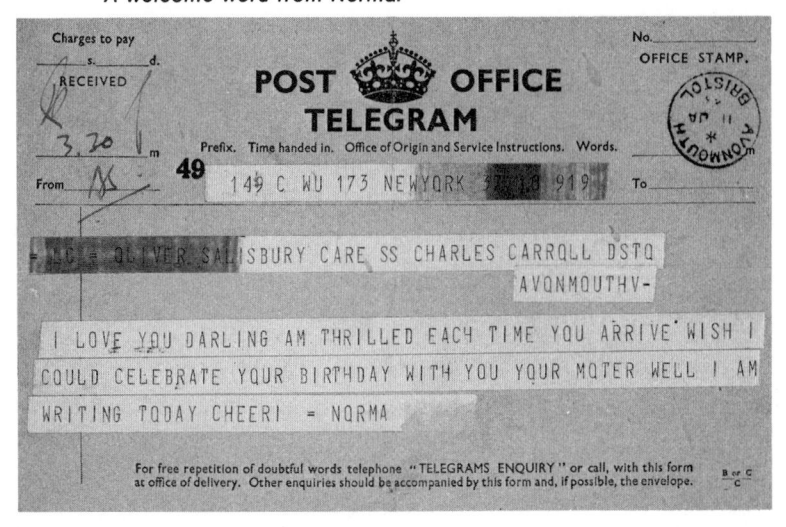

> LT OLIVER SALISBURY CARE SS CHARLES CARROLL DSTQ
>   AVONMOUTHV-
>
> I LOVE YOU DARLING AM THRILLED EACH TIME YOU ARRIVE WISH I COULD CELEBRATE YOUR BIRTHDAY WITH YOU YOUR MOTER WELL I AM WRITING TODAY CHEERI = NORMA

Portrait of Norma before I met her but a very good reason why I wanted to. These pictures were my pin-up girls.

WAR SHIPPING ADMINISTRATION TRAINING ORGANIZATION
UNITED STATES MARITIME SERVICE
(IDENTIFICATION CARD)
MS 9B

SIGNATURE (TO EXTEND ACROSS PHOTO): *Oliver M Salisbury*

NAME (TYPED): Oliver M. Salisbury
RANK OR RATING: Lt.(j.g.)
DATE OF BIRTH: 3-8-06
SERVICE No.: 4330-02482
HEIGHT: 71"
WEIGHT: 190
DATE ISSUED: 6-5-43
TITLE: L. F. LIVINGSTON, Lt.Comdr., USMS
16—31212-2

NAVY LEAGUE
MERCHANT OFFICERS CLUB
HALIFAX, N. S.
MEMBERSHIP CARD

2709

Mr. O. M. Salisbury

C. N. TAYLOR
SECRETARY
N. S. (MAINLAND) DIV.
NAVY LEAGUE OF CANADA

MANAGER

THE STARS AND STRIPES

U. S. Army Newspaper
Published Weekly in Africa

Through Facilities of Stars and Stripes and Yank

Vol. 1 - No 1 - Wednesday, 9 December, 1942 — ALGIERS — TWO FRANCS

First Army Strikes At Two Cities In Tunisia

Light Forces Held Up For Reinforcement But Air War Still Rages

Four weeks after Allied forces under the command of Lieut. Gen. Dwight D. Eisenhower moved into French North Africa, a campaign in the protectorate of Tunisia, about 400 miles across the Mediterranean from Italian-owned Sicily was shaping up.

This campaign centered around Tunisia's two largest cities—Bizerta, the big French naval base, and Tunis, the capital. Shortly after the Allies set foot in North Africa, the British 1st Army, having landed at Bone and Philippeville, moved across the Algerian border into Tunisia. This was admittedly a not-too-heavily equipped but very large force, but at that time it was hoped that it might get to Bizerta and Tunis before the Germans arrived in strength.

The Nazis, however, quickly landed air-borne troops, took over important airdromes at «both» these cities and began shifting a considerable part of the Luftwaffe to this new theatre of war. They were able to operate on the coastal plains of Tunisia, whereas Allied forces had to cross difficult mountains in which roads ...

A Message From The C-in-C

Lt. Gen. Dwight D. Eisenhower

I welcome the publication of *Stars and Stripes* in Africa, as will every man of the Allied Forces. We are a long way from home. Only people who have experienced the isolation inherent in extended military operations can fully appreciate the value to the soldier of news from home and friends. We have come to depend on *Stars and Stripes* for...

FDR Bans Volunteers Between 18 and 40

Washington — Men between 18 and 40 can no longer volunteer for the Army or Navy, according to an executive order issued by President Roosevelt. Hereafter, both civilian and military manpower needs will be met through a special commission headed by Paul V. McNutt. Selective service is to be transferred to the commission.

Secretary of War Stimson announced that hereafter no men over 39 years old would be drafted. The War and Navy secretaries have been ordered to determine and present their estimates to this new commission. Certain enlisted men particularly those over age who are unable to perform military service satisfactorily may now be honorably discharged from the Army.

Clark Gets D.S.M. For His Part In Secret Trip

Huddles In Cellar With Bribe Money And Gun Unused

U. S. War Output Shatters Record One Year After

O. W. I. Warns 1943 Means More Sacrifice And More Goods

Washington, Dec 7—This first anniversary of the Japanese attack on Pearl Harbor has been a time here at home for checking up on our accomplishments during the last twelve months.

The Office of War Information released impressive figures of American war production, but added the sober warning that the year 1943 would entail still further sacrifices. Donald Nelson, chief of the Office of War production, estimated that the United States alone was now producing twice as much war materiel as all our enemies combined.

Here were the OWI figures for 1942:
49,000 airplanes, with emphasis on heavy bombers.
32,000 tanks and self-propelled artillery.
17,000 anti-aircraft guns of more than 20-mm. calibre.
8,200,000 tons of merchant shipping.

The miracle of American rearmament is that ...

Facsimile of Vol. 1—No. 1, Stars and Stripes. I bought this in Arzew where we were supply ship to the First United States Rangers who took that port from the Darlan/Vichy French, suffering some casualties. Dec. 1942.

Facsimile of the Gibraltar Chronicle. I bought this paper in Gibraltar where we were anchored for thirty days awaiting convoy escort. Many ships were lost there at anchor from assaults by Italian one-man submarines. The HMS Rodney and the HMS Nelson were inside the breakwater undergoing battle damage repairs. The war did not look good at this time. March 1943.

SACCONE & SPEED Ltd.
(Established 1839)
130 Main Street
Gibraltar
The firm with a Century's experience in
WINES, SPIRITS
CIGARS, CIGARETTES and TOBACCO

MONDAY, MARCH 15, 1943.

Gibraltar Chronicle

Vol. CCIX.—No. 32,658. Price: One Penny.

INSIST ON Fino Catalina

A Fine Light Dry Sherry
Obtainable Everywhere

Berlin Claims Fall of Kharkov, Moscow Says:
TENSE BATTLE GOES ON, FLANK BLOW HELD

"IN THE AREA OF KHARKOV HEAVY FIGHTING CONTINUES. NORTH OF THE CITY OUR TROOPS YESTERDAY CONTINUED INTENSIVE ACTION AGAINST ENEMY INFANTRY AND TANKS."

THAT was Moscow's official reply at midnight to a special German High Command communique last night claiming Kharkov's recapture after a southern German army group had thrown back the Russians across the Donetz after a week of hard fighting.

Said Berlin: "Units of the armed S.S., well supported by the air force, have retaken the city in an encircling attack. Russian losses have not yet been ascertained."

SMOLENSK FRONT:

Moscow radio broadcast the following account of the battle: "Fighting for Kharkov is growing constantly fiercer, especially in the sectors ...

Nazi Key 'Dromes In France Raided

LONDON, Sunday night.—Whirlwind bombers this afternoon attacked the Nazi-operated airfields at Abbeville and Maupertus in Cherbourg peninsula.

In addition to covering the Whirlwinds, Fighter Command aircraft made several sweeps over northern France and Belgium, destroying two German fighters in air ...

R.A.F. POUNDS AXIS ARMOUR

BRITISH FIGHTERS AND BOMBERS THIS WEEK-END HAVE BEEN SWEEPING THE NORTHERN, CENTRAL AND SOUTHERN SECTORS OF THE TUNISIAN BATTLEFIELDS, POUNDING ARMOURED UNITS AND TROOPS. OUR BOMBERS MADE ANOTHER ATTACK ON THE MARETH LINE, FOUR ENEMY FIGHTERS BEING DESTROYED.

LIBERATORS and other bombers of the United States air force attacked Naples on Saturday night and Sunday morning, concentrating the raid on the harbour area.

Malta-based aircraft are also hitting hard at Axis shipping. On Saturday night fighter-bombers blew up a ship in convoy west of Sicily and damaged another vessel. On Sunday a third ship was damaged by R.A.F. bombers and in another raid a ship and schooner were hit with cannon fire in ...

WAR SHIPPING ADMINISTRATION

This is to certify that

Lt. Oliver M. Salisbury

HAS BEEN AWARDED

The Merchant Marine Combat Bar

confirming active service with THE UNITED STATES MERCHANT MARINE *in a ship which was engaged in direct enemy action*

E S Land
ADMINISTRATOR

16—35373-1

WAR SHIPPING ADMINISTRATION

This is to certify that

Lt. Oliver M. Salisbury

HAS BEEN AWARDED THE

Mediterranean Middle East War Zone Bar

confirming active service with THE UNITED STATES MERCHANT MARINE *in that war area.*

E S Land
ADMINISTRATOR

16—35373-1

WAR SHIPPING ADMINISTRATION

This is to certify that

Lt. Oliver M. Salisbury

HAS BEEN AWARDED THE

Atlantic War Zone Bar

confirming active service with THE UNITED STATES MERCHANT MARINE *in that war area.*

E S Land
ADMINISTRATOR

16—35373-1

Postcard of the inn where I stayed in Grasmere. A group of British Commandos were spending their last night there before being flown to the great battle of El Alamein in Egypt. They really whooped it up late into the night. Not quite the quiet and peace I was looking for, but I was not unsympathetic. Nov. 1942.

Poem written by John Ackerson during the wolf pack attack. John was purser on the ship and had published much verse.

RADIO OFFICER

His sturdy jaw lifts from the rubber suit
    Loose at the throat; to 'phones looping his neck,
    His ears are cocked; boots on the butt-strewn deck
    Sway wide apart; and a fresh-lit cheroot
His lips clamp tight. He flashes a grave glance
    As I fill up his doorway. 'One more hit,
    'Broke off her S.S.S. —' Well, bit by bit,
    Our convoy melts in the cold sea's expanse !
'Sparks' had a berth ashore, vice-president
    Of his brave front-line union; soon he'd wed;
    But Freedom for all men he coveted,
    And in her cause he holds his days well spent.
There slam our guns ! — shipmate, a fond farewell
Till we dig through this latest patch of Hell !

                           — John Ackerson.

North Atlantic Convoy,
November, 1942.

CHAPTER TWENTY SIX

Insurmountable Adversity

Shortly after the SS Front Royal arrived again in Rahway, New Jersey, I returned to my apartment to spend a few hours with Norma before making another voyage. I understood this time it would be across the Atlantic, again out of convoy and unescorted.

Navy Lieutenant Morris, in charge of the armed guard on the Front Royal, called on me in my apartment and said, "I want to tell you in a friendly way that Navy intelligence has been quizzing me about your conduct aboard ship and your competence as a radio officer. I told them, 'Salisbury's conduct was exemplary and his performance as a radio man was 100% efficient. I see no reason to question his loyalty.' I said, 'I think the drunken Captain has said something that brings this question about.' I feel that I might be helping you avoid some unnecessary embarrassment by telling you this."

I began to feel that if this stupid kind of harassment was going to follow me around, there were other places where I could support the war effort and be more appreciated and even make a greater contribution to my country. Radio operators by now were being trained in great numbers by all different branches of the services and by the Maritime School at Hoffman Island. There was no longer any shortage of men with these skills. True, the men coming out of the schools were not thoroughly trained and lacked experience, but they were serving the purpose.

I would not want to deny that the continuing narrow escapes with my life that I was experiencing were also on my mind. I asked myself, "How many times must a man lay his neck on the block for his country?" I had higher skills in communications, skills that were very much needed. Why not use them? Furthermore, why should I continue to expose myself to behind-the-back inquisitions?

I went back to the ship and quit. The War Manpower Commission had a policy of allowing merchant seamen so many days of rest between ships before their names were turned in to the draft board. Whatever the figure, I had the maximum coming and it amounted to several weeks.

I decided to try to get into one of the "crash" radar programs. The big electronics companies were running radar engineer schools: they would take a man with a lot of basic radio communications experience and put him through a nine months' course in radar engineering and pay him very well while he went to school. They were "live-in" programs and required that you study 12 hours a day. When you came out you were given a Navy commander's uniform, though still a civilian, and assigned to the fleet to maintain the radar equipment that was rapidly being installed on our warships. It sounded like good work and a fine place for me to make a maximum effort. I also felt that I would be on the ground floor of a new phase of communications and would be fitting myself for a good-paying postwar job. Several of my close friends had been through the program and all had done very well, receiving several promotions. My friends knew my qualifications and felt that this was a good program for me personally and certainly a maximum effort for the war.

I launched myself into this effort. First, I went to one of the big companies hiring such men and took their examination to see what would be required. I went to the company my friends thought the least of and made application. After passing through several personnel people I ended up getting a written examination on basic radio. With no preparation and no recent study I did not do at all well. However, I then knew what I was expected to know. I bought some radio books and began a cramming, grueling few weeks of study. I then applied at another company. I was almost accepted, but the examination was tougher than the first one. I decided to hire a tutor. I was able to engage a young Cuban Army lieutenant who was taking very advanced courses at the RCA Institute and whom the Institute highly recommended as being well qualified to tutor me in the subjects that I needed help with.

After about three weeks of this tutoring, several days each week and a lot of midnight oil burned studying, I applied to the company that I really wanted to work for. I went through the same process of applying and interviews and finally the examination by the chief engineer. Again I took a written examination, going deep into basic radio theory involving logarithms and the very things my Cuban lieutenant had been tutoring me on. The chief engineer was very pleased with my examination results and said, "Mr. Salisbury, you have done better than a man with an engineer's degree to whom I have just given this same examination." I felt very proud of my achievement and happy that I still had the ability to study and learn a tough subject. I held some trepidations as to whether I could succeed if I got into such a program. Having successfully studied and passed the examination satisfied me that I could. My confidence was up.

Mr. Orr, the Chief Engineer, told me I was hired subject to clearance by Naval Intelligence at 90 Church Street, N.Y.C. Well, I was naive enough to think that having been cleared as a security risk by no less a person than Secretary of the Navy Knox, I would have no trouble there. I felt that the minor harassment I was getting on the ships was petty stuff being handed out by incompetent officers. I spent a couple of days being processed and prepared for final indoctrination and then the blow fell. Mr. Orr told me that Naval Intelligence had rejected me as a bad security risk without any explanation to him. I could go down and talk to them if I liked. He seemed as disappointed as I was. He said, "No doubt it has something to do with your union activities."

I did go down and talk to them at 90 Church Street. The Intelligence officer told me, "While the Navy has cleared you to sail on merchant ships as a result of union pressure, the unions have no influence in the U.S. Navy fleet, and I could hardly accept you in that sensitive radar work." It didn't make any sense but I decided that I didn't want to make my major war effort that of fighting the U.S. Navy. There must be other places where my skill would be needed.

The Army Air Transport Corps, a quasi-military arm of the Army Air Corps, was flying military cargo all over the world wherever the war called for it. The were using C3's which were the largest cargo plane at the time. They made long flights out to India, the South Pacific or wherever the military had cargo that could not wait for slow convoy surface transportation. These planes carried a flight radio officer, an FCC-licensed civilian with special technical training for that particular type of work.

American Airlines was a government contractor in this service. I applied there for appointment as a flight radio officer. The pay was good. We were required to wear an Army lieutenant's uniform. There was a two months' training course in the school located at La Guardia Field; after graduation you would be assigned to flight duty. I was readily accepted, passing all the interviews and required tests with flying colors. I went through the two months' training and graduated from the school with good marks. They then told me I had to to have a State Department passport before I could be assigned to a plane. I applied to the State Department for a passport and they turned me down. I had the radio operators' union intervene for me. The lady at the State Department said, "We cannot have a man like that whom we suspect of being a subversive flying around the world." She ended up giving me a "seaman's passport." It was o.k. for me to come into any foreign port by water but not by air. Again a fatal decision made by a person who had reached her "highest level of incompetence." I lost my job as flight radio officer.

The policy was plain. I was not going to be able to work anywhere except where I was protected by the union. I knew men who stood on street corners selling the Daily Worker and wore the hammer and sickle emblem on their lapel, but yet were not on any black list. I was an effective union leader, associated with the militant left in the labor movement. For that I was banned from giving my best to my country. In retrospect it was no worse than the treatment of people of Japanese ancestry on the West Coast. I was not the only radio operator to receive this treatment either.

This left me nothing to do but go back to Mackay Radio and beat my brains out working as a radio telegrapher, which I did. The international circuits were so piled up and so far behind that the mails often beat delivery of telegrams. In fact, about 200,000 "GI" telegrams that I knew about were mailed to our fighting men overseas. They hired clerks to copy them off on telegraph and cable forms. The circuits overseas were so loaded with essential wartime traffic that this type of message should never have been accepted for transmission. No harm done, but the radio and cable companies picked up a few million dollars from the unknowing public under false pretenses. I say false because if they didn't know better, they should have. The operators were working 12, 16, and 20 hours a day. When you went to work you never knew when you would ever see your bed again. It was punishing work. There were plenty of "goof-offs" among the workers, too. Card games for big money stakes were going on in the locker rooms with all participants being on overtime pay at time and a half.

We were highly unionized and the practice during the war was to set up labor/management committees to handle production problems. Because I was well known to all of the employees in the company and because of my experience in the union I was quickly elected to the shop chairmanship and to the labor/management committee and found myself heavily back in the union work. I worked many long and hard hours on trans-Atlantic radio circuits and then worked on these activities. The company, anxious to keep production going smoothly, would take me off the circuits with other members of the committee and we would spend hours solving production problems. We devised an incentive system that the company and the union accepted which went a long way in increasing efficiency.

One day I was contracted by Mr. Alexander, an officer of the company, and offered a job as personnel manager at a good salary. It was explained that this offer was made in all sincerity as being in the best interest of the union and the company, and not an effort to divert me from my loyalty to the union. I said that I would give it serious thought.

Insurmountable Adversity

After a couple of days I met with the officer of the company again. I suggested that the company write a letter to the president of the union asking his consent to my appointment to this job and explaining in writing their reasons; then only if the president of the union agreed would I accept this appointment. They agreed to write such a letter and did. It was approved by the highest officer in the I.T.&T., President Sosthenes Behn.

To my surprise the president of the union rejected the proposal, telling me that he and the members of the union would look upon it as a "sellout." Of course, I didn't take the job under those circumstances, though I didn't agree with him about how the members would feel. I think the president of the union made a tragic error, not his only mistake. Three years later the man the company did hire smashed the union, with a company-provoked strike that was part of a diabolical plan.

The company officials were made up of 'doves' and 'hawks.' Our union president's decision tilted company authority in favor of the 'hawks.' They hired a vicious anti-labor man from South Carolina right out of intensive training in union busting. The company decided it was cheaper to fight a union than make peace with it. The ACA/CIO lost out in that company forever and then lost jurisdiction after jurisdiction. The company 'doves' were sent overseas and scattered through out the I.T.&T. System. We have the I.T.&T. interfering in the domestic affairs in Chile and the other big stories of 'power plays' that we read in the press. It might have been different had the 'doves' prevailed. In the end the ACA/CIO lost its C.I.O. charter, being expelled by Philip Murray, president of the C.I.O. That might have been different too. Of course this is pure conjecture on my part.

About this time I was offered another opportunity of an entirely different nature. I was contacted by an officer of the O.S.S. (Office of Strategic Services, U.S. Army) and asked if I would come to a certain office building in downtown Manhattan. I was told by a certain union official whom I trusted that I should go. The O.S.S. officer told me that this time my radical, militant history was working for me and that they had an opportunity for me to make a maximum contribution to the war effort, possibly meaning my life. It seemed the Army was preparing several demolition units to be parachuted into Jugoslavia to Marshal Tito's headquarters and to operate under his direction. Each unit of five men had a radio operator. I would be one. I would receive special training in demolition work at an Army location outside of Washington. My rating would be that of a sergeant and I would be given $300 per month extra which would be deposited to a New York bank account in my name. They wanted me, as Tito would accept me because of my radical history. They knew that I could ride a horse, I was raised in a rugged part of western Montana as a rancher's son, I'd seen and helped use dynamite, I was familiar with firearms, had military training in Alaska and was an experienced radio operator. It seemed that my life had trained me for this assignment. I asked my interviewing officer, "What happens after victory in Europe?"

The officer said, "You would be in for the duration. You might be dropped by parachute into China."

"It sounds kind of terminal, but I'll do it," I said.

I was given reams of security forms to fill out. They wanted references right back to kindergarten age, ex-wives' names and addresses and the names of anyone who knew me well. As time went on I found they checked every last one of them and probably others, too.

One day I was called into the OSS office and told that I had been rejected by the top brass, Colonel Donovan. The officer said, "The one thing the Colonel could not accept was the fact you were living together for some time before you were legally married to Norma. Everything else about you is fine." (Norma and I had waited for her Jewish divorce to become final in order to get her ex-husband's cooperation in the court divorce.)

It seems all was not lost. The OSS officer who was to go in on the demolition unit wanted me so badly that he was willing to make another arrangement. They had money for hiring local people on the scene. The OSS would arrange for me to go as radio officer on the next merchant ship bound for Cairo, and I would by pre-arrangement jump ship in Cairo and meet a contact that the OSS would have arranged, and go into Jugoslavia that way. I would not be in the Army, but I would be well compensated. The OSS would have me released from my job in Mackay Radio and would have my relief in Cairo arranged without any repercussions for jumping ship. Again I said, "Yes."

It was real cloak-and-dagger stuff, sort of James Bond style. I was waiting for the next ship to Cairo when I was called into OSS and told that the whole program had been cancelled. Marshal Tito didn't want any American units. This was a great disappointment.

I stayed on in Mackay Radio, continuing to pound out telegrams and to serve on the Union commitees. I understand that none of the OSS demolition units ever got further than Bari, Italy. The men sat the war out there in boredom. I was glad to have been spared that.

On January 3, 1945, my son Tom was born. Norma and I lived in a big apartment house in Gramercy Park. No children allowed. During the long war and the housing shortage several babies had been born in the building and the people could not move, as there was no housing available. The young mothers, most of them war brides like Norma, would park their perambulators in the sun in front of the building on 22nd Street. The landlord would come out and say, "You can't park those carriages here, you must keep moving!" Norma would have the baby dressed in blue ribbons and satin comforters and she wouldn't be out on the street fifteen munutes before the finery would be covered with soot and filth.

When the war ended, we decided that New York City was no place for a man from Montana to raise a family. I asked for a transfer to WSL, Southampton, Long Island, N.Y., the big shore-to-ship coastal radio station that had been a subject of controversy with the Navy at the start of the war. The men there were glad to have me and I was happy to be there. Norma and I moved out to Sag Harbor, Long Island, a few miles from the station, and a new life began.

Chapter Twenty Seven

The Saga Of Sag Harbor

The move to Sag Harbor was a good one for us. Sag Harbor was nine miles from the town of Southampton. Sag Harbor is an old, old colonial whaling village. The house we were able to buy there was built before the American Revolution. It was made of oak and cypress, the oak beams and joists all being hand hewn and hand joined. The original cypress shingle was still on the exterior, being three inches thick at the butt end and thinner at the weathered end. The only nails in the old house were hand forged similar to those used in horse shoeing. There was a fireplace in every room, though some of them were boarded up. I made a hobby of restoring the old Dutch oven in the ancient kitchen. The oven had nice lines and the original wrought iron fixtures still in place. The house sat on a big corner lot on Sag Harbor's main street.

We liked the atmosphere of this village and its historical lore. I liked my work and the men I worked with very much.

Eastern Long Island in 1946 was still quite rural. Boating, swimming, fishing, clamming, digging oysters were popular sports. Sag Harbor was becoming an art colony and many interesting people were buying and renting summer homes in the area. I took an adult education course in painting and sculpture and made many friends through that association, even winning a first prize in amateur sculpture at the Parish Museum in Southampton.

Norma was busy being a young mother to our two small children. Our second child, Lois, was born to us the first year we lived there. Norma was a good tennis player and enjoyed that game and the friends she made through it. With the big house we had many guests all year around. Norma and the children and I look back on Sag Harbor as being the happiest years of our lives. It was indeed a great place to live and we were at the right age to enjoy the things it offered.

We had ceased all political activism, though we had by no means abandoned our principles and consciousness. When we moved into Sag Harbor we both went down and registered to vote as members of the American Labor Party, which in New York State was a large legal third party. The editor of the little Sag Harbor paper saw fit to editorialize on "How did two members of the American Labor Party happen to sneak into our town?" We didn't exactly sneak in, and if we had, we would not have gone down and registered American Labor Party.

At that time the little village was embroiled in a duel between two real estate brokers. One owned a lot of property on the beach which well-to-do black middle class and professionals were interested in developing as a beach site and the other broker owned a lot of the property inside the town. Both suddenly became great Lincoln Republicans. The one owning suburban beach property supported zoning laws in the town that banned any but Caucasians from owning property. The other broker opposed annexing the suburban property claiming the city water system would not support the new homes. This comic debate went on for some time. I had several chuckles seeing local merchants reverse their positions from one of militant racism to going around saying, "The color of the money is the same no matter the color of who's carrying it!"

The town of Southampton, where most of the radio station

personnel lived, was another story. Southampton was a wealthy beach colony dating back to the turn of the century. All the biggest names of American industry were there as well as much of the lesser nobility of Europe. The place was divided into about four social and economic classes: the estate owners, the doctors who cared for the rich patrons, the merchants and the tradesmen, plumbers, electricians, carpenters, etc., and by no means the least, the gardeners. Then there were the radio men who had their own economy and were completely independent of the politics and economy of the town. There were about fifty of them, so their existence could not be ignored. This atmosphere didn't exactly set up what one would call a labor town. The first radio station strike there in 1935 was a shock to the community. By the time the second strike took place in 1948, the people were more or less inured to the existence of the radical radio operators—which was the way they looked upon us.

I had made a good decision in picking Sag Harbor as a place to live. We were accepted and the pace was slow and easy, something Norma and I were both ready for.

We worked short hours at the radio station, working five seven-hour shifts in four days, thus having three days every week to enjoy our homes and the wonderful recreation activities available to us. This was particularly delightful in the summertime. My last shift would end at 7 a.m., say on a Friday, and then I would not be due back on duty until three in the afternoon the following Monday. Coming off duty at 7 a.m. and coming home just as Norma and the babies were awakening made it a tough time for me to get sleep. As the day went on the household became noisier as the kids' little playmates began to show up in our huge yard, with barking puppies and bicycle bells and all that goes with those little darlings. The wife would start running household equipment all over the place and I recognized that it was just no place to sleep. Failing to get some rest after the grueling five shifts in four days would leave me grumpy for the first 24 hours off, and therefore nothing was gained.

So I started the practice in the summertime of coming home at 7 a.m., having breakfast and then taking my boat and motor and going fishing. Generally, the morning fishing was the best and we had some very good fishing in Long Island Sound, weakfish, bluefish, some striped bass, porgies, sea bass, king fish and a wide variety besides lobsters, crabs, clams and oysters. A morning out like that was relaxing and fun. When the sun began to get high along about 11 o'clock I would pull up on the nearest beach, lay out my blanket and have a good snooze. When the sun started to get low and cool, or I was slept out, I'd awaken and come home, rested and ready for a good couple of days with my wife and kids and the houseful of guests that we seemed to always have.

On one particular morning, a beautiful day in June, I followed that procedure. Along about 11 o'clock I felt drowsy as the sun warmed and I found myself alongside a small uninhabited island near North Haven, L.I. The island was beautiful, lush with foliage, fragrant with wild honeysuckle, and full of birds of all descriptions. I pulled the boat up on the white sandy beach, pushed the anchor into the sand, took my blanket and spread it out under a shady oak tree that was half covered with wild cucumber vine. I was in a small inlet and my boat could not even be seen from out on the bay. I flopped on the blanket and was instantly asleep, having by that time been up for at least 30 hours, from about 6 a.m. the day before. I had a beautiful sleep, waking late in the afternoon. As I opened my eyes and became aware of what world I was in I noticed a sign on a nearby tree—a professionally painted sign which read, "NO TRESPASSING, VIOLATORS WILL BE PROSECUTED. This island is patrolled! Signed, Mary Gerard."

You had to be my age and be from the Bitterroot Valley in Montana to know who Mary Gerard was and how I felt. Mary Gerard was the daughter of Marcus Daly, the Montana Copper King, and one of the richest men in America in the early part of this century. Mary Daly had married Ambassador Gerard, the American Ambassador to Germany at the time of the outbreak of World War I. Being a small boy with big ears I had picked up that bit of gossip listening to conversations between my mother and my elder sister. (I had always had a great talent for retaining information of no consequence to me.)

When I was a teenage lad living in Hamilton, Montana, my brother and I were great hunters and fishermen; consequently our friends were also hunters and fishermen. We had been trained to handle guns and our mother didn't object. There were all too many hunting accidents in that valley and many parents wouldn't permit their sons to indulge in this sport. Our mother found that we actually were a source of supply of meat and fish for the table and I really felt like a provider more than a sportsman. We were trained in good manners and sportsmanship and knew the rules. As a matter of fact, even in that day in Montana we had to have hunting and fishing licenses at the age of twelve.

Marcus Daly had an estate of some five thousand acres in the Bitterroot Valley, most of it fenced. There was an artificially created five-acre duck pond which was fenced with a high hurricane fence with strands of barbed wire around the top. There were also deer and elk in this area. When the duck season was open the hunters shooting up and down the valley, along the Bitterroot River and the lagoons and ponds, eventually spooked the wild ducks and they were quick to find this sanctuary that Marcus Daly provided. He and his friends hunted there when they were at the mansion so it was not a game refuge. I'd go in there with my brother or my chum Chuck Stanton or his brother Harold. We'd crawl under the fence, sneak up to the edge of the pond and fire into the flocks of ducks that were feeding on the beach, dash down and pick up the kill and make a fast retreat for the hole under the fence. The private game warden, employed by Mr. Daly, would come out of his shack on the other side of the pond shooting. Shooting at us, too, with a 12-gauge automatic shotgun. We were too far away to get hurt by the light bird shot, but it would shower around us, adding to the excitement. Once a bird shot stuck in the skin of my hand but I flicked it out as it was barely a flesh wound. We felt justified—wrong, but justified. It was his pond, but they were wild ducks—not his.

Five thousand acres is a lot of square miles and it seemed like no matter where we went, rabbit hunting, duck hunting, coyote hunting or just hiking, I could always look at the nearest tree and see a "NO TRESPASSING, Marcus Daly," sign. My brother and I used to say, "How far do you have to go to get off that man's land?"

Well, when I looked up from my happy nap on the beach on Long Island Sound and saw that "NO TRESPASSING, Mary Gerard" sign, I thought, "My God! Three thousand miles and I'm not off that man's land yet." Pushing my boat back into the water, I saw fresh jeep tracks in the sand. They were still patrolling, only having changed from horses to jeeps.

I was constantly working in our big yard in Sag Harbor. One spring morning about the middle of May a hot dry spell set in. I was raking the old leaves up and started studying the honeysuckle hedge around our place. We lived on a corner lot with about 150 feet fronting on Main Street and running back about 250 feet. The hedge went clear across the front and down the side. I noticed that the hedge was about four feet thick and there was an old picket fence in the center of it. The honeysuckle had not started to leaf out yet and was dry and brittle. It came up new every year from the root, the new vine climbing on the old. I thought, Now if I could clean that off and get down to that old picket fence, probably a hundred years old at least, I could restore the fence, paint it and have a nice white picket fence around this old colonial home.

I tried pulling the honeysuckle vines loose but they didn't come loose very well. Then I thought, Why not burn it? No sooner had the thought surfaced than I'd thrown a match into it. It was as if I had taken a barrel of gun powder and sprinkled it the length of my fence. The fire just took off with a crackle and a ten-foot high flame. Looking down the side fence I saw the honeysuckle had climbed over onto a maple tree and from the tree to the roof of my house. It was high time to call the fire department.

Son Tommy, then about two and a half years old, always enjoyed seeing the big red fire trucks go racing down Main Street past the house as he ran to the front gate to cheer them on. He was not so happy when the trucks stopped at our house with engines roaring, bells ringing and sirens sounding. He had been excited by the fire running along the fence, thinking that was a great show.

After I ran into the house and called in the alarm I raced back to the yard to see if the fire had reached the roof yet. All credit to the fire department, they were there in three minutes from my calling in. The fire had then climbed across the tree and to the dry shingle roof. As his men went to work, the fire chief jumped off his truck and asked where my phone was; another alarm had come in. I yelled, "In the kitchen, go right in!" The day had been full of grass fires similar to mine. About the time the fire chief was in the kitchen on the phone, the firemen started playing a big stream of water on the roof. In all the excitement of the fire, my son screaming, and having to pick him up to keep him out of the way of the firemen, I had forgotten my wife was sleeping in the nude in the back room underneath the fire and the huge stream of water pouring on the roof. She woke up, frightened by the racket, came running into the kitchen stark naked, and bumped into the fire chief.

We never quite lived that down. Every time my wife passed the fire hall, which was also on Main Street, the firemen would ask, "How's that incendiary husband of yours?" I'm sure too, they said, "Woo, woo!" under their breaths, as you can be sure the chief had described his collision in the kitchen.

Norma and I were enjoying these years with the small children and the nice pace. The postwar years were pleasant while the country readjusted for a period of peace.

CHAPTER TWENTY EIGHT

Caught In The Backlash

By 1947-1948 a backlash to wartime progress had set in. Reactionary forces were at work throughout the country. Senator Taft was out to make a name for himself and win the Republican nomination for President. He introduced the Taft-Hartley Act which amended the more liberal Wagner Act. President Truman vetoed the Taft-Hartley Act but the Congress overrode his veto. The big corporations and the anti-labor element in the country were girding themselves to take away labor's wartime gains.

Mackay Radio and Telegraph Company, a wholly-owned subsidiary of I.T.&T., was no exception. The company had employed a labor relations director who was schooled in the latest techniques of union busting. He was vicious and anxious to sink his teeth into our union. Settling local grievances became difficult. A new contract was in the offing. All of us knew a storm was coming. There was, as always, a shortage of radio operators qualified to work at our skills and requirements. When the union couldn't furnish men, the company by our contract was allowed to hire outside. They started sending men out to our station to work who weren't even needed. We had a closed shop, so they joined the union. Any radio operator with the experience to take one of these jobs at Southampton who had not yet joined the union was "suspect." He had to have been running from the union by going to the few non-union jobs that still existed, such as the airlines at that time. Some men sent out were notorious finks, that is, men who were slow to join the union at the beginning and only joined after labor agreements were signed compelling them to. We could see the preparations for a battle.

During this time the company's labor relations director went overseas and called on the British Wireless and Cable Operators' Association and was allowed to address a membership meeting. He told the British Operators' Association that if they were called upon to support a strike by American Communications Association/CIO they should not do it, as they would be supporting Moscow and world communism. In the past, when the British operators had had a strike our members had refused to work the New York end of their circuits until they had settled their labor problems. They had reciprocated by doing the same for us when asked. This company union buster then went on to Paris and made the same presentation to the French Radio and Cable Operators' Association. Those good unions wrote our union president and asked that he send an officer over or come himself to address their members and tell them our answer to the company's lie. The cold war had begun by 1948 and Western world hostility was accelerating against that ideology.

Joseph Selly, president of ACA/CIO, made a grave and tragic error by not going overseas or sending over our National Director of Organization, Joe Kehoe. Selly did go as far as getting a passport for Kehoe, and made plans for him to go to London and Paris on this mission. Something else came up that in Selly's opinion was more important, and he cancelled Kehoe's trip.

The result, when the strike came: the British and French operators worked our circuits manned by company officials and strikebreakers at this end. After three long hard winter months on the picket lines the members went back to work without a union contract. That was a tragic error on the part of President Joe Selly, one that we never recovered from. Subsequently, this same dogged intransigence led our union to expulsion by the

CIO because of its alleged communist leadership. This was the beginning of the McCarthy period.

Out at our radio stations on Long Island at Southampton, Brentwood and Amagansett, we had conducted a perfect strike. Not one single member out of nearly 100 men had gone back to work during this entire three months. We had set up strike headquarters, at Southampton, in what was Paton's Wild Duck Inn. It was the old mansion of Elsie Ferguson, the early day silent movie star. We had been great patrons of this inn and loved Jim Paton, its owner and proprietor, who had been an oldtime locomotive engineer and union man. He enjoyed our business before the strike. It was a favorite stopover for us on the way home from the evening shifts, as well as a good place to take our families for a Sunday dinner. Jim Paton made his great dining hall available to us as strike headquarters, a meeting place, and a hangout. Our strike headquarters were deluxe.

The company had recruited a few strikebreakers but none from our ranks. Even those the company had sent out in advance of the strike stood with us when they saw our solidarity. The strike collapsed in New York City. The union represented the All American Cables and the Commercial Cable Company employees through the affiliation of their associations and they had joined the strike, both these companies also being I.T.&T. affiliates. Because of the large numbers involved, holding the people in New York City together was a difficult job. Strike benefits were meager. I was strike chairman at Southampton and I like to think that I did a good job of it. Everyone said that I had. I'm sure the company thought so.

There was a spirit of camaraderie out on Long Island that was beautiful. We all knew each other well and each other's wives and children. When a family had a problem we had a committee that sat down with them and worked it out. The company resorted to every dirty trick known to strikebreaking. They contacted men who had pregnant wives and cancelled their hospitalization Blue Cross benefits; they contacted men that were known to be badly in debt and put pressure on them through their creditors. The company had promoted a manager from our ranks a year or two before the strike, expecting that he would be more effective in breaking the strike because he knew us all so intimately. He had been popular among us, and as a matter of fact had been fired and reinstated by the 1935 U.S. Supreme Court case, becoming a union hero to the men. He was popular as a manager until he started resorting to extreme means to break our strike. When the strike broke in New York City it left the men at the Long Island stations no choice but to go back to work. The company took us all back, having had their lesson in discrimination by that now famous court decision.

It wasn't long before layoffs began. Business had suffered from the prolonged strike. They laid off by seniority so that we didn't have resort to labor board charges. The company no longer recognized our union or any union, so we were at their mercy.

It is sad to see men lose their dignity. One of the greatest things working men gain in being represented by a good union is dignity. They have their rights and can hold their heads high. In an open shop where the union has been beaten, the company moves in vindictively. Many men cannot stand up under this. I saw that happening here to good men—men who before had been brave and militant.

We had two strikebreakers that tried to stay on after the strike. Not one man would speak to them. A week or two after the strike one of them was walking home through the woods. He was beaten up, so the company claimed. Not one of us ever saw him after the alleged incident, so we didn't know if it really happened. No one ever walked to work the three miles from the station to Southampton. If this fellow was walking he probably was put up to it and paid for doing so. Possibly he was beaten, I do not know, but if one of our members was tempted, it is not too hard to understand. I never condoned violence as a union man. It was, and is, my belief that aside from being wrong it is not the way to win.

I came to work at three o'clock in the afternoon a few weeks after the strike to find the station parking lot full of sheriff's cars, at least three or four of them. I thought, "Oh, oh! Here it is." No sooner had I entered the operating room than the chief operator said, "You are wanted in the manager's office."

I went in and Mr. Eldridge , the manager, said, "The sheriff wants to talk to you."

A clown in civilian clothes putting on an act like a Hollywood comedian playing the role of a detective, slamming a sloppy hat on his head and then on the table, started in on me in the most provocative way. He said, "An employee is near death in the local hospital with possible concussion of the brain; we have reason to believe you are the one that did it."

I asked, "What time and where did it happen?"

The sheriff's deputy said, "At ten minutes past 11 p.m., the exact time that you'd, a been passing the point of the assault, which is just at the Sag Harbor turnoff. The victim claims the assailant took the Sag Harbor road. You are the only one on that shift that goes that way."

I said, "I was still in the station at that time. I'd been in to New York to union headquarters and the three men that came on duty relieving our shift asked me to stay and tell them what was going on in New York. Though I was tired, I stayed a good half hour filling them in on the latest developments."

The sheriff said, "Can you prove it?"

"Yes, call in the supervisor. I see he's here."

He had always been a staunch union man, but when he came in he couldn't remember that I had stayed over, though he was the one that asked me to stay.

The sheriff called in the second man. I couldn't believe it, but he couldn't remember what had happened the evening before either.

The atmosphere was intimidating with all these deputy, uniformed, heavily armed men standing in the small office towering over you. I can always tell the truth and my friends' sudden lapse of memory was a loss of dignity in my book. They had ceased to be men and were crawling like creatures.

The third man who had been present the evening before was still at home. He lived next door to me in Sag Harbor. The sheriff said they would escort me home and be sure in that way that I did not call him before they had a chance to talk with him. With a police escort home you can imagine the curiosity that two sheriff's cars in front of my house created. The sheriff went next door to Joe Maus's house and asked him, "What time did Salisbury leave the station last night?"

Joe answered, "At 11:30. I remember as I made the first entry in my radio log as he left. You can verify that with the log."

The sheriff and his deputies left, driving away without an apology. I escaped what appeared to be the classical attempt to frame me, jail me, and throw the key away.

As time went by things simmered down; we licked our wounds and looked to the union to revive its efforts to put the pieces back together. Another union appeared in the picture—at the company's invitation, I suspected. Their organizers contacted me and tried to convince me to switch my loyalties. The organizer said, "We don't know if you are a communist or not but that is not enough. You'll have to be an active anticommunist."

This kind of chicanery was not a part of my character. I knew some members who were said to be communists and they always seemed to stand for programs that were good for the membership.

The union began to breathe life again, but so did the other group, and we seemed to be dividing about evenly. I think some very good and honest men went for the new union believing that it would be impossible to put the old one back together. They were probably right as it worked out.

Because I continued to stand by the old union, most of the militants did likewise. The new union was not able to get a majority, apparently because of me. I began to get pressure from the company manager in subtle and not-so-subtle forms. The manager called me into his office and said, "Salisbury, your fist (my telegraph sending with a hand key) is deplorable, and unless you can rapidly improve I will have to let you go."

I had been there going on seven years and suddenly this developed. I had spent a great deal of time handling land line telegraph keys. The style of sending on land line and the difference between the American Morse code and the International Morse developed somewhat different characteristics in sending from that of a ship's telegrapher. The land line telegrapher tends to shorten his dashes and thereby accelerates his sending speed. Ship's telegraphers are generally working through static and interference from other ships so they elongate their dashes and drag the Morse signals out. We called it "salty" sending. The manager had a very salty style of sending and he was a good operator. His sending was so styled that many operators out on the ships knew when they were working with him.

I asked "What do you mean by rapid improvement?"

"Thirty days!" and he got up and quickly walked away.

In some respects I have not always acted intelligently. It had been my feeling always that in this business the company should furnish all of the equipment we were asked to use, as it was so specialized it couldn't be used elsewhere.

Many good operators used a "bug," a vibrating key which made sending Morse code more rapid, easier and—if the operator was skilled at it—produced nicer signals for the receiving operator to read. In my super militancy I had always said, "I'll use a bug when the company furnishes me with one." I had owned them long ago, but on the trans-Pacific and trans-Atlantic radio circuits most sending was from a typewriter-like keyboard, only using the hand key to break into the circuit for corrections or circuit instructions.

I wanted to keep my job so I bought a "bug," a good one, and had the station machinist make some fine changes in it so that my fellow operators said my sending really was superb. Then I emulated the manager's style of sending until operators on the ship were asking, "Is this Johnny?" meaning the manager.

Johnny Eldridge had a super ego, and when he listened to my sending in his style, he loved it. He congratulated me on having made a miraculous transition. I asked him if he would give me a letter to that effect, which, in his enthusiasm, he did. I never had to worry about being fired because of my work again.

Years passed. The strike had been in the winter of 1948; it was now 1951. Mr. Ellery W. Stone was again president of Mackay Radio, having risen to the rank of full admiral in the U.S. Navy during World War II and been Allied security officer for Italy during the occupation after surrender. He had married an Italian countess, according to the society columns in the New York papers. If you recall my difficulties with Mr. Stone in the early chapters of this book, and if you will recall my father's admonitions about my having written a vituperative bulletin attacking Mr. Stone and his comment that men like that have much power and long memories and can be vindictive, then you must recognize my father to have been a very wise prophet.

About 16 years after my first confrontation with Mr. Stone he came into the radio station at Southampton. I was working at my radio position and he came in with other high company officials on an inspection tour of the company's facilities. He recognized me, came over and very cordially told me how glad he was to see me, to see me looking so well and to have me on the staff. Mr.

Stone himself was a fine-looking gentleman and it was not hard to understand his marital successes—not at staying married, but at marrying several beautiful young heiresses. I really felt flattered that he remembered me, but then why shouldn't he have? Hadn't I given him enough trouble?

Soon after this visit, and I have no proof that it was related, an order came out that all coastal radio station operators employed by the company must have radio officer's licenses issued by the U.S. Coast Guard. This was a way of forcing us through a screening process without the company getting the blame. I could see the purpose: it was aimed at me. This was 1951 and the beginning of the McCarthy period. The cold war was on, the Korean War was on and an hysteria had been whipped up to where a great many people looked for a "red" under the bed each night.

Obtaining a radio officer's license was a nuisance. We already had F.C.C. (Federal Communications Commission), first class radio telegrapher's license which attested to our skills, technical and legal knowledge of international laws governing radio communications. During the war Congress, in recognition of the heroic services being performed by radio operators in the U.S. Merchant Marine, had passed a law making radio operators line officers aboard ship. Heretofore, they had been staff officers and some of our membership felt "status" was a very important thing and had passed resolutions in the union asking the union officers to support passage of such a bill. This was all right, but it wasn't long after the war before the ship owners and radio service companies saw this as a chance to get the militant union members off the ships. In effect a good thing boomeranged. That was not all, either. Being a ship's radio operator had always been a good job for the physically handicapped. Crippled men and other unfortunates had been able to master the skills required and become useful, happily employed citizens as a result. Now the Coast Guard called for a rigid physical examination as well as security clearance. They also required that a ship's radio officer obtain a First Aid Certificate from the Surgeon General's office before he could even apply for the radio officer's license.

I delayed as long as I could, perhaps six months, before the company gave me an order that I must have that license within 60 days or be discharged. I then went to see my lawyer, Leonard Boudin, who achieved national prominence as a civil defense attorney. Leonard and Victor Rabinowitz had represented me any number of times down through the years during the difficulties I have been relating. Leonard said, "You again? Aren't you ever going to get clear of trouble?"

I said, "Not while people keep pickin' on me." I related my predicament. Leonard Boudin, incidentally, is a genius at his profession.

He looked up the law and read: "It is against the law and a misdemeanor for anyone to require others to or to obtain a Radio Officer's License for any reason other than to serve on a U.S. Merchant ship as a Radio Officer." He wrote the company a letter calling this to their attention. The company posted a notice on our bulletin board rescinding the order.

All was peaceful again for some time. Then Admiral Stone went to Washington, using his I.T.&T. clout to have Congress amend the law to apply to coastal radio stations.

Now it was the spring of 1952. It is presumption on my part that Mr. Stone went to Washington; perhaps he only had to write a letter. Maybe it was not Stone. The I.T.&T. was full of admirals, Admiral Halsey not being the least.

In any event, immediately a directive was issued by the company instructing those who had not obtained their radio officer's licenses to get them within three months. I started the procedure: first, the physical exam, then the First Aid Certificate, and finally the security check. Each phase called for a 125-mile trip into New York City on my day off.

The Coast Guard denied my radio officer's license: "Because you are known to associate with known Communists."

Under the law I could appeal my case to the federal courts if I wished; I wished. I went to see Leonard Boudin again, but he advised me to forget it and take my bath even if that meant losing my job. He thought that to go into court would only result in further difficulty; the people who wanted me out of my profession would furnish the government with perjured witnesses that would testify to whatever they directed and my denial would result in perjury charges against me and possible imprisonment. Senator Joe McCarthy was really whipping the country into a frenzy and few voices were speaking up against him.

I followed Leonard's advice and sent in my resignation to the company. I have always been a little sorry that I didn't stay and fight it. Some of the ship operators who had been denied their radio officer's licenses took the matter to court and the screening was eventually thrown out as unconstitutional by the U.S. Supreme Court. Friends told me that after I resigned no one was ever asked to show or obtain a radio officer's license to work at a coastal radio station.

Leonard Boudin has been right so many times in his long legal career, largely representing people fighting for their constitutional rights, that I must presume his advice was good and that he saved me from even worse treatment.

This brought about a radical change in my life and I left the communications field forever.

CHAPTER TWENTY NINE

First Phase Of Transition

Norma and I began to think in terms of doing something else for a livelihood. We had saved a little money and had our equity in the Sag Harbor home. It not only appeared that the forces against me were finally going to win and I would be fired, but Norma and I were becoming weary of the harassment. After all, I had been standing up to it for 15 or 20 years.

As a hobby I had been sharecropping eight acres of land near Bridgehampton in my spare time as well as having a large vegetable garden in our back lot. Norma knew that I liked farming and said, "Oliver, wouldn't you like to be a farmer?"

"It has not occurred to me that this is a possibility for us," I answered.

Norma was born and raised in Brooklyn, the daughter of a luggage manufacturer—not exactly the background to fit her for a farmer's wife. Still, she was strong of will and strong of body. She said, "The idea of a family effort appeals to me, as it must to you."

In talking this idea over some very fine and generous friends volunteered, "If you need financial help to buy what you find that you like, we'll be glad to help you." We had a lot of sympathetic friends who gave us moral encouragement. We made a clear-cut decision and I resigned from my job at the radio station.

The decision to become a farmer having been made, we began careful research on the kind and size of farm that we should look for. I wrote to Cornell University and asked for all the information and advice they could give me. Their advice was to buy a family-size dairy farm, as I had had some experience as a youth with livestock. I was now 46 years old, healthy and in fine physical condition as was Norma, though Norma was 11 years younger than I. We had a son, Tom, 8, and a daughter, Lois, 6, who would before long be a great help around a farm and would love it. What Cornell called a family-size dairy farm was enough acreage to grow your own feed with proper buildings to support a 20-cow herd plus a growing replacement herd, avoid hiring labor, and operate a Grade A dairy within the New York City Milk Shed—a marketing area arbitrarily established by the state and federal governments.

We put the kids in the car when school was out and spent the next seven weeks looking at what I believe must have been every farm that was for sale in New York State. Eventually, we got to Seneca County in the Finger Lakes country of upstate New York. As we looked, we learned. We met by chance some lovely people named Stewart who lived in Oneonta, N.Y. They took a fancy to our children, who by then were getting a bit travel-weary, and invited us to leave the youngsters with them for a rest while we continued our search. They loved the kids and our son and daughter still talk about the Stewarts to this day.

We wrote several earnest-money agreements that didn't stick for one reason or another and finally settled on a 120-acre dairy farm eight miles out of Waterloo, N.Y. in the Township of Junius. This farm had a brand new polished aluminum 40 by 80 dairy barn, and a nine-room brick house built in 1790. The house had once been an inn and, despite its age, had a lot of charm, even having a beautiful circular staircase and three fireplaces. It was located on Whiskey Hill Road. "Whiskey Hill Farm" was the name we adopted for registration of our purebred Holstein cattle.

First Phase of Transition 241

The Finger Lakes country is a beautiful part of New York State. There are five great long lakes lying like the fingers of a man, running north and south and forming limestone ridges. The soil is sweet and seldom needs to be irrigated. Cornell University at Ithaca is located at the south end of Lake Cayuga, near enough to enable me to attend dairy seminars there.

We would be able to raise all the feed for our dairy herd, corn for the silo, corn for grain, soy beans, oats and alfalfa hay. There was a pear orchard for a cash crop and a big vegetable garden. This was a good farm. The owner had fallen from the barn roof in building the new barn and injured himself so that he wasn't able to continue with the heavy work of dairy farming. He had sharecropped his land that year and dispersed his herd. Our deal included the owner's share of the crops thus assuring us of having feed for the herd we planned to buy. We checked the place out with the bank, with the county agent and with Cornell University.

We proceeded to get a mortgage from Equitable Life Assurance Society and their agent checked out the farm thoroughly and our credit as well. We applied to the Federal Farmers' Home Administration for a $10,000 loan to buy a herd and equipment. They took a dim view of making a farmer's wife out of a Brooklyn girl, but Norma's beauty and charm carried her through that crisis and we were approved for a long-term low interest federal loan. I got a chuckle out of the irony of this. Our government would not let me have a radio officer's license that would permit me to sail on some rusty tramp freighter, but they would loan me $10,000.

The farmer had given me a big pitch on the thousands of dollars' worth of manure he was leaving me. This was piled ten feet deep in the barnyard and in the loafing shed. After I bought the farm I called the local milk inspector from the plant where I would be shipping my milk and asked him what had to be done before I could put a herd on and ship milk. He came out, took a look at the manure in the barnyard and said," Get all of that out of here, right down to bare ground and then call me again!"

I had to buy a tractor with a fork and a manure spreader with a power takeoff and get to work. It took me three months to accomplish that little feat that the inspector called for. Of course, it was great stuff on the land. Had I been a little more exerienced I would have told that farmer to put the manure on the land and then I would buy the farm.

I moved onto the farm first, leaving Norma in Sag Harbor with the children while I readied the house. There was a lot of work to be done in that old house to make it acceptable to Norma. I sanded the floors down to bare wood, varnished and painted the interiors of all rooms. Fortunately, the house was full brick and didn't need anything on the exterior, and the roof was good. After a month of this work, Norma and the kids came up in time for the children to start school in Waterloo. Lois was in the first grade and Tommy in the second. A school bus picked them up at the door. They loved the whole experience.

Norma was able to get a job as purchasing agent for a large electronics plant in Seneca Falls and that gave us income to survive until we got a milk check coming in. I applied for New York State unemployment benefits, which I had been paying into for many years though I had never been unemployed except during several strikes. My conscience was clear; the law read that you were eligible if you were "able, ready and willing to take a position at your previous classification and wage." Most people, especially inland, had no idea what the duties of a radio operator were. It was my bad luck that the manager of the N.Y. State Unemployment Office in Geneva, N.Y. was an ex-radio operator. In fact, he had been employed many years earlier at the very radio station where I had been working when it was owned by the German Telefunken Corporation during World War I. He spent the early World War I years intercepting messages from the Canadian Marconi Company being transmitted to London and monitoring Atlantic shipping. When America entered the war he was interned. After the war he elected to become an American citizen. In New York State the unemployment benefits are governed by a "merit system." If a company maintains a good record of steady employment they benefit by a cheaper rate of participation in the portion that the employer pays. Employers watch this zealously and in my case, I believed, with a certain vindictiveness. At any rate, this bureau manager in Geneva seemed, somehow, to have all the information on the circumstances of my leaving Mackay Radio.

Perhaps he was just doing his job. I admit that by this time I was possibly a little supersensitive. He asked, "How do you expect to get employment as a radio operator in this locality?"

I said, "Well, the law simply states that I be 'able, ready and willing to work at my old classification and wage or comparable classification and wage,' and since Waterloo is my home, this is the logical place for me to seek employment."

He couldn't argue with this but there were several large electronic plants in the vicinity, General Electric and Sylvania, and some smaller ones, and he insisted that I apply at one of those places each week to comply with the law. I almost had to go to work once. A company was interested in me because of my FCC license which would permit them to use me in a supervisory capacity testing transmitting equipment. However, they were not prepared to pay the kind of wages that I had been receiving and never forced the issue of my coming to work at their scale and I never pressed it. I was being paid $52.50 per week, the maximum benefit at that time, and was able to spend six days a week hauling manure to the land from my barnyard. The unemployment bureau manager would have me in each week for a personal interview and he never let an assistant conduct that interview. He had been advised by higher-ups that the minute I put milk cows on the farm and started drawing a milk check my eligibility for benefits would end. So he would grill me about what I was doing about getting a herd. I drew this for 11 weeks and then started buying cows and was no longer eligible.

By this time my loan from Farmers' Home Administration had been approved and I was ready to buy cows and equipment and start farming. It was all very exciting. My friend Wesley Engst helped me pick a herd of grade Holsteins that were all carrying calves and ready to freshen at the season when the price of milk would be the highest. I received $5.20 per cwt. for the first milk I sold. Four years later I received $3.20 cwt. for milk sold at the same time of the year to the same market. The first thing President Eisenhower did when he was elected was cut the support price from the dairy farmer. All the things that I had to buy had gone up in price.

I kept close touch with the county agent, who was a Cornell graduate, and he was a great help. The agent for the Farmers' Home Administration was very cooperative and helpful, but at some points, restraining. My friend Wesley Engst was the greatest help, as was his mother. I joined the Dairy Herd Improvement Association (DHIA), eventually becoming local vice-president, and brought my herd to 17th place out of 155 herds in Seneca County under DHIA test. At the time of my dispersal auction I had 10 out of 20 milking cows on the County Honor Roll for high production. By that time, four years after buying the farm, my herd was about 90% registered Holstein and I had some very fine stock.

With all that manure on the land, the crops in my first full year on the farm were bumper. Neighbors stopped and congratulated me on having the best crops they had ever seen on that farm.

We bought a 24-foot deep freeze and Norma and the kids filled it with produce from the garden, 50 fat young roosters, lambs, beef and frozen fruits. Of course we had our own milk, raw milk and cream. Norma worked hard driving ten miles to her job in Seneca Falls, which in winter snows and ice was hazardous and frightening to her. However, she stuck it out for over two years. The company she was working for as purchasing agent received a big electronic contract from the Navy to make transformers for an aircraft carrier that was under construction. After the work started the Navy sent an intelligence officer around to run the highest type security on the people that would be handling this highly classified work. Norma, having heard all my stories and experiences with the Navy, decided she did not want any part of Navy security screening and quit her job to stay home on the farm. She has always been a pacifist and building battleships was just not her thing anyway. The kids and I were glad to have her home even though we missed her weekly pay check.

I weighed 210 pounds when I bought the farm and within a few months was down to 160 pounds. I could eat everything and anything and I couldn't gain a pound. John L. Lewis, famous ex-president of the United Mine Workers of America, once said, "There's only one man in America that lifts more tonnage in a year than a miner and that's America's dairy farmer." I will testify to the weight of that statement. I did toughen up to the work, though friends coming up from New York City to visit were always shocked at the transition from a corpulent person to a sinewy, skinny, weather-beaten farmer. I got up at 4:30 a.m., went to the barn and had the milk on the milk house platform for the truck to pick up at 6 o'clock. If it wasn't there he didn't wait. Then you had to load it up and take it 20 miles to the plant. I never let that happen.

First Phase of Transition

At 9 p.m. you made the last check-up of the barn, bedding down and stuffing hay in front of those big cows that do such a great job of converting fodder into delicious sweet milk. If a cow was calving or sick I might make another trip to the barn before the night was over; she could need help.

We had automatic water cups in the barn, but the pump to the well and the water tank were in the basement of the house. I could hear through the pipes when a cow was sick or calving; she would start hitting the water cup and taking long drafts of cold water to quench her fever.

Our farm was only 20 miles from Lake Ontario and the severe winters made it necessary to keep the cows in the barn seven months of the year. Come May, when the pastures were ready and I could let them out, the work on the land began. Whoever invented lights on a tractor didn't do the dairy farmer any favor.

In recalling my boyhood in the Bitterroot Valley in Montana I remembered that a farmer with four or five cows making butter, cheese, and selling milk and eggs to his neighbors, feeding the whey to the pigs and chickens, seemed to have a good life. He had time to hunt and fish and ride with his children and never seemed to want for anything. This was quite a different life.

Norma felt that she should go into New York City and work as a court stenographer transcriber, a skill that she had mastered and would be well paid for. She would free-lance and that way could come home every few weeks and spend a week with me and the kids. Needing the money and seeing her nervous unrest made me agree to this plan. Norma did this for nearly a year. The kids and I made out the best we could. Lois and Tommy were wonderful. They learned to cook and do chores and be cheerful about it. They missed their mother but she called them often and they wrote cute letters to her.

This was obviously not the "family way of life" we had had in mind when we bought the farm. It is not easy to get out of a situation like that once you are in it. It's like "grabbing the proverbial bull by the tail"—you don't dare let go. It always looks like maybe next year is the the year to get out and then it becomes the year after.

Norma's sisters and father were prevailing on her to get me off the farm and by now her friends were, too. Norma's doctor said, "You will have to get her off that farm or she will have a breakdown." It came to the point where my choice was Norma or the cows, which was no choice. We agreed to start planning the exodus. The decision was made at Thanksgiving time. I had been able to get a man to milk for me and took the only four days off I ever had in four years. I took the kids and caught a plane from Syracuse into La Guardia. Over the holidays I got the pressure from the family that convinced me to sell the farm and get off no matter what the cost.

Norma went back to the farm with me. Once having accepted defeat I began to look forward to the surrender—an auction of the cattle, equipment and crops still on hand. We got in a fine auctioneer by the name of Wilcox who specialized in auctioning registered Holstein herds. He had a reputation of never taking a bad auction. Dairymen knew that if he was doing the auctioning the stock was good, and he was zealous of that record. Wesley Engst said that at Cornell, where they had been classmates, "Wilcox was voted the most likely not to succeed in his class, but he was the first one to become a millionaire." He had talent and was honest to the penny.

We called Mr. Wilcox in and went over our Dairy Herd Improvement records and the registration certificates of the herd. He went over the land and he made an inventory of the crops in the barn, the silo, corn cribs and granary. We asked him to give us his most optimistic figure and the lowest figure. Also, we wanted the farm auctioned along with everything else. With the set of figures he gave us, we felt we could leave solvent without debts behind us. He would "bid the farm in" at a certain low price. It meant Mr. Wilcox would buy it if we didn't get a higher bid than his bid.

He allowed us six weeks to prepare for the auction, setting the date for February 4th, 1956. We had to get the registration papers all straight, and there was much work about the farm to have all the equipment and livestock looking good by that date.

Luckily, I had been able to hire a very good man that fall to help with the crops. He stayed on during the winter to help me get ready for the auction. We had experienced odd weather all fall, and we picked the corn Christmas week in bitter cold, eight-to-ten-degree weather. I had 40 acres of corn and it was no small job. A neighbor custom picked it with his big self-propelled corn picker but my man and I ran the wagons and did the hauling and cribbing.

First Phase of Transition

This man I had hired had been a herdsman and was an expert at "fitting" cows (clipping, combing and beautifying them). He started that fitting process a week before the auction and had them looking like show animals the day of the sale.

Having your own farm auction can be one of the most exciting and emotional experiences in life. Norma and the kids and I found it so. The auctioneer said, "I never tire of it and always find each one exciting." Having people recognize the care you have taken with your livestock, their feeding, breeding and health—and having them recognize this fact with good hard money on the auctioneer's table—is very gratifying, perhaps like an artist selling his work.

A bull calf was born out of a very fine cow the day before the auction. Most dairymen use artificial insemination, one bull serving many cows and siring great numbers of calves. Few farmers raise bulls today and therefore they are most often immediately sold to the butcher for veal. This day I was going to call the butcher with this fine big calf but then I thought there will be butchers at the auction and I was too busy to make the call anyway. That little fellow sold for $120 at the sale and the butcher would have given me only $20. It just happened a 4H boy was there with his father to buy a bull calf to raise for breeding and this calf's pedigree was right and his mother's production record tremendous. He was a handsome big calf with great legs. Lois and Tommy's yearling heifers brought big prices because of their blue ribbons won at the county fair. We were all emotionally involved with the animals.

It was a beautiful, warm, thawing, February day. The winter had been tough, with people unable to get out because of cold and deep snow. There had not been an auction in the area all winter. My friends and neighbors were not able to buy anything. With buyers coming from as far away as Buffalo, Rochester and Syracuse, attracted by the reputation of the auctioneer, the local people never had a chance. Those from far off felt that if the locals, who knew the farmer and knew his stock, thought it was good enough to bid heavily on, it must be very good and they went higher.

Some of the equipment went for more than I paid for it new. I had assembled a hay wagon, buying a chassis here, the wheels there and a steel-bound oak frame elsewhere. It all cost me $100, and the wagon sold to a dealer for $150. It was a good wagon and probably well worth it. The dealer didn't have the time to shop as I had done.

We sold everything in the house but what we would be able to get into the car after packing ourselves and the kids in. We kept blankets, linen and silverware and our clothes. The rest went under the auctioneer's gavel. When the sale was over, the house, the barn, the barnyard and everything were as bare as a desert. My little daughter was sitting in a corner of the empty house weeping great tears. Finally, after the hurricane of the auction had passed, her mother noticed her and queried the cause. They had sold her dolls' china tea set that her aunt had given her for Christmas. Norma had to check with the auctioneer's secretary and determine the name of the purchaser who, fortunately, lived only a few miles away. Norma took Lois with her big tears and went and bought the little dishes back. The people had paid $7.50 for them, which was probably more than they cost new, and wanted them for their little girl, but they were kind enough to let Lois have them back.

Of the many hundreds of large and small items sold that day there was not one dollar that was not paid in cash to the auctioneer's secretary that evening. There was not one item on the inventory that did not sell for cash. Not one thing was stolen. It confirmed my faith in humanity.

Norma and the kids took off in the car for New York City, where they would stay with Norma's sister until I joined them. I stayed behind and lived with a neighbor friend and his family until the crops were hauled away. The man who bought all the crops—grain, corn, hay, soy beans and oats (the silage was sold to a local farmer)—had the biggest trailer tractor I had ever seen. He paid a higher price than local people would pay and he wrote a check for it all and took his first load that night. I asked him what he was going to do with it. He said there had been a drought in Georgia and he would drive south as long as the price kept going up. When he got out of the drought area and the price started declining he would turn around and return to the highest point. Pretty smart, I thought. When he came back for his second load of corn I asked him how it worked. He said, "I'd pull up in front of a beanery and go in for lunch. When I came out there'd be a gang of hungry farmers around. I'd say, 'How much am I bid?' I'd write down the name and address of the highest bid and climb in the cab of my rig and wheel on. When I finally reached the highest bid I sold the load for cash and came back here for more." He did the same with the beautiful green alfalfa hay.

It's quite an experience to see a living, breathing, vibrating thing like a dairy farm shut down and cleaned off so fast. It will twist your old thumper a bit and make you gulp as you walk off the last time.

We far exceeded the auctioneer's most optimistic estimate and were able to pay off all of our debts and buy a new Oldsmobile and head for Seattle, Washington. When Norma said she wanted to move back to a city, I said, "O.K., let me pick the city."

She said, "O.K." I picked Seattle, where my brother and his family and my elder sister lived, a city where I had once lived and loved it.

Our Sag Harbor home. This house was built before the American Revolution, had five fireplaces, a Dutch oven and a bond-slaves' room in the attic. The style had been marred from the front by the addition of a modern-day ranch-type veranda. I preferred this exposure. 1946.

Some grapes that never made it into the wine crock. Me, Tommie and Lois. 1949.

Son Tom was born. Jan. 3, 1946

Seneca County FARM BUREAU, HOME BUREAU, and 4-H CLUB NEWS

MARCH 1954

SPECIAL ISSUE ON SOIL CONSERVATION

VOL. XXXVII   WATERLOO, N. Y.   NO. 3

A SPRING CHORE

Tommy and Lois were in the 4-H Club. I was active in the Farm Bureau and was a director of the Dairy Herd Improvement Association. This picture was taken by Seneca County Agent.

Milking time on Whiskey Hill Farm. Nephew Robert, Lois, Tommy and me on a hot August day—haying time. 1955.

Whiskey Hill Farm near Waterloo, upstate New York. This house was built in 1790 as an inn—a place for drivers to stop for one for the road. In those days roads followed the ridges, avoiding swamps and mud holes. We lived here for nearly four years, 1952 to 1956.

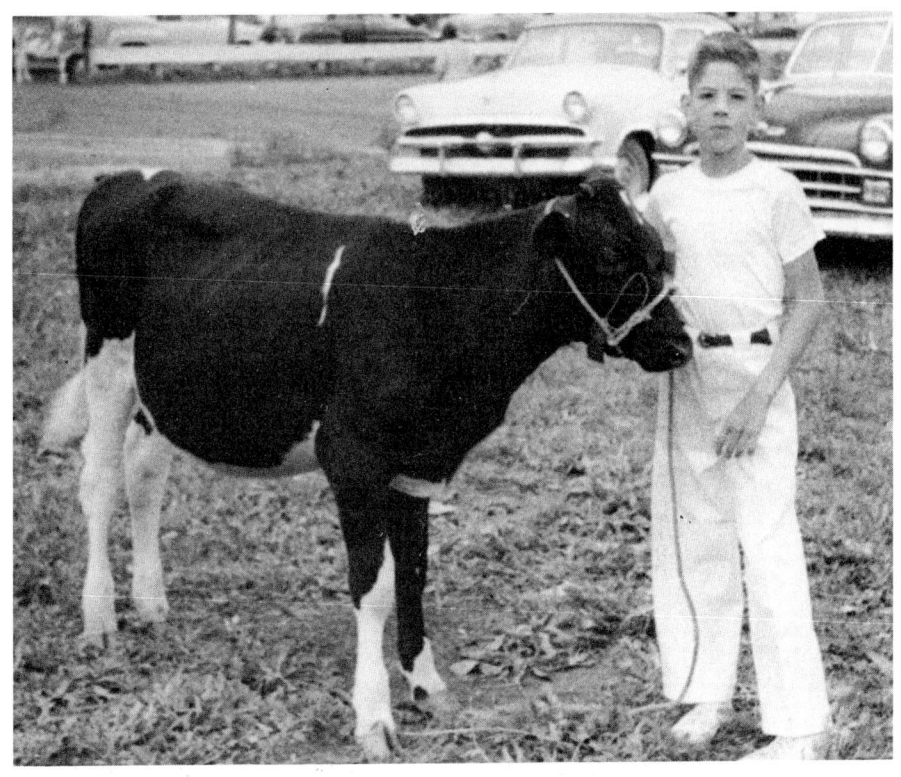

Lois and Tommy Salisbury with their prize-winning Holstein heifers. Both won first prize in the 4-H senior heifer class. Lois won the grand championship with hers. Both heifers were born on the farm and brought big prices at our auction the following February. Sept. 1955.

CHAPTER THIRTY

We Settle In Seattle

After paying debts and cleaning up the final details I said goodbye to my Waterloo friends and went into New York City to join Norma and the children. Norma and I had paid cash for the new Oldsmobile. We would leave for Seattle with no debts, a little cash and a fresh start at my age of 50.

In New York I said goodbye to my old union and communications friends whom I hadn't seen in several years. As they greeted me they said, "How are you, Oliver?" I had been listening only to the lowing of cattle and the chatter of children for so long that I had forgotten how to carry on a conversation. My hearing was dulled from years of radio telegraphy and now from lack of listening. Several times I heard that question of "How are you, Oliver?" as "How old are you, Oliver?" And I answered, "I'm fifty!" My friends answered, "So what?" After the question had been asked me several times I finally tumbled to what they were saying. I was a few days from my fiftieth birthday and had it on my mind.

We Settle in Seattle

On the first of March, 1956, we loaded all our worldly possessions, except two cartons of linen and bedding which we shipped ahead, into our car and headed west via Washington, D.C. and the southern route across the country. We felt the children were old enough to absorb some history of this land and might not get a chance for such a tour of it again for some time. We visited the Lincoln Memorial, the White House, the Capitol and the sights of Washington. Then we went on to Monticello, Thomas Jefferson's home in Virginia, and then crossed to Memphis and stopped at the replica of the Parthenon. We crossed Arkansas and Texas and went into Mexico at Juarez, then on to California. We were caught in a sandstorm in Arizona, ruining the paint job and glass on our new car. I visited my old friends in San Francisco for a few days and then on to Seattle and a new life.

The children were 10 and 12 years old. At the end of the trip the things they remembered most were the swimming pool motels and the big dishes of ice cream served in the South. However, Norma and I really enjoyed seeing the sights on the leisurely 14-day trip.

Leaving San Francisco we stopped off in Healdsburg to visit my daughter-in-law, Beth Salisbury, the wife of my son, Robby, who was then a sergeant in the Marine Corps aboard the carrier Hancock on China Sea patrol. This was my son by my first wife. I got acquainted with my one-year-old grandson, David, and his mother Beth.

The happy marriage of Robby and Beth has produced four grandsons who are now young men. It has been my pleasure to visit them from time to time over the years since then.

Arriving in Seattle with $500 and no employment, we accepted my brother Al's and sister-in-law Jane's invitation to live in their basement until we could do better. It was exciting to see my brother and sister and their families, whom I had not seen for over 14 years. Getting employment was something else. Before leaving New York City I had called one of the large companies that were getting into computer production in a big way and who were advertising for men with electronic backgrounds to attend their schools for service men and salesmen. They said over the phone that they would be glad to hire a man with my background. I had noticed in a Seattle paper that they had a similar school in Seattle, which they had verified. It was my plan to seek such employment in Seattle. Upon applying in Seattle I was told, "We cannot hire a man over 40."

I applied other places where my background would be of help, always receiving the same answer. I even applied for a job as a grain and feed salesman in one of the big mills; though my farm experience fit me for such a job, my age kept them from hiring me. This was the first time I realized that people could look on me as an old man. Actually, I was thin and in excellent physical condition from the farm work. It occurred to me to lie about my age. The next time I applied for a job, I told them I was 40. I got the job.

It was with a nationally advertised paint company as a paint salesman. I got along fine for three months. Because I handled money a bond was required. When the bond finally came through, the company called me in and fired me for lying about my age, saying that I was too old to fit into their organization. They would not be able to do that under today's laws.

I had walked to work that day. In walking home and tripping on my chin as I did so, I thought, This'll never do! I must get a job before I go home! I stopped and bought a paper and read an ad. It said, "Real Estate Salesmen Wanted. Earn $1,000 per month." I went on home and got my car without going into the apartment. (On the strength of my job and Norma's work as a free-lance court stenographer, we had been able to move out of my brother's basement.) I drove out to the address of Mr. Dana Brown, who had run the ad. I told Mr. Brown my experience in losing the paint salesman's job because of my age. Mr. Brown said the right thing: he said, "Why, Mr. Salisbury, in this business age is an asset. People will respect you for it." Dana Brown was an excellent teacher, and a part of his duties as general manager of a big real estate company was to train the salesmen. He taught by slogans, proverbs and cliches. They were very effective, especially with me, for this had been my mother's method of teaching; and I had a good memory. Mr. Brown taught me hundreds of these slogans: "In this business you cannot afford one enemy"; "Never overestimate your competitor's lethargy"; "Don't forget Aunt Hannah" (Aunt Hannah being the White Angel that can help with the down payment). With Mr. Brown as a teacher I became within a year the top salesman in a company employing 75 men, winning permanent possession of the "Oscar" given to the salesman winning the honor three times in one year. I made Mr. Brown an honest man, always earning at least $1,000 a month or more in this profession over a period of many years.

Norma had come through as usual. She had gained employment as a free-lance stenotype operator and was getting all the work she could handle. I was a little shaky about taking a job on straight commission, but my brother and sister told me, "Take it. We will back you up if you need it." They showed their sincerity by each giving me a check for $250. With that kind of support, how could I fail? And I didn't.

I was fortunate in working under a good manager, too: Mr. Bjorne Theusen, a postwar Norwegian immigrant, a young man who recognized the opportunities this country offered and was making the best of them. He was a hard working, hard driving, demanding kind of manager, unpopular with lazy salesmen; but I quickly noted that listening to him and doing what he said made me money. The fact that this also made money for him was inconsequential to me. We got along just fine. I worked hard, so did he, and we both made out well.

I had always looked upon salesmen as parasites on society, feeling that if anyone wanted to buy something they needed they would go out and buy it. In selling paint I had overcome this erroneous feeling and realized that if you were selling a good product for the good purpose it was intended you were performing a service that the buyer needed. As Mr. Brown had said, "If it wasn't for real estate salesmen we would all still be living east of the Mississippi. It took creative promotion to convince people they should settle the West."

I found great satisfaction in finding a suitable first home for young people or in relocating older people looking for a smaller home or whatever the need. I made many friends, and found the more honest I was the more successful I was. I'm sure that I am welcome in the home of anyone I sold to or for during my real estate career. As Mr. Brown had said, "In this business you cannot afford one enemy." I tried to live by that.

A year after arriving in Seattle we bought our own custom-built house in a very nice wooded suburban area. I had sold 17 houses for Ray Anderson and sold myself on having him build a home for us. On Christmas morning Ray rang my doorbell and handed me a check for $75 saying, "Oliver, this is not because I owe you anything, but this is in appreciation of your working so hard on my houses." This was real reward.

I eventually became a broker. I'd done quite a bit of land development work with builders, so I began specializing in that field, ending up working land out in the hinterland all over the state of Washington. I always liked cow paths better than streets, and I preferred cow dung on my shoes to dog dung. Raw land became my specialty, real estate brokers my best customers. River fronts, lake fronts, ocean fronts, mountains, valleys, swamps became my business and my playgrounds. I sold riverfront land to the Game Department of the state of Washington, which is like selling snowballs to the Eskimos. I sold gravel deposits and timberlands. It is a fascinating business for one who likes being outdoors and will take the time to develop some expertise in that phase of the real estate business.

During this period I had been hired by a small mortgage and escrow company to start a real estate land brokerage company for them. This worked out very well for me since Don Leech, the owner, was anxious to get into land investments. Don was a good businessman in the field of finance and management where I had the land knowledge. We each had confidence in the other's ability within our specialties. The brokerage worked out fairly successfully.

Don and I started buying land and, in some cases, developing it. We made some very good deals and some poor ones, but the good more than offset the bad and the whole relationship would have to be termed successful.

CHAPTER THIRTY ONE

Fight For My Life And Conclusion

In selling and listing raw land all over the State of Washington and sometimes even in Canada (I had American investors who owned land in British Columbia), it was my practice to hike over the land. I enjoyed doing this, and familiarity with the acreages involved was, of course, a big aid in selling.

Sometimes these inspections involved crossing the state, doing a lot of hiking, and making a few other side trips; though enjoyable, they could be quite strenuous by the time I had been out two or three days and returned to Seattle. Often after returning I ran a high fever and was sick in bed as if I had influenza or old fashioned "grippe," as my mother used to call it.

Norma remarked that this was becoming a pattern with me after these trips. I would usually be too sick to go to the doctor and after I began to recover would then go see him. The doctor would give me antibiotics to kill the fever and I would get well.

In July of 1968 this occurred again and this time I went to the doctor immediately. The doctor x-rayed me, saw a spot on my lung, and told me that I had pneumonia. He gave me the usual antibiotics and sent me home to bed.

I got well as usual and went back to work. Norma had gone to Florida to see her 85-year-old father, who was in a nursing home in Miami Beach, and to meet her sisters from New York there. I made one of my tough land inspections, came home feeling lonely and neglected, and decided to go out on the town. I returned to one of my old "watering holes" and hoisted a few. I got mixed up with a group of Czechoslovakian refugees who thought the U.S. should have declared war against the Soviet Union over the Red Army's invasion of their country. This became a pretty heated argument. I felt rather strong on the subject of foreign involvement; among other reasons, my son was then in the Navy on "Tonkin Bay Patrol," known as "Yankee Station" to Navy personnel in the Viet Nam war.

The "Pentagon Papers" had not yet been published, but there had been some stories in the papers casting dark clouds over President Johnson's decision to make a major war of it. The argument with the Czechoslovakians ended up with me getting left with a $50 tab for the drinks. I think I lost that war to the interventionists.

Though I had quite a lot to drink, I could handle them pretty well and was never subject to serious hangovers. However, next morning I awoke feeling fuzzy and needing to cough. I went to the bathroom and started coughing violently, coughing up copious amounts of blood, at first dark and then bright red. It frightened me, especially as I was alone. When I was able to stop the coughing, I called the doctor, who told me to go to the emergency room of the hospital. I met him there and he put a "bird" on me, a breathing apparatus. He said, "One lung is collapsed. I'll take spittle samples for the laboratory tests. It will be a few days before I'll hear from the lab. I'll call you if there is anything wrong." He gave me some medication and I began to feel all right. He sent me home.

The following Friday afternoon, just at 5 o'clock, the doctor's nurse called and said, "The doctor would like to see you. Can you come right up?"

I said, "Yes, it'll take me 20 minutes." Before I could get out of the house the phone rang again and the nurse said, "No, the doctor thinks it will be all right if you come in Tuesday morning,

Monday being Labor Day."

I said, "O.K." After a few minutes the meaning began to register. The doctor had said, "I'll call if anything is wrong." Well, he had called. Something must be wrong.

Norma was in Florida. I began to worry and called her about my problem for the first time. I told her she was on the wrong side of the country, to get a plane and come home, and why. She was home the next morning and we sweated it out together until Tuesday.

Tuesday morning Norma went to the doctor's office with me. The doctor said, "Do you want it straight?"

I said, "After you ask a question like that, what am I supposed to say? No, Doc, tell me a big lie."

Doc said, "Your tests show cancerlike cells. If it is cancer, you have a 5% chance that it will be operable and a 5% chance of survival if the operation is successful."

The surgeon found a malignant tumor on the "Y" of my right lung which had already made the lower lobe collapse and had impaired the function of the upper lobe. I lost most of my right lung. There were some complications due to a secondary infection, and I spent 35 days in the hospital and four months recuperating.

The doctor who gave me the anesthesia was the most beautiful woman. I thought, At least they give you a pretty picture to go out on. She gave me something to relax me and then said, "Now, what I'll give you will be quick and the next thing you know you'll be awaking back in your room." Right after I awakened, the doctor came into the room and said, "Oh! You are all right. I was afraid for you." That was the last time I ever saw her. Even though she was very beautiful, I'm not ready to sacrifice the remaining lung just to see her.

During my illness I learned some things. I learned what it is to be loved. I know that had I been a lonely man in a hospital in that condition without the expressed love of my wife, son and daughter, my brother and his family, and the many flowers and cards from loving sisters and friends, I would never have survived. I thought, Gee! All these people love me so much I must get well to justify it. I really never thought I was going to die; but neither did I think much about living until I felt the need to justify the love and faith my family and friends held for me. If you ever have a loved one in the hospital, don't hesitate to express your love in some way. Believe me, love is a great healer.

In my several months of convalescence I had an opportunity for the first time since boyhood to think philosophically about life in general. I wanted some answers. I decided that when I was well, rather than concentrating on making money I would think on more spiritual levels, try and find some answers. Why was I here? What did I do with sixty-some years in this world? I decided that I had a right to feel good about my role in life, that I had been a person who stood for good. I now reject all dogmas although following a dogma can be a good discipline in life. Being dogmatic to extreme can be a horrible waste. I do believe that we humans have great sensitivities yet to be explored and developed.

In spite of all the strife, struggle and tragedy in the world, I feel the world is a better place than it was when I arrived in it and that it will continue to be a better place. I am sure there is a universal harmonious scheme of things and that if people live within that harmony things go well. When they depart from the harmony and allow themselves discord they get in trouble.

I am now retired. Friends urged me to write this book. I would not want to live it over again. I think I did things the way I thought was right at the time they were done.

Life can be like the bitterroot, the Montana State flower—the root and growth bitter, the mature blossom beautiful.